Migrating to Fortran 90

Migrating to Fortran 90

Jim Kerrigan

O'Reilly & Associates, Inc.
103 Morris Street, Suite A
Sebastopol, CA 95472

Migrating to Fortran 90
by Jim Kerrigan

Editor: Andy Oram
Production Editor: Leslie Chalmers

Printing History:

November 1993:   First Edition.

ISBN: 1-56592-049-X

Dedicated to the memory of
William M. Kerrigan

Table of Contents

List of Figures

List of Tables

Preface

A huge volume of scientific and engineering code is developed and maintained by an extensive community of Fortran programmers. Since the last ANSI standard was delivered fifteen years ago, sixty books specifically targeting the "Fortran 77" readership remain in print, attesting to the vigor of the language. Since microprocessors first became a viable computing platform, well over a dozen commercial Fortran compilers for PCs have come to market, proving a demand for the language.

Fortran 90 has many features not found in the previous standard. Individually, these features are sufficiently "new" to require full and detailed description. Collectively, they extend the functionality of the language and broaden its applicability.

This book is tailored to the current Fortran practitioner. It includes dozens of full program examples. Fortran programs have always balanced the need of implementing some algorithm against an independent need to acquire information, communicate with the user, and generate reports and output files. Both the formula translation need and the data management need are addressed by the examples in this book. Algorithms are drawn from the natural sciences, mathematics, and operations research. Data management and program control are illustrated by the demands of the interactive prompt/response cycle, data structures, linked lists, and input/ output error handling.

Reader experience encompasses not only Fortran 77 but many extensions that have spread throughout the industry; this book recognizes that. Comparisons to popular extensions and work-arounds as well as Fortran 77 can be found here. Furthermore, perfect knowledge of standard Fortran 77 is not assumed; recapitulations are included for obscure features.

Finally, this book lists additional Fortran 90 resources. It includes pointers to available full and partial Fortran 90 compilers, addresses from which to order the actual Fortran 90 standard, and detailed instructions on how to get machine-readable copies of the source code for the examples in this book.

Who Should Read This Book?

This book is for programmers who are already working with large applications in some dialect of Fortran. This community knows Fortran essentially as implemented by compilers subscribing to Fortran 77, the ANSI standard published in 1978. Fortran 90 is the next step in the evolution of the language.

This book is a comprehensive explanation of every new feature that the 1990 ANSI/ISO standard has added to the language. The text describes every change from the Fortran 77 standard, and grounds new concepts in the readers' current needs and experiences.

How This Book Is Organized

This book is structured to deliver the information in the order that busy programmers would most likely want it. Simple enhancements and widely useful features come early in the book. Features that require a lot of time and program redesign to implement, or that are less useful to the majority of programmers, come later. But every change between Fortran 77 and Fortran 90 is covered somewhere in the book.

Following the above criteria, Chapter 1, *Compatibility*, offers a brief look at the whole language and the effect of migration on current Fortran programmers. Chapters 2 through 7 offer the most substantial new features, while Chapters 8 through 10 offer miscellaneous enhancements that are useful in particular situations. Chapter 11 covers any new intrinsic functions that were not fully described in earlier chapters.

Arrays are the essential repositories of data in Fortran, and their use has been widely enhanced with a number of powerful extensions over the years. These extensions, now standardized, are fairly easy to learn and useful in almost every programming situation. They are the subject of Chapter 2, *Array Operations.*

Derived types—also known as records in VAX FORTRAN and structures in C—complement arrays well. They are not as widely useful as the new array features, but have many applications in grouping different types of data. They are covered in Chapter 3, *Derived Types.*

Chapters 4, 5, and 6 form a progression, taking the reader through features of increasing complexity and power. The overall subject is program organization, involving the grouping of data and subprograms. Chapter 4, *Subroutines and Functions Revisited,* starts the process by examining the common model for the subdivision of programs. It offers some new ways of handling subprograms with minimal disruption of current practice. Along with program structure, it is useful to look at the option of invoking user-defined functions and subroutines through operators, so that feature comes next in Chapter 5, *Overloaded Operators.* Finally, Chapter 6, *Modules,* offers a full solution to the problems addressed in Chapter 4, promoting the use of modules for new programs and for major changes to old ones.

Chapter 7, *Dynamic Memory Management,* discusses the last major feature introduced by Fortran 90, the dynamic management of memory through allocatable arrays and pointers. While not central to program structure like the features of the previous chapters, the features in this chapter have important uses.

Chapter 8, *File Handling,* is rather disjointed. Here, all the new features for file handling and I/O are presented in one place. Fortran 90's changes in these areas are small but in some cases long-desired, such as the ability to specify whether a file is opened at the beginning or the end.

Numeric precision has been hard to specify in a portable manner up to now. The new features of Fortran 90 standardizing this area appear in Chapter 9, *Numeric Models.*

The special programming topic of bit manipulation is covered in Chapter 10, *Bit Functions.*

New intrinsic functions (75 of them) intertwine with the other new programming capabilities offered by Fortran 90. Most of the new intrinsics, because they interact heavily with other features, appear in the first 10 chapters of the book. Chapter 11, *Intrinsic Functions,* serves as a summary and clean-up, covering the less important intrinsics or the subtler features that did not appear earlier.

Finally, several appendices list full Fortran 90 compilers, partial Fortran 90 compilers, ordering procedures for the standard itself, and the complete source code of some of the larger example programs.

How to Improve This Book

Fortran 90 is very new. There is very little practical experience with the full language anywhere. Some of the lack of experience is due to the availability of compilers. Several compilers have been delivered to the marketplace, one available as early as mid-summer 1991, and more scheduled for delivery in late 1993 and early 1994. But they have been used primarily in an experimental role. Only now are they being gradually adopted for production use. Hardware and software vendors will probably migrate existing compilers towards Fortran 90 in direct response to their users' discovery of how new Fortran 90 features assist in research and development.

Some of the lack of experience is due to the limited exposure Fortran 90 has had in the press. This book is one of few devoted entirely to Fortran 90. Others are:

Aberti, Christophe

1992   Fortran 90: Initiation à partir du FORTRAN 77. Série Informatique Éditions. 144 pages. Menton, France.
ISBN 2-090615-00-6

Adams, Jeanne C., et. al.

1990   Fortran 90 Handbook: Complete ANSI/ISO Reference. McGraw-Hill Publishing Co. 740 pages. New York, NY.
ISBN 0-070004-06-4

Brainerd, Walter S. et. al.

1990   A Programmer's Guide to Fortran 90. McGraw-Hill Publishing Co. 410 pages. New York, NY.
ISBN 0-070002-48-7

1993   (German edition) R. P. Oldenbourg Verlag gmbh. Munich, Germany.

Counihan, Martin

1991   Fortran 90. Pitman Publishing. 309 pages. London, England.
        ISBN 0-273030-73-6

Delannoy, C.

1993   Programmer en Fortran 90: Guide Complet. Edition Eyrolles. 413
        pages. Paris, France.
        ISBN 2-212087-23-2

Gehrke, Wilhelm

1991   Fortran 90 Referenz-Handbuch: der neue Fortran-Standard. Carl
        Hanser Verlag. 964 pages. München, Germany.
        ISBN 3-446163-21-2

Heisterkamp, Manfred

1991   Fortran 90: eine informelle Einführung. BI-Wissenshaftsverlag. 202
        pages. Mannheim, Germany.
        ISBN 3-411153-21-0

Langer, Erasmus

1993   Programmieren in Fortran 90. Springer-Verlag. 320 pages. New
        York, NY.
        ISBN 0-387824-46-4

Lignelet, Patrice

1993   Fortran 90: Approche par la Pratique. Série Informatique Éditions.
        240 pages. Menton, France.
        ISBN 2-090615-01-4

Meissner, Loren P.

1994   Fortran 90. PWS-KENT Publishing Company. 650+ pages. Boston,
        MA.
        ISBN 0-534933-72-6

Metcalf, Michael and John K. Reid

1990   Fortran 90 Explained. Oxford University Press. 294 pages. Oxford,
        England.
        ISBN 0-198537-72-7

1993   (French edition) AFNOR. Paris, France.

1994   (Russian edition) Mir. Moscow, Russia.

1994   (Japanese edition) Kyoritsu Shuppan. Tokyo, Japan.

Morgan, J. Steve and J. Lawrie Schonfelder

1993   Programming in Fortran 90. Blackwell Scientific Publications. 360
        pages. Oxford, England.
        ISBN 0-632028-38-6

Überhuber, C. and P. Meditz

1993   Software-Entwicklung in Fortran 90. Springer-Verlag. 426 pages.
        Berlin, Germany.
        ISBN 0-387824-50-2

Wojcieszynski, Ranier and Brigitte Wojcieszynski

1993   Fortran 90 Programmieren mit dem Neuen Standard. Addison-
        Wesley Publishing Co., Inc. 344 pages. Reading, MA.
        ISBN 3-893196-00-5

Four college-level textbooks cover both Fortran 77 and Fortran 90 in an
integrated way:

Bronson, Gary J.

1992   Modern Fortran 77/90. Scott/Jones Inc. 595z pages. El Granada, CA.
        ISBN 0-962423-05-X.

Ellis, T. M. R.

1990   Fortran 77 Programming with an Introduction to the Fortran 90
        Standard. Addison-Wesley Publishing Company. 641 pages.
        Wokingham, England.
        ISBN 0-201416-38-7.

Koffman, Elliot B. and Frank L. Friedman

1993   Fortran with Engineering Applications. Addison-Wesley Publishing
        Company. 664 pages. Reading, MA.
        ISBN 0-201558-75-0.

Zirkel, Gene and Eli Berlinger

1993   Understanding Fortran 77 and 90. PWS-KENT Publishing
        Company. 608 pages. Boston, MA.
        ISBN 0-534934-47-1

In journals, Fortran 90 has received significant coverage only in the Fortran Journal published by the Fortran User Group (Fullerton, CA) and in Fortran Forum published by the Association for Computing Machinery (New York, NY). Fortran 90 reached the "popular" press only in short articles in BYTE (Doris Appleby, "FORTRAN", Volume 16, Number 9, pages 147-150, September 1991 issue), the New Scientist (Michael Metcalf, September 12, 1992 issue, pages 30-33), and Scientific American (Paul Wallich, "FORTRAN Forever", Volume 265, Number 1, page 112, July 1991 issue).

Your experience is invited. New examples, better examples, clearer examples are urgently sought. If you discern an application of Fortran 90 features that isn't even hinted at in this book, speak up. As you discover shortcomings in the text, note them and send them in. Mistakes? Some remain regardless of the care that went into rooting them out: please let the publisher know so that they can be corrected in a future edition.

Further Developments on the Fortran Front

It is still not clear what kinds of problems are best solved with Fortran 90. Certainly Fortran 90 will inherit a whole universe of applications from Fortran 77. Fortran 90 might gain ground for Fortran by providing a viable alternative for problems that would have been tackled in C or C++.

Extensions to Fortran 90 for parallel programming are the objective of the High Performance Fortran Forum organized at the Center for Research on Parallel Computation at Rice University (Houston, TX). Their "High Performance Fortran" (HPF) facilitates writing data parallel programs where the distribution of data impacts performance. It supports high performance programming on a wide variety of machines, including massively parallel SIMD and MIMD systems and vector processors. The HPF Forum is on target to complete the specification of this extended Fortran by late winter, 1993. In fact, a subset of this high performance Fortran called xHPF will be available commercially in early spring, 1993, as a joint product of Applied Parallel Research (Placerville, CA) and Kuck and Associates, Inc. (Champaign, IL).

System level Fortran 90 bindings are planned as the POSIX 1003.19 standard by the Institute of Electrical and Electronics Engineers, Inc. (Piscataway, NJ). This effort was scheduled to complete in 1996. Basically, the committe was charged with a mission to recast the Fortan 77 language interface (POSIX 1003.9) to system services (POSIX 1003.1) into the "best practices" of Fortran 90. Work began in 1991 but stopped in July 1993. Further development has been postponed because vendors cited incomplete experience in development of Fortran 90 compilers and users cited a lack of widespread experience in using the new Fortran 90 constructs. As such, the project to develop POSIX 1003.19 has been withdrawn, but is likely to be reintroduced as broad-based industry Fortran 90 experience grows.

Examples Online

The source code and input files for all examples in this book are available free from UUnet (that is, free except for UUnet's usual connect-time charges). If you have access to uunet, you can retrieve the examples using UUCP or FTP. For UUCP, find a machine with direct access to uunet, and type the following command:

```
uucp uunet\!~/nutshell/fortran90/fortran90.tar.Z yourhost\!~/yourname/
```

The backslashes can be omitted if you use the Bourne shell (sh) instead of the C shell (csh). The file should appear some time later (up to a day or more) in the directory **/usr/spool/uucppublic/yourname**.

You don't need to subscribe to UUNET to be able to use their archives via uucp. By calling 1-900-468-7727 and using the login "uucp" with no password, anyone may uucp any of the UUNET's on line source collection. (Start by copying uunet!~/ls-lR.Z, which is a compressed index of every file in the archives.) As of this writing, the cost is 40 cents per minute. The charges will appear on your next telephone bill.

To use ftp, you will need to find a host with direct access to the Internet. A sample session is shown, with commands in boldface:

```
% ftp uunet.uu.net
Connected to uunet.uu.net.
220 uunet FTP server (Version 5.99 Wed May 23 14:40:19 EDT 1993) ready.
Name (uunet.uu.net:yourname): anonymous
331 Guest login ok, send ident as password.
Password: yourname@yourhost.xxx
230 Guest login, ok, access restrictions apply.
ftp> cd nutshell/fortran90
250 CWD command successful.
ftp> binary
200 Type set to I.
ftp> get fortran90.tar.Z
200 PORT command successful.
150 Opening ASCII mode data connection for fortran90.tar.Z
```

```
226 Transfer complete.
ftp> quit
221 Goodbye.
%
```

The file is a compressed tar archive. To extract the files once you have retrieved the archive, type:

```
% zcat fortran90.tar.Z | tar xf -
```

System V systems require the following tar command instead:

```
% zcat fortran90.tar.Z | tar xof -
```

All of the examples have been run on a Sun 3/50 system under SunOS 4.1 with Version 1.1(392) of the f90 compiler from the Numerical Algorithms Group Ltd. If you notice behavior on your system that show the examples to be in error, please contact the author through the publisher at nutshell@ora.com.

Acknowledgments

I am grateful to many people for their help during the course of this book's development.

Tony Nilles of the Numerical Algorithms Group championed my request within NAG for an extended loan of their Fortran 90 compiler. In addition, the assistance of Karl Knapp and Malcolm Cohen of NAG's technical support staff was prompt and comprehensive whenever I posed a question.

Bob Bonocore and Rich Bateman of Sun Microsystem's local office came to the rescue with much needed advice when my aged, but serviceable, Sun 3/ 50 system threatened to give up the ghost.

Dick Arscott (Software Associates), Walt Brainerd (Unicomp), John McCalpin (University of Delaware), Loren Meissner (University of San Francisco), and Mike Metcalf (CERN), all generously gave their time to review the completed manuscript. It has profited immensely from their knowledge and experience.

Mike Loukides and Steve Talbott at O'Reilly & Associates took a chance on my proposal and approved the book's development. I thank them for accepting the risk of publishing a book by an unknown author on a subject that in and of itself contained a large number of unknowns.

Edie Freedman, Leslie Chalmers, and Chris Reilley at O'Reilly & Associates handled all the design, production, and illustrations, respectively. Although

I am responsible for what this book contains, they deserve the credit for how good it looks. Linda Walsh and Jane Appleyard put immense energy into marketing the book among vendors of Fortran 90 compilers.

Andy Oram at O'Reilly & Associates edited this book. That is a brief statement of his role, but falls far short of Andy's influence. Andy is an expert in organizing written material to convey complex ideas: the flow of topics in this book is testament to his skill. Furthermore, his knowledge of the subject kept the treatment on an even keel. Finally, throughout the process, Andy made every effort to produce the best book possible, and, like a director, he suggested, cajoled, requested, and demanded the same from me. Andy's influence is the foundation of whatever measure of quality this book achieves.

My family invested so much in this book. My boys—Ian, Phillip, and Evan—watched me work all hours on this project and never complained. My wife, Ellen, missed my company as I became more and more involved, but she understood my commitment. This book would never exist were it not for my family's support.

1

Compatibility

Fortran 90 is different from Fortran 77. It is a superset by any measure: more statements, new data types, additional decision constructs, etc. Looking at a program written with the full-blown Fortran 90 syntax and a functionally compatible Fortran 77 version is as striking a difference visually as laying a Fortran 77 program next to its Fortran 66 counterpart. It took a long time for the Fortran community to merge the then "new" Fortran features with existing practice and build a Fortran 77 idiom. It will take some time to do the same for Fortran 90.

But there is a big difference. Standard conforming Fortran 66 programs could prove incompatible with the Fortran 77 standard in two dozen ways. Conversely, all standard conforming Fortran 77 programs are standard conforming Fortran 90 programs.

That is such a strong statement that it is worth a straight-forward interpretation. It means that if a program was designed and programmed with strict adherence to the previous Fortran standard, then it will compile, link, load, and execute the same way under this new Fortran standard.

So many extensions have been added to Fortran implementations that it is sometimes hard to remember what is "standard Fortran 77"—covered under upward compatibility to Fortran 90—and what is not. As a reminder of what is "standard" and what is not, it would be prudent to pass existing code through a Fortran 77 compiler and let that compiler flag nonstandard constructs.

Upward compatibility allows Fortran programmers to integrate new Fortran 90 features into existing code in a controlled, evolutionary manner. There is no need to convert existing code. Upward compatibility permits each Fortran 90 feature to be introduced in situations where and when it proves useful.

Why Was Fortran 90 Developed?

One premise of this book is that integrating Fortran 90 features into existing code is an easy, incremental job. Each programmer can choose the features that are useful for particular tasks and ignore the rest.The changes in Fortran 90 vary widely, from standardizations of common extensions to entirely new programming models. To convey the scope and variety of the new features, some history is useful. This section will explain just enough historical background to show what is part of Fortran 90, and why. Several references listed in the preface were consulted for this history.

Three major goals drove the ANSI committee (X3J3) that standardized Fortran 90. First, they wanted to introduce array manipulations that would raise runtime performance, particularly to achieve the maximum benefit from parallel architectures. This goal was probably achieved (perhaps not fully) because the new language contains constructs that have proven valuable as extensions, such as array operations and array sections. Second, the committee wanted to standardize some practices that did not make it into Fortran 77. Finally, they wanted to modernize the language in order to keep up with others, such as C and Ada.

The entire standardization effort for Fortran 90 represented a stand-off, and ultimately a compromise, between two schools of thought. One side wanted to introduce the most advanced features of modern programming languages, essentially transforming Fortran into a sophisticated instrument with the maximal assured value to scientific programmers through the next several decades. The other side wanted to preserve existing practice while making modest extensions in order to fill gaps in the current Fortran 77 standard. The first side in the debate can be thanked for several valuable additions to Fortran, including:

- Modules, which encapsulate data and subprograms.

- KIND, which standardizes the specification of numeric precision.

- Overloaded assignment statements and operators, which permit some knowledge domains to be coded in a more natural and self-documenting way.

- Pointers, which provide data structures that can grow and shrink.

The other side mandated the addition of less spectacular features with long popularity, such as:

- INCLUDE statements

- MIL-STD-1753 bit manipulation functions

- DO WHILE loops

- NAMELIST input/output

Backward compatibility formed the issue around which the two groups clashed. Both knew, at the beginning of the Fortran 90 effort, that many features of Fortran were old-fashioned and increasingly hard to manage. The question was how to deal with the many millions of lines of code that were still in regular production use.

The first side in the debate, with its leaning toward change, tried to institute gradual but radical replacement. Through the process of deprecating features, declaring them obsolescent, and then removing them from the standard, they hoped to prod programmers to remove problematic features over a period of decades. Among the language features on the hit list were several mainstays of current practice: some awkward features of DO-loops, COMMON blocks, EQUIVALENCE statements, and the arithmetic IF. Each were to be replaced by more flexible and maintainable constructs.

The second side defended fiercely the viewpoint of the busy engineer who is working with dozens of inherited Fortran modules containing thousands of lines that represent the very features the committee was planning to eliminate. While opposing efforts to change the historical foundations of Fortran coding style, the second side lobbied for the inclusion of the existing extensions mentioned above, which had achieved the status of *de facto* standards. The modernizers resisted the temptation to include what had long been available but never standardized before, pointing out that the extensions were halfway measures and presented some long-term problems.

While the modernizers dominated the ANSI X3J3 committee, pressure from the more conservative forces was extremely evident outside it. The battle between these two sides played some role in lengthening the process of finalizing Fortran 8X until (as one committee member put it) the X turned out to be a hexadecimal digit.

The compromise affords the best result that an existing Fortran programmer could have requested. Existing practices were all preserved, except for some minor features with known maintenance or portability problems. For instance, floating-point variables are no longer recommended as DO-loop variables, and arithmetic IF statements have been declared obsolescent. On the positive side, both types of requested features—popular existing extensions, and new methods for solving problems—have been incorporated.

The result is a large but forgiving language. Dusty decks can persist so long as they prove useful, while programmers can introduce new features when permitted by their schedules and dictated by organizational goals. A section of newly minted code can incorporate all the newest features, while still interacting with more static sections of the program that have not changed in years.

Thus, COMMON blocks can be preserved, while more flexible implementations of global data can be experimented with. EQUIVALENCE can be tolerated where it has appeared for years, while newer methods such as TRANSFER statements or pointers can be employed for all new code. DO WHILE can be used out of habit because it is now in the standard, but EXIT and CYCLE statements can be used instead, where the programmer recognizes an advantage in doing so.

Some concerns have been expressed about the size of Fortran 90, as well as the complex web of restrictions or cautions resulting from the necessity to let old and new features coexist. But, emergence of several compilers shows that parsing and implementing the new language is indeed possible.

Where a great number of restrictions exist, it clearly signals that the programmer should attempt to replace old features entirely in the function or module being newly programmed. But the language is fully consistent and can be used robustly.

The upshot is that every reason exists to learn about and start taking advantage of Fortran 90 features. There is no reason to hold back, save for concerns about the robustness and optimization capabilities of the new compilers; these will probably not take long to fall into place.

Fortran 90 is now a standard, and one that code providers will be asked to conform to. In the United States, ANSI has declared Fortran 77 to still be a standard as well, but that is not the case internationally. Well-supported compilers will soon be available from any computer vendor who has a commitment to scientific and engineering communities.

Will My Code Still Work?

Yes. Standard conforming Fortran 77 programs are standard conforming Fortran 90 programs. So, existing code that adheres to the former standard will continue to work. Formal caveats are few:

REAL constants initializing a DOUBLE PRECISION variable in a DATA statement. Fortran 77 allowed more precision to be carried by the REAL constant than the REAL data type could hold in this circumstance. Fortran 90 is not so forgiving. So code the REAL constant with the appropriate DOUBLE PRECISION indicator (i.e., DATA D / 1.23d0 /).

NonCOMMON variables initialized in a DATA statement. A variable that is not in a common block, but which has been initialized in a DATA statement, always keeps its last value when the subprogram is called again, just as if a SAVE statement were used. The question of whether to SAVE the variable was left open in Fortran 77, but is clearly specified in Fortran 90.

User-written procedure conflicts with the name of a new intrinsic subprogram. Fortran 90 introduces seventy-five new intrinsics. The name of one of these new intrinsics might conflict with the name of a user-written procedure. One solution is to change the name of the user-written procedure. The other solution, leaving the user written procedure alone and declaring it EXTERNAL, has the disadvantage of sacrificing the use of the new Fortran 90 intrinsic for its intended purpose.

Informal problems could be more serious. Many programmers inherit code containing extensions added by compiler vendors, and do not always know what adheres to the standard and what does not. Some of the most popular extensions have been included in Fortran 90, in order to respond to pressure from the user community. Code containing these should port with minor syntax changes. Less popular extensions remain nonstandard.

Also, there is less likelihood of automatic data initialization and saving. For decades, programmers relied on the compiler to initialize local variables to zero or blank by default, and to preserve their values between subprogram calls. The new memory management flexibility offered in Fortran 90 puts pressure on compilers to use the stack for storage, thus eliminating this hidden service. The prudent course is to initialize all variables before they are referenced, and put in SAVE statements where the old values are needed again.

Existing Fortran programs should also be audited in regard to two categories. First, Fortran 90 creates a "deleted" category for any feature of the previous standard that does not appear in the new standard. This category is empty. However, it is likely that the next Fortran standard will "delete" some features carried over from Fortran 77, or even Fortran 90 features that turn out to be less useful.

Second, the Fortran 90 standard has a formal category—obsolescent—for features of the previous standard that should be avoided. Various reasons might land a feature in this category: better Fortran methods exist, poor programming practices have grown up around its use, etc. Less than a dozen features are declared obsolescent. The features are listed in Table 1-1.

Table 1-1: Obsolescent Features

Feature	Example
Arithmetic IF	`if (x), 100,200,300`
Alternate return from subroutine	`call sub (x,y,*400,*500)`
ASSIGN statement	`assign 600 to i`
Assigned FORMAT specifier	`assign 700 to i; write (6,i)`
Assigned GO TO statement	`assign 800 to i;` `  goto i,(800,900)`
DO loop control variables that are not integers	`do 1000,x=1.1,9.9`
DO loop not ending on CONTINUE	`do 1100,i=1,5;1100 x=x+1.0`
Branch to END IF from outside IF block	
H edit descriptor	`1h+ or 13hColumn Title`
PAUSE statement	`pause 1200 or` `pause 'Mount tape'`

Existing code containing any of these features should be rewritten to avoid them. They will compile, they will work, but they are prime candidates for being left out of the next Fortran standard.

Fortran 90 Statement Census

There are eighty-five statements in Fortran 90. All Fortran 77 statements are represented as well as new Fortran 90 statements. Most of the Fortran 77 statements are incorporated without change in Fortran 90. The remaining Fortran 77 statements are roughly split between those having undergone a minor change and those that have had some major change. A census of Fortran 90 statements using this classification follows.

26   Fortran 90 statements have not changed from Fortran 77

8   Fortran 90 statements have a minor change from Fortran 77

12   Fortran 90 statements have a major change from Fortran 77

38   Fortran 90 statements are entirely new

This classification scheme is visual; it is not an assessment of the power or functionality of each change or new feature. The classification allows a Fortran programmer to focus on those statements that have changed and recognize new statements. It reflects the differences in syntax between a Fortran 77 statement and its Fortran 90 counterpart. All Fortran 90 statements are classified according to this scheme in Table 1-2 through Table 1-5.

Table 1-2: Statements Classified By Degree of Change in Fortran 90

Statement	Remark
ASSIGN	Declared obsolescent
BACKSPACE	
BLOCK DATA	
CLOSE	
COMMON	
CONTINUE	
DATA	
END	
END IF	
ENDFILE	
EQUIVALENCE	
EXTERNAL	
GO TO (ASSIGNED)	Declared obsolescent
GO TO (COMPUTED)	
GO TO (UNCONDITIONAL)	
IF (ARITHMETIC)	Declared obsolescent
IF (LOGICAL)	
INTRINSIC	
PAUSE	Declared obsolescent
PARAMETER	

Table 1-2: Statements Classified By Degree of Change in Fortran 90 (Continued)

Statement	Remark
PRINT	
PROGRAM	
RETURN	
REWIND	
SAVE	
STOP	

Table 1-3: Minor Differences From Older Fortran Statements

Statement	Remark	Page
ELSE	Can use name of IF construct	15
ELSE IF	Can use name of IF construct	15
ENTRY	RESULT name	-
FORMAT	Binary, octal, hex, engineering, generic G	205,209
FUNCTION	RECURSIVE, RESULT name	102
IF... THEN	Can give name to IF construct	15
IMPLICIT	IMPLICIT NONE added	13
SUBROUTINE	RECURSIVE	103

Table 1-4: Major Differences From Older Fortran Statements

Statement	Remark	Page
CALL	Keywords in argument list	100
CHARACTER	Select precision, initialization in type statement	221
COMPLEX	Select precision, initialization in type statement	217
DIMENSION	Undeclared array limits	-
DO	Named, DO WHILE, CYCLE, EXIT	15
DOUBLE PRECISION	Select precision, initialization in type statement	217
INQUIRE	Size RECL, file POSITION	188
INTEGER	Select precision, initialization in type statement	216
LOGICAL	Select precision, initialization in type statement	281
OPEN	READONLY, PAD, STATUS=REPLACE	176

Table 1-4: Major Differences From Older Fortran Statements (Continued)

Statement	Remark	Page
READ	Nonadvancing input, end-of-record, namelist	190 191 202
REAL	Select precision, initialization in type statement	217
WRITE	Nonadvancing output, namelist	194 202

Table 1-5: New Fortran Statements

Statement	Remark	Page
ALLOCATABLE	Declare dynamic arrays allocatable	138
ALLOCATE	Allocate array	139
CASE	SELECT structure element	15
CASE DEFAULT	SELECT structure element	15
CONTAINS	Mark procedures internal to subprogram or module	122
CYCLE	DO structure element	15
DEALLOCATE	Deallocate allocatable arrays and pointers	140
ELSEWHERE	WHERE structure element	47
END BLOCK DATA	Concludes BLOCK DATA	-
END DO	Concludes DO	15
END FUNCTION	Concludes FUNCTION	104
END INTERFACE	Concludes INTERFACE	89
END MODULE	Concludes MODULE	122
END PROGRAM	Concludes PROGRAM	88
END SELECT	Concludes SELECT	15
END SUBROUTINE	Concludes SUBROUTINE	90
END TYPE	Concludes TYPE	67
END WHERE	Concludes WHERE	47
EXIT	DO structure element	15
INCLUDE	Insert source code from external file	90
INTENT	Classify arguments	89
INTERFACE	Define procedure interface	89
INTERFACE ASSIGNMENT	Redefine =	113

Table 1-5: New Fortran Statements (Continued)

Statement	Remark	Page
INTERFACE OPERATOR	Define new or redefine intrinsic operators	108
MODULE	Package data and subprograms	122
MODULE PROCEDURE	Identify subprogram for defined operator	132
NAMELIST	Flexible input/output specification	199
NULLIFY	Disassociate pointer	143
OPTIONAL	Classification of subprogram arguments	100
POINTER	Data type qualifier	142
PRIVATE	Restrict data access	125
PUBLIC	Expand data access	125
SELECT CASE	Decision/branch construct	15
SEQUENCE	Data alignment declaration	81
TARGET	Target of pointer	142
TYPE	User-defined data structure	67
USE	Declare access to module data and/or subprogram	122
WHERE	Array decision construct	47

Look and Feel: Programming Logistics

Fortran 90 programs can look very different from earlier Fortran programs. Most of these differences arise from new statements, new decision structures, new instrinsic functions, etc. Indeed, such differences are the subject of this entire book. But there are variations on a smaller, mechanical scale including additions to the character set, synonyms for the relational operators, name length, free format source code, and the incorporation of external source code files.

Fortran 90 recognizes all the letters, digits, and special characters from Fortran 77. However, the underscore character, _, is introduced and permitted in symbolic names (i.e., names for constants, constructs, subprograms, types, and variables). A few new special characters are added but are not allowed in symbolic names, these are listed in Table 1-6.

Table 1-6: New Characters

Symbol	Name	Purpose
!	Exclamation mark	Sets off a comment from executable code
"	Double quotation mark	Delimits a character constant
%	Percent sign	Separates components in a derived type
&	Ampersand	Signals that continuation line will follow
;	Semicolon	Allows multiple statements to appear on one line of source code
<	Less than symbol	Used in synonyms for some relational operators
>	Greater than symbol	Used in synonyms for some relational operators
?	Question mark	May appear in source code but has no special use, just like the dollar sign in Fortran 77

Fortran 90 establishes synonyms for relational operators. The traditional relational operators listed in Table 1-7 can also be written symbolically.

Table 1-7: Symbols for Relational Operators

Relational Operator	New Symbolic Representation
.EQ.	==
.NE.	/=
.LT.	<
.LE.	<=
.GT.	>
.GE.	>=

Both forms of relational operators can be intermingled in the same source code file. These synonyms ease the tangled typing necessary to surround traditional relational operators with periods.

Fortran 90 increases the maximum length of variable and subprogram names from 6 to 31 characters. Furthermore, the underscore can now be used in variable and subprogram names, which increases program clarity.

New Source Form

Fortran 90 introduces free form source code. When this form is used, the traditional interpretation of column one for comments, column six for continuation lines, and columns seven through 72 for code, no longer applies. A line of source code can now be 132 characters long rather than limited to 72 characters. Up to 39 continuation lies can extend a line of source code instead of the old limit of 19 continuation lines. New continuation lines are signalled on the initial line rather than on the continuation line. Traditionally, a mark in column six showed that a line of source code was a continuation line.

```
    if ( i .ge. 123 .and.
  -     i .le. 456      ) j = 789
```

But, Fortran 90 free form source code signals a continuation line by placing an ampersand on the initial line

```
    if ( i .ge. 123 .and.              &
         i .le. 456      ) j = 789
```

Each individual source code file must conform to either the new free form or the traditional fixed form; the two styles can not be mixed in a single source code file.

In either the fixed or free format, comments are preceded by an exclamation point and can appear anywhere on a line of source code, such as:

```
! Compute factorial.
  factorial = product ( (/ ( k, k = 2, n ) /) ! OVERFLOW alert
```

Of course, in fixed format source, comments are still recognized by either a C or c in the first column. Finally, in both fixed and free modes, multiple statements can be packed on a single line of source code as:

```
    total = 0.0; do i = 1, 10, 1; total = total + x(i); end do
```

Fortran 90 permits a source code stored in one file to be incorporated into another file through the popular INCLUDE statement. Since the source form to be used by the including file might not be known when the included file is written, the included one should adhere to all restrictions of both source forms. Thus, included files should be written following this strategy:

1. Limit statement labels to columns one through five.

2. Confine code in columns seven through 72.

3. Use only the exclamation point as the comment indicator.

4. Begin a comment anywhere except in column six.

5. Place an ampersand in column 73 of the initial and each continued line.

6. Place an ampersand in column six of each continuation line.

7. Pay close attention to significant blanks.

This book has stayed true to the fixed format style. Fixed format was chosen for two reasons. First, the focus of this book is on the features of Fortran 90 rather than on the mechanics of program design or style. Keeping to a familiar format seemed to suite that focus because it did not introduce a stylistic element that could prove a distraction. Second, the typographic convention of this book limits each line of source code to no more than sixty-seven characters. Any benefits of a wide line for source code would be lost in that restricted space.

What Can Fortran 90 Do?

Presenting small snippets of code is a good way to introduce the diversity of Fortran 90's new features. None of the following code fragments stand alone as an application, and few real programs would concentrate on just one new feature, but these tiny examples show how far Fortran has evolved.

Declaring All Variables: IMPLICIT NONE

This well-worn extension, which brings Fortran into the ranks of modern languages so far as type-checking goes, has now finally been standardized. If the following statement,

```
IMPLICIT NONE
```

appears at the beginning of a program unit, all variables referenced in the program unit must be declared. The statement eliminates a large range of trivial but dangerous errors, and is highly recommended.

Programming Mechanics: Including Files and Long Names

A familiar extension to Fortran is the ability to incorporate one source code file into another. A classic use of this extension is to document which file unit numbers refer to the terminal or specific files:

```
integer :: crtin  = 5
integer :: crtout = 6
```

so that a program can refer to them by variables rather than constants:

```
      include 'units_include.f'
      write ( crtout,100 ) crtin, crtout
100   format ( 1H , 'Keyboard and display units:', 2i2 )
```

This bit of code displays:

```
Keyboard and display units: 5 6
```

The ability to include one file into another is so prevalent that it has sometimes been wrongly assumed to have been part of the ANSI standard leading to Fortran 77. Although it was part of MIL-STD-1753, it is only now part of the new ANSI standard.

Self-documenting Programs: Long Names

Long variable and subprogram names both help and hurt the goal of readable code. They certainly improve the "self documenting" aspect of source code,

```
      relative_humidity_prior_to_dawn = 37.0
      print 100, relative_humidity_prior_to_dawn
100   format ( '6:00 AM humidity was ', f4.1, '%' )
```

which displays:

```
6:00 AM humidity was 37.0%
```

But, carried to extremes, they bloat a program and make it hard to understand. Fortran 90's free form source code format with lines up to 132 characters seems to pair naturally with long variable and subprogram names.

Transfer of Control: DO, IF, and CASE

The mainstay of Fortran processing constructs, the DO loop, has benefitted from two major advances in Fortran 90. Finally, a "do while" syntax is permitted.

```
io_stat = 0
do while ( io_status .eq. 0 )
   read ( 5,*, iostat=io_status ) x
end do
```

DO loops also can cycle and exit early, and both DO loops and the IF construct can carry labels.

```
integer :: decades = 0
integer :: year    = 0
age: do
        year = year + 1
        if (    year      > 130 ) exit age        !END LOOP
        life_span: if ( mod(year,10) /=  0 ) then
                        cycle age                  ! ITERATE
                    else
                        decades = decades + 1
        end if life_span
end do age
```

All three of these changes to the venerable Fortran DO loop help document the flow of control. Another typical Fortran extension, a CASE construct, has also been standardized.

```
character ( len = 7 ) prime
number = 7
select case ( number )
        case ( :1 )                         ! ANYTHING <=  1
            prime = 'unknown'
        case ( 10: )                        ! ANYTHING >= 10
            prime = 'unknown'
        case ( 3, 5, 7 )
            prime = 'yes'
        case default
            prime = 'no'
end select
print 100, number, prime
100   format ( 'Is the number ', i1, ' prime? ', a )
```

The output is:

```
Is the number 7 prime? yes
```

Array Handling: Construction, Manipulation, and Dynamic Sizing

Array handling is significantly enhanced in Fortran 90. Once an array is declared, Fortran 90 provides many array-oriented intrinsics. Just a few of these new intrinsics are enough to extract the diagonal from an array.

```
      real, dimension(3,3) :: array
      real, dimension( 3 ) :: diagonal
      real, dimension( 9 ) :: linear
      array = reshape ( (/ 1,2,3,4,5,6,7,8,9 /), (/ 3,3 /) )
      print 100, transpose ( array )
100   format ( 'Array row 1 ', 3f5.2
    -         / 'Array row 2 ', 3f5.2
    -         / 'Array row 3 ', 3f5.2 )
      linear   = pack    ( array, .TRUE. )
      diagonal = linear ( 1:9:4 )
      print 200, diagonal
200   format ( / '.. diagonal ', 3f5.2 )
```

New Fortran 90 intrinsics populate the array with RESHAPE, transpose it with TRANSPOSE, and collapse it into a one dimensional vector with PACK.

```
      Array row 1  1.00 4.00 7.00
      Array row 2  2.00 5.00 8.00
      Array row 3  3.00 6.00 9.00

      .. diagonal  1.00 5.00 9.00
```

The diagonal is isolated by stepping through the single dimension vector from the lower to upper limits of the subscript with a stride that follows the original array's main diagonal.

Vector subscripts are another way to isolate parts of matrix. Here, a list of subscripts, VECTOR, is used to reference an array by columns and by rows.

```
      real,    dimension(3,3) :: matrix
      integer, dimension( 3 ) :: vector = (/ 1, 2, 3 /)
      matrix = reshape ( (/ 1,2,3,4,5,6,7,8,9 /), (/ 3,3 /) )
      print 100, transpose ( matrix )
100   format ( 'Matrix row 1 ', 3f5.2
    -         / 'Matrix row 2 ', 3f5.2
    -         / 'Matrix row 3 ', 3f5.2 )
      print 200
200   format ( ' ' )
      do j = 1, 3, 1
        print 300, j, matrix ( vector, j )
300     format ( '... column', i2, ' ', 3f5.2 )
      end do
      print 200
```

```
      do i = 1, 3, 1
        print 400, i, matrix ( i, vector )
400     format ( '...... row', i2, ' ', 3f5.2 )
      end do

      Matrix row 1  1.00 4.00 7.00
      Matrix row 2  2.00 5.00 8.00
      Matrix row 3  3.00 6.00 9.00
```

Here by columns:

```
      ... column 1  1.00 2.00 3.00
      ... column 2  4.00 5.00 6.00
      ... column 3  7.00 8.00 9.00
```

And here by rows:

```
      ...... row 1  1.00 4.00 7.00
      ...... row 2  2.00 5.00 8.00
      ...... row 3  3.00 6.00 9.00
```

Fortran 90 has plenty of intrinsics to manipulate whole arrays. Just as simply as the diagonal was extracted, other intrinsics make short work of computing an average.

```
      real                   :: average
      integer                :: n
      integer, dimension(3) :: scores = (/ 81, 92, 79 /)
      integer                :: total
      n       = size ( scores )    ! NUMBER OF ELEMENTS IN SCORES
      total   = sum ( scores )
      average = real ( total  ) / real ( n )
      print 100, scores, total, average
100   format ( 'Sum of {',3i3,' } is ',i3,' ... average = ',f4.1
```

The result is:

```
      Sum of { 81 92 79 } is 252 ... average = 84.0
```

Using these and other array-oriented intrinsics in combination can create very powerful, compact programming tools.

Since Fortran was invented, arrays have always had fixed sizes. Now, an array's size can be set at run time.

```
      integer                       :: length = 99
      real, dimension (:), allocatable :: list
      integer                       :: status
100   continue
      write ( 6,200,advance='NO' )
200   format ( 'Enter length of list (1 to 99): ' )
      read (5,*,err=100) length
      if ( length .lt.  1 .or.
```

```
      -      length .gt. 99      ) go to 100
      allocate ( list(length), stat=status ) ! CREATE ARRAY SPACE
      if ( status .ne. 0 ) then
            print *, "Can not allocate LIST!"
      else
            list(      1) = 1.2
            list(length) = 3.4
            print 300, list(1), length, list(length)
300         format ( 'Dynamic array (01) = ', f3.1,
      -                ' array (', i2.2, ') = ', f3.1 )
            deallocate ( list )
      end if
```

Asking the user to enter the length of the list:

```
Enter length of list (1 to 99): 50
```

yields the following display:

```
Dynamic array (01) = 1.2 array (50) = 3.4
```

As with many runtime facilities, housekeeping is left up to the programmer. It is prudent to check the status of the array with the ALLOCATE statement when creating the array and to DEALLOCATE the array at the end of the subprogram.

User-Defined Data Structures: Derived Types

Derived types are Fortran 90's implementation of a data structure. Fortran programmers can now declare an object containing several data types. Thus, information on elements in the periodic table can be contained in a derived type:

```
type mendeleyev
      character (len=32 ) :: name
      real                :: atomic_weight
end  type mendeleyev
type    ( mendeleyev )      periodic_table(106)
periodic_table(92) = mendeleyev ( 'uranium', 238.03 )
print 100, periodic_table(92)
100   format ( 'Element ', a7, ' has an atomic weight of ', f6.2)
```

and then displayed.

```
Element uranium has an atomic weight of 238.03
```

All or part of a derived type can be referenced in a single stroke irrespective of the data types contained in it.

Explicit Subprogram Calling Conventions

Calling conventions for subprograms can now be made explicit. Variables that are input to or output from a subprogram can be defined in a separate INTERFACE block to establish a subprogram prototype.

```
interface
   subroutine convert ( a_unit, b_unit, rate, new_rate )
      real,    intent (in)              :: a_unit
      real,    intent (out)             :: b_unit
      real,    intent (in)              :: rate
      integer, intent (in), optional :: new_rate
   end subroutine convert
end interface
```

The distinction between input and output arguments can be checked by a Fortran 90 compiler to enforce the planned use of the arguments.

When a subprogram is called, some arguments can be OPTIONAL and appear only in those calls that need them. They are identified by user-defined keywords in a style similar to the keywords in the standard CLOSE, INQUIRE, and OPEN statements.

```
program change
call convert ( 2.97, value, 0.94                     )
call convert ( 2.77, value, 0.94                     )
call convert ( 2.83, value, 1.02, new_rate = 1 )
call convert ( 2.89, value, 1.02                     )
end program change
```

The receiving program can even detect when an OPTIONAL argument is present:

```
    subroutine convert ( a_unit, b_unit, rate, new_rate )
    real,    intent (in)              :: a_unit
    real,    intent (out)             :: b_unit
    real,    intent (in)              :: rate
    integer, intent (in), optional :: new_rate
    b_unit = rate * a_unit
    print 100, a_unit, b_unit
100 format ( / f4.2, ' converted to ', f4.2 )
    if ( present ( new_rate ) ) print 200
200 format (   'NOTICE: new rate in effect!' )
    end subroutine convert
```

and take special programmatic action.

```
2.97 converted to 2.79

2.77 converted to 2.60
```

```
2.83 converted to 2.89
NOTICE: new rate in effect!

2.89 converted to 2.95
```

Cursor Control in the Prompt/Response Cycle

Prompting the user for input has always been awkward in Fortran. Now, the prompt can be displayed and the response read all on the same line.

```
        write ( 6,100,advance='no' )
100     format ( 1H , 'Enter temperature: ' )
        read  ( 5,200,advance='no',size=i ) degrees
200     format ( f4.1 )
        write ( 6,300 ) i, degrees
300     format ( 1H , 'OK ... ', i2.2, ' characters entered'
        -       / 1H , 'and temperature is ', f4.1 )
```

Furthermore, a count of characters in the user's response is automatically produced.

```
Enter temperature: 98.6
OK ... 04 characters entered
and temperature is 98.6
```

Binary, Octal, and Hexadecimal Formats and Constants

Fortran has always had a strong bias toward decimal numerals. Now, with new Fortran 90 edit descriptors, a single number:

```
        number = 345
        print 100, number, number, number, number
100     format ( i3, 'd ', b9, 'b ', o3, 'o ', z3, 'z' )
```

can be displayed in decimal, binary, octal, and hexadecimal:

```
345d 101011001b 531o 159z
```

Furthermore, variables can be initialized with constants in other bases in a DATA statement (i.e., B'101011001', O'531', or Z'159').

Parameters of Numeric Model Accessible

For pure numerical work, Fortran 90 allows programmers to query the parameters in the underlying model used to represent numbers. New intrinsics are provided, such as:

```
      print 100, precision ( x ), huge ( i )
100   format ( 'Numeric models: REAL precision is ',i1, ' digits'
      -         / '                   largest INTEGER = ', i10 )
```

to query the limits of numeric data types.

```
Numeric models: REAL precision is 6 digits
                largest INTEGER = 2147483647
```

These intriniscs will help a programmer tailor code to Fortran 90 implementations on particular computer systems.

Attributes in Type Declarations

Because of the many new features that variables can take on—ALLOCAT-ABLE, INTENT, and so on—a new syntax for type declarations has been added to the language. The type can be followed by an attribute list, separated by commas and terminated by a double colon:

```
real, allocatable, dimension(3,3) :: array
```

This allows all relevant information about a variable to be declared in one statement. Attributes include ALLOCATABLE, DIMENSION, EXTERNAL, INTENT, INTRINSIC, OPTIONAL, PARAMETER, POINTER, SAVE, and TARGET.

The length of CHARACTER variables can also be declared with a LEN selector instead of the old asterisk convention. Thus, the following statement declares a 32-character variable:

```
character (len=32 ) :: name
```

The Focus of This Book

From the previous whirlwind tour it might be easy to get the impression that most of Fortran 90's new features are simple conveniences. Yes, conveniences abound, but the new language also implies new habits in problem-solving. The deeper changes in programming practice is what the rest of this book will focus on.

Many old problems that were imperfectly solved by Fortran 77 or vendor extensions can now be addressed in a more satisfactory way. Each classic area of difficulty—operating on array sections, maintaining related data of different types, and so on—receives a chapter or a section in this book.

By concentrating on the areas that require new thinking as well as new syntax, this book chooses to spend more time on some features than others. For instance, flow control (such as the new DO-loop features) and file handling receive less attention than array operations and memory management. However, every new feature is touched on somewhere. The index can help you find particular features.

2

Array Operations

Arrays are the only data structure recognized in Fortran 77. Being one of a kind, they are put to ingenious uses. Most programs will manage linear lists of numbers as well as row-and-column oriented tables. More adventurous programs might consolidate several data types into an array of character strings and access individual elements as an internal file using READ and WRITE statements. And on the furthest edge of array manipulation, context-sensitive runtime FORMATs may be retrieved from arrays according to a program's needs. In every case, handling of arrays is limited. Two major limitations are that arrays contain only a single data type and that arrays can be referenced in just two ways: as the whole array or by individual elements. It is exactly these limitations that Fortran 90 overcomes.

Three areas of array operations are new. First, Fortran 90 permits an array to be submitted to almost all operations that were previously restricted to single data elements. In conjunction with this entirely new programming model involving whole arrays, Fortran 90 offers great plasticity in sizing and shaping arrays. Familiar Fortran 77 sequences of:

```
      real      sums
      dimension sums(2,3)
      do 200 j = 1, 3
         do 100 i = 1, 2
            sums(i,j) = 0.0
100      continue
200   continue
```

can be replaced with the single clear, concise Fortran 90 statement:

```
      real, dimension (2,3) :: sums = 0.0
```

Second, functions now can return an array. Many intrinsic functions work if the argument is a scalar, a vector, or a multi-dimensional array.

```
print *, sin ( angles )
```

This works no matter what shape ANGLES might be. Other Fortran 90 intrinsics perform array reduction operations that eliminate the need for hand-crafted DO loops. Even user-written functions can be created to handle arrays.

This facility of Fortran 90 almost blurs the line between subroutines and functions. Functions used to be thought of as producing a single, scalar variable. It used to be thought that subroutines affected one or more scalar or array arguments. Now, this distinction is not so clear. Programmers are free to choose either model depending on programming design and style.

Third, the programming tyranny of referring to either an entire array or to individual elements is over. Fortran 90 array sections let the programmer isolate parts of an array, such as:

```
real, dimension ( 2,3 ) :: array
real, dimension (   3 ) :: first_row
real, dimension ( 2   ) :: last_column
first_row(:)   = array(1,:)
last_column(:) = array(:,3)
```

The results are shown in Figure 2-1.

These array sections are also valuable in passing slices of an array to subprograms, such as:

```
program slice
real, dimension ( 2,3 ) :: array
.
.
.
call list ( array(1,:) )
.
.
.
end program slice
subroutine list ( vector )
real, dimension ( 3 ) :: vector
```

.
.
.
```
end subroutine list
```

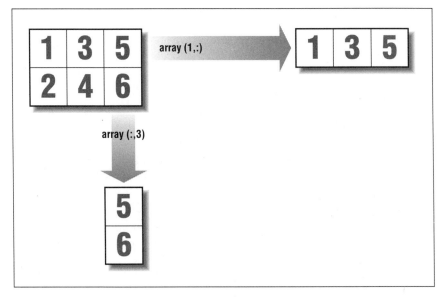

Figure 2-1: Array sections

Additional features support even more specific selections of elements, by location (vector subscript) or by value (logical masks and the WHERE statement).

All three areas of Fortran 90 array operations receive attention in this chapter and are demonstrated in several full length programs and some short code fragments. Later chapters examine two other powerful features that affect array handling: derived types (user-defined data structures) and the ability to allocate the size of an array dynamically (i.e., at run time).

Aggregate Array Operations

Arrays come in all sizes and shapes. Size refers to the total number of array elements measured for the entire array, or along a particular array dimension. Shape refers to the number of elements along each dimension of an array. In addition, the number of dimensions is called the array's rank. For instance, a vector has rank 1, while a matrix has rank 2.

Fortran 77 and 90 have the same upper limit—seven—for the rank of an array. Fortran 90 offers intrinsics to find out the size and shape of an array:

```
real,     dimension ( -3:4, -5:6 ) :: array
integer, dimension ( 2 )           :: array_lower
integer, dimension ( 2 )           :: array_shape
integer                            :: array_size
integer, dimension ( 2 )           :: array_upper
array_shape = shape  ( array )
array_size  = size   ( array )
array_lower = lbound ( array )
array_upper = ubound ( array )
```

SHAPE will set ARRAY_SHAPE to {8,12} because ARRAY has two dimensions, the first of which contains eight elements, and the second twelve elements. ARRAY_SIZE results from multiplying together the number of elements in both dimension: 8 times 12 is 96. In general, SIZE is the product of mutiplying each element in the vector returned by SHAPE. Whereas SHAPE returns the number of elements per dimension, the two "bounds" intrinsics—LBOUND and UBOUND—return limits of each dimension: ARRAY_LOWER is {-3,-5} and ARRAY_UPPER is {4,6}.

This information can be used in novel ways including customizing runtime FORMAT statements to "fit" an array or computing the memory requirements of an array. Later sections will show how arrays can be pushed and pulled into quite a variety of shapes to fit the task at hand.

Array Initialization

Arrays can be initialized and assigned values concisely in Fortran 90. When declared, an array can be given an initial value:

```
real, dimension ( 3 ) :: array = 0.0
```

This zeros all three elements of ARRAY in a single stroke. Two full colons are used to separate declaration attributes (i.e., REAL, DIMENSION, etc.) from the variable name.

Alternatively, the array could be set to a regular sequence of values such as the even numbers, either explicitly:

```
real, dimension ( 3 ) :: array = (/ 2.0, 4.0, 6.0 /)
```

or using one of the following implied DO-loop array constructors:

```
real, dimension ( 3 ) :: array = (/ ( 2 * i, i = 1, 3 ) /)
```

or

```
real, dimension ( 3 ) :: array = (/ ( i, i = 2, 6, 2 ) /)
```

The syntax is complicated enough to deserve some parsing here. First all specifications of constants in vectors must be enclosed in the "(/" and "/)" delimiters. Within these, constants can appear as a single list or as an implied DO-loop, a construction familiar to programmers from DATA, READ, or WRITE statements.

These statements can be thought of as a compact combination of type declaration, DIMENSION, and DATA statements all rolled up into one. In either case, ARRAY could then be converted to the odd numbers by an equation:

```
array = array - 1.0
```

or by either of these assignment statements:

```
array = (/ 1.0, 3.0, 5.0 /)
array = (/ ( i, i = 1, 5, 2 ) /)
```

or even set to a scalar:

```
array = 9.0
```

These last three examples highlight how scalars and arrays can be mixed in equations and assignments. This flexibility is a boon to certain application development areas (i.e., operations research, parallelizing algorithms, etc.).

Array Sections

Fortran 90 also allows access to array sections. Array sections select part of an array consisting of regularly spaced array elements taken parallel to the dimensions of the source array.

Regular spacing means that a repetitive selection of elements from some dimensions are drawn out of the source array and placed into the target array. Regular spacing also requires that the sequence of dimensions in the source and the target remain the same. So, if the first five elements were extracted from the first column of a target array, then those same five elements need to be extracted from other selected columns. Array sections require that the starting and stopping be the same along each dimension. It rules out diagonals as boundaries to the sections.

Array section syntax is very similar to accessing groups of characters in a
string. Recall that Fortran uses the full colon (:) to mark character substrings
such as:

```
character*12 string
string = 'alphanumeric'
print *, string(:5), '(', string(5:7), ')', string(6:)
```

which displays:

```
alpha(anu)numeric
```

Fortran 90 uses this same syntax with arrays:

```
integer, dimension ( 5,5 ) :: array
integer, dimension ( 3,3 ) :: array_interior
integer, dimension ( 5   ) :: array_left_column
integer, dimension (   5 ) :: array_top_row
integer, dimension (   5 ) :: diagonal
integer, dimension ( 25 ) :: linear
array_left_column = array(:,5)
array_interior    = array(2:4,2:4)
array_top_row     = array(1,:)
linear            = pack ( array, .TRUE. )
diagonal          = linear ( 1:25:6 )
```

Extracting the diagonal of a matrix poses a challenge, because the desired
elements are regularly spaced, but parallel to the edges of the matrix. So, a
special work-around must be used. The PACK instrinsic collapses ARRAY
into a vector called LINEAR. This is done so that the main diagonal of
ARRAY can be itemized by seeking every sixth element of the LINEAR
vector. Using a triplet for the array section of DIAGONAL extracts the
desired elements.

If ARRAY was initialized from 1 to 25 in storage order, then the LINEAR and
DIAGONAL vectors would be as shown in Figure 2-2.

A Fortran 90 array index triplet is comprised of the lower and upper range
of array indices to be affected and the "stride" or quantum by which the
array should be traversed. Here, the syntax of (1:25:6) sets the lower and
upper index limits and the stride across the single dimension of LINEAR. As
such, it can be interpreted as an implied DO-loop such as (I,I=1,25,6). Note
that triplets are valid in higher dimensioned arrays. For example, if OTHER
is an array declared as a 4-by-4 matrix, then a 2-by-2 matrix, EVERY, could
be created containing only the odd rows and columns of OTHER using the
statement EVERY = OTHER (1:4:2,1:4:2).

This brief sample demonstrates how Fortran 90 programs can extract
sections of an array—a row, a column, or a plane—by "sliding" an adjust-

able window over the original array and specifying the size and shape of the view.

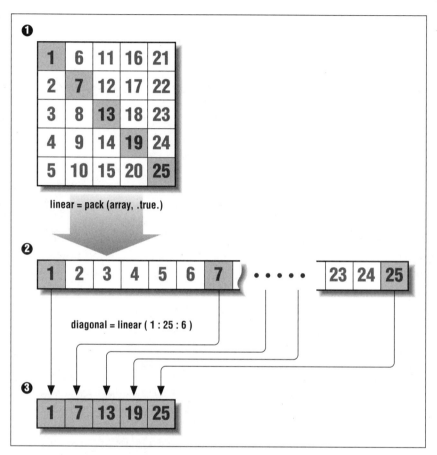

Figure 2-2: Extracting the diagonal from an array

Vector Subscripts

Relaxing the regularity required of array sections, vector subscripts allow elements to be extracted in any order. An array can be turned topsy-turvey with vector subscripts:

```
program topsyturvey
integer, dimension ( 3, 3  ) :: array
integer, dimension ( 3     ) :: rows    = (/ 3, 2, 1 /)
integer, dimension (   3   ) :: columns = (/ 3, 2, 1 /)
array = reshape ( (/ 1,4,7,2,5,8,3,6,9 /), (/ 3,3 /) )
do i = 1, 3, 1
```

```
    print *, ( array(i,j), j = 1, 3 )
  end do
  array = array(rows,columns)
  print *, " "
  do i = 1, 3, 1
    print *, ( array(i,j), j = 1, 3 )
  end do
end program
```

This will display the array right-side up and then both up-side down and inside-out as:

```
1 2 3
4 5 6
7 8 9

9 8 7
6 5 4
3 2 1
```

The RESHAPE intrinsic helps to initialize the base array. Here, a vector containing the first nine whole numbers is structured into a 3-by-3 array. RESHAPE works in a fashion similar to reading an entire array in one statement. In the same sense that a READ statement would fill an array in array element order, so will the RESHAPE command. If ARRAY was brought in from a file, a statement like

```
read (5,* ) array
```

would grab the first nine elements and store them in ARRAY(1,1), ARRAY(2,1), ARRAY(3,1), ARRAY(1,2), ..., ARRAY(3,3). RESHAPE works in the same way: the first element from RESHAPE's first argument is deposited in ARRAY(1,1), the second in ARRAY(2,1), the third in ARRAY(3,1), etc., in Fortran's standard "column-major" storage order. Figure 2-3 illustrates how the use of RESHAPE is accomplished.

Vector subscripts can reorder the elements if an array is required. When ARRAY(ROWS,COLUMNS) is written, it signals a new way in which to order ARRAY

```
ARRAY(ROWS(1),COLUMNS(1))    ->    ARRAY(3,3)    =    9
ARRAY(ROWS(1),COLUMNS(2))    ->    ARRAY(3,2)    =    8
    .
    .
    .
ARRAY(ROWS(3),COLUMNS(3))    ->    ARRAY(1,1)    =    1
```

This corresponds to the values in vectors ROWS and COLUMNS. Note that if the same value is used multiple times in the vector, the same row or

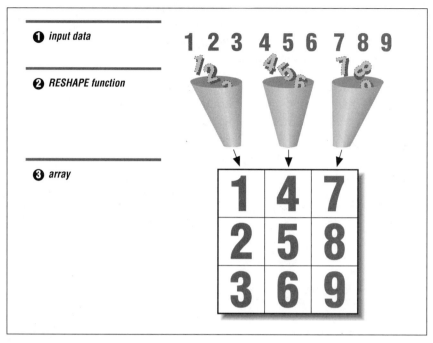

Figure 2-3: RESHAPE intrinsic

column can be harvested repeatedly. The statement assigning ARRAY to itself in a different order also shows that the left-hand and right-hand sides of an assignment statement are independent; changes on the left cannot contaminate the right. Thus, array aggregates make in-place operations easy. Creative use of array sections, vector subscripts, and the index triplet permits an array to be whittled down into a piece of virtually any size and shape.

While this section has introduced the possibilities of extracting array elements by location, Fortran 90 is equally versatile at extracting by value. Such features—masks and the WHERE statement—appear later in this chapter.

Shifting Elements Within Arrays

Fortran 90 introduces some shift functions, CSHIFT and EOSHIFT, to rearrange arrays. CSHIFT performs a circular shift and EOSHIFT performs an end off shift of one or more dimensions.

Circular shifting can be illustrated by a program to simulate the one-armed bandit at so many casinos. The program begins by initializing BANDIT, the analog of a "three disk" slot machine, with numbers from zero to nine:

```
program casino
integer, dimension (10,3) :: bandit
integer, dimension (3)    :: pull
real,    dimension (3)    :: spin
bandit(1:10,1) = (/ ( i, i = 0, 9 ) /)
bandit(1:10,2) = (/ ( i, i = 0, 9 ) /)
bandit(1:10,3) = (/ ( i, i = 0, 9 ) /)
print *, " "
print *, "Original BANDIT configuration"
print *, " "
do i = 1, 10, 1
   print *, ( bandit(i,j), j = 1, 3 )
end do
print *, " "
```

This displays the starting configuration.

```
Original BANDIT configuration

0 0 0
1 1 1
2 2 2
3 3 3
4 4 4
5 5 5
6 6 6
7 7 7
8 8 8
9 9 9
```

Then, draw three random numbers from the numbers 0 to 10 and randomly change their sign. The RANDOM_NUMBER function, described fully in Chapter 11, *Intrinsic Functions*, produces an array of numbers greater than or equal to zero but less than 1:

```
do k = 1, 1000, 1
   call random_number ( spin )
   pull = nint ( 10.0 * spin )
   call random_number ( spin )
   where ( spin .lt. 0.5 ) pull = -pull
```

The three numbers represent how much "spin" to put on each disk of the one-armed bandit using the CSHIFT intrinsic.

```
bandit = cshift ( bandit, pull, dim=1 )
```

Negative numbers push a column down, zero numbers leave a column alone, and positive numbers pull a column up. Figure 2-4 shows the machine. So, the first two spins

```
if ( k .le. 2 ) then
    print *, "After PULL number", k, "by", pull
    print *, " "
    do i = 1, 10, 1
        print *, ( bandit(i,j), j = 1, 3 )
    end do
    print *, " "
end if
```

look like this:

```
After PULL number 1 by 7 -8 4

7 2 4
8 3 5
9 4 6
0 5 7
1 6 8
2 7 9
3 8 0
4 9 1
5 0 2
6 1 3

After PULL number 2 by 8 -2 1

5 0 5
6 1 6
7 2 7
8 3 8
9 4 9
0 5 0
1 6 1
2 7 2
3 8 3
4 9 4
```

If the same number appears across any row, the program declares a winner.

```
        if ( bandit(1,1) .eq. bandit(1,2) .and.
   —         bandit(1,2) .eq. bandit(1,3)          ) then
            print *, "WINNER on spin", k, ":", bandit(1,:)
```

```
      end if
   end do
   print *, " "
   end program casino
```

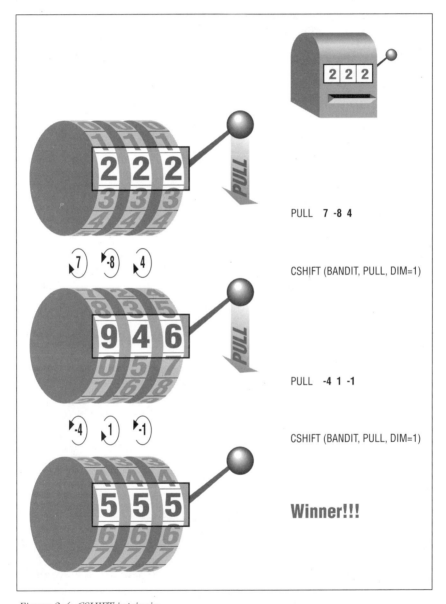

PULL **7 -8 4**

CSHIFT (BANDIT, PULL, DIM=1)

PULL **-4 1 -1**

CSHIFT (BANDIT, PULL, DIM=1)

Winner!!!

Figure 2-4: CSHIFT intrinsic

In one instance of a thousand random plays, the casino won 987 times and the lucky gambler won on these 13 plays:

```
WINNER on spin 164 : 6 6 6
WINNER on spin 174 : 9 9 9
WINNER on spin 468 : 6 6 6
WINNER on spin 547 : 4 4 4
WINNER on spin 663 : 1 1 1
WINNER on spin 757 : 7 7 7
WINNER on spin 781 : 4 4 4
WINNER on spin 810 : 3 3 3
WINNER on spin 854 : 9 9 9
WINNER on spin 865 : 8 8 8
WINNER on spin 866 : 0 0 0
WINNER on spin 902 : 6 6 6
WINNER on spin 906 : 1 1 1
```

Whereas CSHIFT rotates the values in a given dimension, EOSHIFT discards values shifted off the end of a dimension. In the following program, ENDOFF, the contents of ARRAY, once initialized

```
program endoff
integer, dimension ( 5 ) :: array = (/ 1, 2, 3, 4, 5 /)
print *,          array
```

and displayed:

```
1 2 3 4 5
```

can be shifted two places to the right and left with the EOSHIFT intrinsic

```
print *, eoshift ( array, -2 )
print *, eoshift ( array,  2 )
```

and back-filled with zeros, as shown in Figure 2-5.

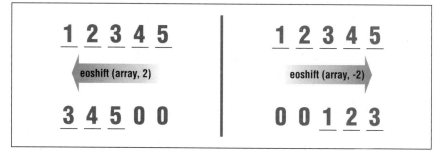

Figure 2-5: EOSHIFT intrinsic

However, sometimes it will be important to mark the positions vacated by the EOSHIFT intrinsic. So, its optional argument, BOUNDARY, can be used to set some value to show which elements have been affected:

```
print *, eoshift ( array, -2, BOUNDARY = 9 )
print *, eoshift ( array,  2, BOUNDARY = 9 )
end program endoff
```

This displays:

```
9 9 1 2 3
3 4 5 9 9
```

Passing Arrays of Unknown Size or Shape

Fortran programmers have developed a variety of techniques to hide array size from subprograms. This is motivated by a desire to build collections of library routines that can be brought to bear on any size of array. There are at least five different ways to pass arrays of unknown size to subprograms: three are inherited from Fortran 77 and the last two are new in Fortran 90. Benefits and drawbacks of each of these techniques are demonstrated in a program called UNKNOWN.

A simple 2-by-3 array called TABLE will be passed to a five different subprograms to illustrate each technique. Initially, TABLE is declared through

```
program unknown
integer, parameter      :: n      = 2
integer, parameter      :: m      = 3
integer, parameter      :: length = n * m
integer, dimension (n,m) :: table
```

and initialized through

```
table = reshape ( (/ 1,2,3,4,5,6 /), (/ n,m /) )
```

which molds the six-element vector into a 2-by-3 array. Then the following code:

```
      print 100, table
100   format ( 1H , 'MAIN PROGRAM           ', 3i5 )
```

would display TABLE as:

```
MAIN PROGRAM           1    2    3
MAIN PROGRAM           4    5    6
```

Traditional Techniques

Three traditional techniques of hiding the array shape are declaring the array as a single-element vector, declaring the array as a vector of unknown length with the * character, and explicitly declaring the array except for the last dimension.

First, a classic technique hides the shape of an array by passing it to a subprogram that redeclares it a vector of unit length. So, when UNKNOWN calls such a subprogram

```
      subroutine ones ( table, length )
      integer table(1), length
      do i = 1, length, 1
         table(i) = table(i) + 6
      end do
      print *, " "
      print 100, ( table(i), i = 1, length )
100   format ( 1H , 'ONES                    ', 3i5 )
      end subroutine ones
```

the entire array is neatly processed:

```
      ONES                     7    8    9
      ONES                    10   11   12
```

True to its objective, this technique hides the shape of the array from the subprogram. But to do anything with TABLE, the total number of elements must be available. Without LENGTH, neither the extent of the DO loop nor the implied-DO in the PRINT statement could be specified. As TABLE is declared in ONES, the subprogram doesn't know that the array is six elements long so it is illegal to rewrite the DO-loop into the more compact "TABLE = TABLE + 6" or to display all values as "PRINT 100, TABLE". None of Fortran 90's whole array constructions or instrinsics can be used in such a subroutine because TABLE in the main program and TABLE in subroutine ONES are the same size but not the same shape.

Second, a related technique is to pass the array to a vector of unknown length. Note that the Fortran 77 standard does not cover arrays declared as a vector of length one. It does permit the use of (*) to create an assumed size array. When UNKNOWN calls such a subprogram in a statement like CALL STAR (TABLE, LENGTH):

```
      subroutine star ( table, length )
      integer table(*), length
      do i = 1, length, 1
         table(i) = table(i) + 6
      end do
```

```
      print *, " "
      print 100, ( table(i), i = 1, length )
100   format ( 1H , 'STAR                    ', 3i5 )
      end subroutine star
```

the program can again treat each elements in storage order:

```
STAR                    13   14   15
STAR                    16   17   18
```

All of the comments made for the subroutine ONES apply here: the array's shape is hidden, but none of Fortran 90's array operators are available.

Third, shape can be reintroduced, but the ultimate size can be left unspecified. These assumed size arrays are declared with explicit size in all dimensions but the last which is unlimited. Calling such a subprogram:

```
      subroutine asize ( table, length, n )
      integer table(n,*), length
      k = length / n
      do j = 1, k, 1
         do i = 1, n, 1
            table(i,j) = table(i,j) + 6
         end do
      end do
      print *, " "
      print 100, ( ( table(i,j), i = 1, n ), j = 1, k )
100   format ( 1H , 'ASSUMED SIZE            ', 3i5 )
      end subroutine asize
```

produces

```
ASIZE                   19   20   21
ASIZE                   22   23   24
```

All of the restrictions discussed for the techniques exhibited by ONES and STAR still apply. One small advantage of this technique is that it permits the use of Fortran 90's LBOUND, UBOUND, and SIZE intrinsic functions to query the range of indices and number of elements in each explicitly declared dimension. For instance, UBOUND(TABLE,DIM=1) would show that the upper bound for the first dimension of TABLE is 2.

Fortran 90 Assumed Shape Arrays

Two related techniques are introduced in Fortran 90 to hide the size and shape of an array from a subprogram. The choice depends entirely on whether the subprogram is internal or external.

A new Fortran 90 construct is the internal subprogram. It easily supports varying array shapes. The interface is implicit between the caller and the internal subprogram. Unlike ONES and STAR, arrays in the internal subprogram must always have the same number of dimensions, but any dimension can have any number of elements. The CONTAINS statement signals the beginning of an internal subprogram, INSIDE, that uses very compact array operations:

```
      program unknown
      .
      .
      .
      call inside ( table )
      .
      .
      .
      contains
        subroutine inside ( table )
        integer, dimension (:,:) :: table
        table = table + 6
        print *, " "
        print 100, table
100     format ( 1H , 'ASSUMED SHAPE (internal)  ', 3i5 )
        end subroutine inside
      end program unknown
```

the output is:

```
      ASSUMED SHAPE (internal)      25   26   27
      ASSUMED SHAPE (internal)      28   29   30
```

In this subprogram, the shape of TABLE is fixed as a matrix of rank 2 because it is declared within INSIDE with the same number of colons as the rank of the matrix. TABLE's size is inherited from the actual argument when INSIDE is called. As expected, all of Fortran 90's array manipulation tools are available.

For a more traditional external subprogram, the assumed shape technique requires another new Fortran 90 feature, an INTERFACE block. These blocks make the interface explicit between procedures.

```
      program unknown
      interface
        subroutine ashape ( table )
        integer, dimension ( :,: ) :: table
        end subroutine ashape
      end interface
      integer, parameter      :: n      = 2
```

```
          .
          .
          .
      call ashape ( table )
          .
          .
          .
      end program unknown

      subroutine ashape ( table )
      integer, dimension ( :,: ) :: table
      table = table + 6
      print *, " "
      print 100, table
100   format ( 1H , 'ASSUMED SHAPE (interface) ', 3i5 )
      end subroutine ashape

ASSUMED SHAPE (interface)    31   32   33
ASSUMED SHAPE (interface)    34   35   36
```

All the evidence clearly favors this last technique as the most flexible way to avoid specifying the array size in a general-purpose service subroutine. Its major advantage is that all of Fortran 90's array handling features are available. A small disadvantage is that it forces the programmer to declare an INTERFACE block in the calling program, but the mechanics of doing this are easy. INTERFACE blocks are discussed in Chapter 4, *Subroutines and Functions Revisited.*

Breaking the Dimension Mold

Surprisingly, subprograms can also be written to accept arrays of unknown shape. Trivial examples of this are treating a multi-dimensional array as a one-dimensional vector, as shown in subprograms ONES and STAR in the previous example. But the limits of these approaches were exposed: whole array references and all of Fortran 90's array manipulation features were sacrificed once an array's actual shape was cloaked.

Zero-sized Dimensions

Fortran 90 introduces enough array intrinsics to facilitate passing arrays of unknown shape and referring to that array in the subprogram. Basically, the concept is to pass the array along with information regarding its declaration (i.e., number of elements per dimension). This would be received by a subprogram that declares a comparable array with zero length for every undeclared original dimension. So, if an array is declared in the main program as MATRIX(2,3) then the subprogram would declare the dummy array as:

```
integer,dimension ( 2, 3, 0, 0, 0, 0, 0 ):: array
```

where the third through seventh dimensions have no size. Zero-sized objects were not prohibited in Fortran 77, but it takes the array intrinsics of Fortran 90 to put them to use.

Example: Computing Array Memory Requirements

A functional application of passing arrays of unknown shape is to calculate the memory requirements for an array. This may be useful for unusual uses involving dynamic allocation, discussed in Chapter 7, *Dynamic Memory Management.* Initially, the program MEMORY creates a three-dimensional array TABLE and ancillary arrays:

```
program memory
integer, dimension ( 7 )                  :: limits = 0
integer, dimension ( -12:34,-56:78,9 ) :: table
```

Then, the number of elements per dimension are found.

```
limits(1:size(shape(table))) = shape ( table )
print 200, "TABLE limits", limits
200   format ( a20, 7i6 )
```

This would display

```
TABLE limits    47   135    9    0    0    0    0
```

This code is a little complicated because the SHAPE intrinsic is aware of TABLE's rank. It returns a vector exactly three elements long corresponding to the three explicitly declared dimensions for TABLE. So, elements 1, 2, and 3 (i.e., SIZE(SHAPE(TABLE))) of LIMITS are set to {47,135,9}. Then the subroutine that computes memory requirements can be called with arguments TABLE and LIMITS.

```
call needs ( table, limits )
end program memory
```

This subroutine uses LIMITS, a seven-element vector defining the extent of each dimension of TABLE, to declare a new, seven-dimensional matrix called ARRAY as:

```
subroutine needs ( array, limits )
integer, dimension ( 7 )                  :: limits
integer, dimension ( limits(1), limits(2),
-          limits(3), limits(4), limits(5),
-          limits(6), limits(7)          ) :: array
```

The interface between MEMORY and NEEDS could have been designed in several ways. At the most basic level, seven integers could be passed indicating the extent of each dimension. At the most advanced level, a 2-by-7 array could be passed indicating the lower and upper ranges of indices for each dimension. In the end, a middle ground was chosen that of passing the seven-element LIMITS vector. Depending on how TABLE would be used in the subroutine, MEMORY and NEEDS could be modified to conform to any level of knowledge about TABLE's dimensions.

After declaring other working vectors and constants, subprogram NEEDS then determines the size of ARRAY along each individual axis:

```
      integer, dimension ( 7 )            :: axes
      real                                :: bytes
      integer                             :: dimensions
      integer                             :: elements
      real                                :: kilo=1024.0
      integer                             :: units
      axes = shape ( array )
      do i = 1, 7, 1
         if ( lbound(array,i) .eq. 1 .and.
    -         ubound(array,i) .eq. 0       ) axes(i) = 0
      end do
      print *, " "
      print 100, "ARRAY axes", axes
100   format ( a20, 7i6 )
```

It displays those sizes as:

```
ARRAY axes     47    135      9      0      0      0      0
```

Creating an array like AXES is redundant: it is identical to the LIMITS argument. AXES is created to illustrate the handling of zero sized arrays. Originally, the SHAPE intrinsic returns a seven-element vector into AXES that defines the number of elements in each dimension of ARRAY. However, if any array dimension is declared with zero size, then by definition, LBOUND and UBOUND will return one and zero, respectively. Using that fact, the subprogram forces AXES to record zero for any zero sized dimension. Computing the number of original dimensions of TABLE is accomplished through:

```
      dimensions = count ( axes.gt.0 )
      print 100, "ARRAY dimensions", dimensions
```

which displays:

```
ARRAY dimensions      3
```

Any logical mask can be used in the COUNT intrinsic. Here, the specific mask determines the number of positive elements of AXES, which corresponds to the number of non-zero sized dimensions of ARRAY. Tying together all the information known by this subprogram, a final calculation of memory requirement can be made.

```
        elements = product ( axes, MASK=axes.gt.0 )
        print 200, "ARRAY elements", elements
200     format ( a20, i12 )
        inquire ( iolength=units ) array ( axes(1), axes(2),
     —          axes(3), axes(4), axes(5), axes(6), axes(7) )
        print 100, "ARRAY storage unit", units
        bytes = float ( units * elements )
        print 300, "ARRAY needs KB", bytes / kilo
300     format ( a20, f12.5 )
        print 300, "ARRAY needs MB", bytes / ( kilo * kilo )
        end subroutine needs
```

The output is:

```
    ARRAY elements        57105
ARRAY storage unit    4
    ARRAY needs KB    223.06641
    ARRAY needs MB      0.21784
```

PRODUCT is a Fortran 90 intrinsic that multiplies together elements of an array. Individually, the computations of KB and MB memory needs are fairly straightforward, but they rely on knowing the memory requirements of an individual element of ARRAY. A new Fortran 90 feature of the INQUIRE statement calculates the number of implementation defined "units" it takes to store its argument in a unformatted, direct access file (see Chapter 8, *File Handling*). It is used here to determine the number of "units" required to store just one element—in fact, the ultimate, last element—of ARRAY.

This subprogram assumes that "unit" is synonymous with "byte" in order to assess the memory needs of ARRAY. Where that assumption is not warranted, an adjustment can be introduced into the calculation of BYTES. Although TABLE and ARRAY are declared as INTEGER in this example, the approach is independent of data type. It will work if both TABLE and ARRAY are declared of CHARACTER, COMPLEX, LOGICAL, or REAL data type.

Realistic Applications of Array Section Operations

Once a single array has been initialized, it can be used to populate other arrays through direct assignment or masked assignment. These masks can be logical tests, Fortran 90 intrinsics, or a selection of array subsets by narrowing a range of array indices.

Example: Climatic Conditions

Both direct and masked assignment method are demonstrated in the program CLIMATE, which reads in facts about the Earth and derives some interesting conclusions from them. It begins by establishing this set of arrays:

```
program climate
real,         dimension(18) :: area
real,         dimension(18) :: fahrenheit
character*1,  dimension(18) :: hemisphere
real,         dimension(18) :: land
integer,      dimension(18) :: latitude
integer,      dimension( 1) :: location
real,         dimension(18) :: temperature
```

Certain basic data about the earth are read from an input file:

```
open ( unit=5, file='climate.input' )
do i = 1, 18, 1
    read ( 5,100 ) latitude(i), land(i), temperature(i)
100 format ( i3, 1x, f5.0, 1x, f5.0 )
end do
```

Each of the eighteen rows corresponds to a ten degree band of latitude, as shown in Figure 2-6.

The input file contains three pieces of information: the LATITUDE band limits in degrees of latitude (i.e., -85 means from the South Pole to 80S, 5 means from the Equator to 10N, etc.); the fraction of the world's surface in that latitude that is LAND; and the average annual TEMPERATURE in degrees Celsius. These data are drawn from around page 109 of James C. G. Walker's fascinating book *Numerical Adventures with Geochemical Cycles* (1991, Oxford University Press, 183 pages, New York, NY).

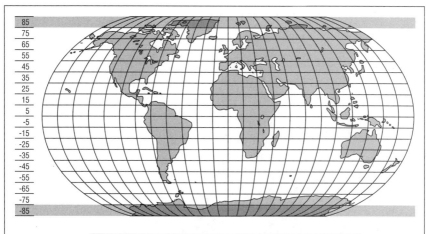

Latitude Band	Percentage Land	Avg. Annual Temp. (degrees celsius)
-85	1.000	- 47.7°
-75	0.754	- 19.3°
-65	0.104	- 10.8°
-55	0.008	1.4°
-45	0.030	8.9°
-35	0.112	13.7°
-25	0.231	19.0°
-15	0.220	23.5°
-5	0.236	25.0°
5	0.228	25.7°
15	0.264	25.3°
25	0.376	20.6°
35	0.428	14.2°
45	0.525	7.7°
55	0.572	0.7°
65	0.706	- 7.7°
75	0.287	- 15.7°
85	0.066	- 23.4°

Figure 2-6: CLIMATE program input file

Now, the fraction of the northern hemisphere's surface that lies in each ten degree band of latitude can now be computed.

```
radians = 57.29578
j = 10
do i = 10, 90, 10
    y = float ( i    ) / radians
    x = float ( i-10 ) / radians
    area(j) = sin(y) - sin(x)
    j = j + 1
end do
```

By symmetry, areas for latitude bands in the southern hemisphere are the same as in the northern hemisphere. Thus, the initialization of the array can be completed by reversing the order of the last half of AREA and inserting it into the first half. Fortran 90's subscript "triplet" with a negative stride accomplishes this reversal in a single statement:

```
area(1:9) = area(18:10:-1)
```

This sets the first nine elements of AREA equal to the second nine elements of AREA, but in reverse order: AREA(1) = AREA(18), AREA(2) = AREA(17), ... , AREA(9) = AREA(10).

So far, AREA has been measured relative to the size of one of earth's hemispheres. Adding together AREA(1) through AREA(9) would equal 1.0, which would signify 100% of the area of the southern hemisphere, and summing AREA(10) through AREA(18) would do the same for the northern hemisphere. Consequently, to have any given element of AREA represent the relative area of the whole earth rather than an individual hemisphere, it has to be halved, which can be done directly through

```
area = 0.5 * area
```

With the data read in at the beginning of the program, the fraction of the area occupied by land in a given latitude band is AREA(I) * LAND(I). Extending this calculation to every element of AREA and LAND allows percentages of the earth's surface covered by land and water to be computed. The DOT_PRODUCT intrinsic performs an element-by-element multiplication of the contents of each vector argument and sums the results:

```
      x = dot_product ( area, land ) * 100.0
      print 200, x, 100.0 - x
200   format ( " Earth's surface is ", f4.1, '% land',
     -                        ' and ', f4.1, '% water' )
```

It then displays:

```
Earth's surface is 29.2% land and 70.8% water
```

Note that Fortran 90 allows literal strings to be enclosed in quotation marks in addition to the traditional apostrophes. So, "EARTH'S SURFACE IS" was used instead of the old style 'EARTH''S SURFACE IS' where a double apostrophe was previously required.

Fortran 90 introduces tools to select array elements by value and by location. Array elements are selected by value when computing the average polar temperature. The polar bands are those where the absolute value of the latitude is greater or equal to 85 degrees. Thus, the values in the LATITUDE array are checked by the expression in an additional MASK argument to the SUM intrinsic:

```
abs(latitude).ge.85.0
```

The effect of this MASK is to limit the sum to those elements that pass the MASK—namely, LATITUDE(1) and LATITUDE(18) as was shown in Figure 2-6. Therefore, in

```
sum ( temperature, MASK=abs(latitude).ge.85.0 )
```

only TEMPERATURE(1) and TEMPERATURE(18) are included.

In addition to a sum of elements, an average requires knowledge of the number of elements. Selection by value comes in useful in another MASK argument, this time to the COUNT intrinsic.

```
count ( abs(latitude).ge.85.0 )
```

Thus, the entire task of calculating the average temperature at the poles can be compressed into a single assignment statement.

```
     x = sum ( temperature, MASK=abs(latitude).ge.85.0 ) /
     -     count ( abs(latitude).ge.85.0 )
     print 300, x
300  format ( ' Average annual temperature within 10 degrees',
     -          ' of poles is ', f5.1, 'C' )
```

It then displays:

```
Average annual temperature within 10 degrees of poles is -35.5C
```

WHERE Statement

While mask arguments apply in intrinsic functions to a single operation, several techniques permit this powerful feature to be applied to large-scale parts of programs. One technique is the PACK intrinsic shown earlier. Another is the WHERE statement, whose syntax resembles block IF. In the CLIMATE program, a WHERE statement clarifies remaining displays by tagging each hemisphere with the appropriate N(orth) or S(outh) designation.

```
where ( latitude .ge. 0 )
        hemisphere = 'N'
elsewhere
        hemisphere = 'S'
end where
```

WHERE operates selectively on elements of one or more arrays of the same shape. In CLIMATE, the mask LATITUDE.GE.0 elects the top nine elements and assigns the corresponding elements of HEMISPHERE to the letter N for north. Conversely, the ELSEWHERE clause operates where LATITUDE is less than zero, so the bottom half of LATITUDE is selected, and matching entries in HEMISPHERE are set to the letter S for south. Short hand versions of the WHERE construct that could have been used in the current example are:

```
where ( latitude .ge. 0 ) hemisphere = 'N'
where ( latitude .lt. 0 ) hemisphere = 'S'
```

Either version would be appropriate in this context. The true power of WHERE lies in the ability to use values from one array to control operations on other similar-sized arrays.

A general Fortran principle underlies the fact that the array mentioned in the WHERE mask may be changed within the WHERE construct. When an array appears in the WHERE statement mask the logical test is executed and the host system retains the result independent of whatever happens inside the WHERE construct. So, in this case:

```
real dimension ( 5 ) :: x = (/ 1,2,3,4,5 /)
where ( x .gt. 0.0 )
        x = -x
end where
```

the sign is reversed for all elements of X because they all pass the initial logical mask. It is as if classic sequence of had been programmed instead of the WHERE construct:

```
do 100 i = 1, 5, 1
     if ( x(i) .gt. 0.0 ) x(i) = -x(i)
100   continue
```

A more ominous and subtle issue surrounds the use of transformational intrinsic functions, which are listed below.

Table 2-1: Transformational Intrinsics and WHERE Statement Safety

ALL	ANY	COUNT
CSHIFT	DOT_PRODUCT	EOSHIFT
MATMUL	MAXLOC	MAXVAL
MINLOC	MINVAL	PACK
PRODUCT	REPEAT	RESHAPE
SELECTED_INT_KIND	SELECTED_REAL_KIND	SPREAD
SUM	TRANSFER	TRANSPOSE
TRIM	UNPACK	

The danger is that when these intrinsics appear in the body of a WHERE construct, the WHERE statement's mask no longer applies. So, in the following example the transformational intrinsic function SUM operates over all five elements of X rather than the two elements of X that exceed six:

```
real dimension ( 5 ) :: x = (/ 2,4,6,8,10 /)
where ( x .gt. 6.0 )
       x = x / sum ( x )
end where
```

So, the new values for X are {2, 4, 6, 8/30, 10/30} rather than {2, 4, 6, 8/18, 10/18}. This standard-conforming but otherwise "unexpected" result should raise a caution for the programmer. A lot of care needs to be taken when transformational intrinsics appear in a WHERE construct to be sure the code implements what was intended.

Maximum and Minimum Elements

A final form of extracting array elements by value comes through the MAXLOC/MINLOC and MAXVAL/MINVAL intrinsics, which return the location and value, respectively, of extrema in an array.

It is hard to believe that every book on a programming language has to work in a Celsius to Fahrenheit conversion, but the following is more appropriate than usual because it is related to the topic of using whole array manipulations.

```
fahrenheit = ( ( 9.0 / 5.0 ) * temperature ) + 32.0
```

FAHRENHEIT can be searched to report the warmest latitude band

```
      location = maxloc ( fahrenheit )
      print 400, abs(latitude(location)), hemisphere(location),
      -          fahrenheit(location)
400   format ( ' Warmest latitude band is near ', i2, a1,
      -          ' at ', f4.1, 'F'                )
```

which displays

```
      Warmest latitude band is near  5N at 78.3F
```

There are two subtle things about the MAXLOC intrinsic function. First, it returns a vector of values, one for each dimension. Thus, it must return a vector even when there is only one dimension. That is why LOCATION is declared as an array of just one element. Second, MAXLOC reports results as if its array argument had lower bounds of one in each dimension. If FAHRENHEIT had been declared with a range of array indices of (-18:-1), then the MAXLOC function would still set LOCATION(1) to 10 instead of -9. Of course, the indices returned by MAXLOC could always be scaled in a subsequent step with the results of the LBOUND intrinsic such as:

```
      incredibly_hot = ( maxloc ( farenheit ) +
      -                   lbound ( farenheit )     ) - 1
```

Similar comments are appropriate for the MINLOC intrinsic used to detect the latitude band with the least land (or most open sea) :

```
      location = minloc ( land )
      print 500, abs(latitude(location)), hemisphere(location),
      -          (100.0-(land(location)*100.0))
500   format ( ' Most water-logged latitude band is near ', i2, a1,
      -          ' with ', f4.1, '% ocean' )
      end program climate
```

which displays:

```
 Most water-logged latitude band is near 55S with 99.2% ocean
```

The second line of the PRINT statement could have been written to show-case the MINVAL intrinsic:

```
      -              ( 100.0 - ( minval(land) * 100.0 ) )
```

Program design will dictate the use of the extract by location or value intrinsic, but it is clear that these intrinsics could replace many Fortran 77 custom DO loops.

This example on Earth facts shows how information can be swapped between vectors of the same size using Fortran 90 intrinsics and methods of manipulating array indices. Array operations make it easy to transfer elements between arrays or to perform a calculation on any entire array all at once. Furthermore, the contents of one array can be queried and that examination used to direct calculations on other arrays.

Example: Matrix Inversion

Fortran 90's ability to extract whole rows, columns, and planes from arrays means that mixing-and-matching data from variously sized arrays is not a problem. A classic case in which these features are required is inverting a matrix, especially the "old fashioned" way of finding minors, cofactors, determinants, and adjoints as outlined early in Ronald E. Miller's *Modern Mathematical Models for Economics and Business* (1972, Holt, Rinehard and Winston, Inc., 488 pages, New York, NY). Many, many texts specializing in numerical programming present inversion algorithms well-tailored to the condition of the matrix, the base accuracy of the target computer system, and the practical uses for any vectors and matrices created as by-products of the inversion algorithm. But this book tries to illuminate the use of Fortran 90. The "old fashioned," slow, inelegant matrix inversion technique selected here satisfies that goal, although it is not necessarily numerically exact:

The program INVERT begins by establishing the names for several key matrices:

```
program invert
real, dimension (:,:), allocatable :: adjoint
real, dimension (:,:), allocatable :: cofactor
real                               :: determinant = 0.0
real, dimension (:,:), allocatable :: identity
real, dimension (:,:), allocatable :: inverse
real, dimension (:,:), allocatable :: matrix
integer                            :: rank = 0
```

where each matrix is declared ALLOCATABLE. Covered in detail in Chapter 7, for present purposes it is sufficient to note that the size of ALLO-CATABLE arrays are set at execution time through:

```
100    continue
       write ( *,200,advance='NO' )
200    format ( ' Enter rank of matrix (2 or 3): ' )
       read ( *,*,err=100 ) rank
       if ( rank .lt. 2 .or. rank .gt. 3 ) go to 100
       allocate ( matrix(rank,rank) )
```

and the matrix is loaded through:

```
      write ( *,300,advance='NO' )
300   format ( / 1H , 'Enter matrix in column order: ' )
      read ( *,* ) matrix
      call echo ( 'MATRIX', matrix, rank )
```

Both WRITE statements include the specifier "ADVANCE=NO", which arrests the cursor at the end of the prompt and suppresses the normal carriage return and line feed sequence. Nonadvancing output is described in detail in Chapter 8.

Then, given this code for subroutine ECHO:

```
      subroutine echo ( name, array, rank )
      integer                      :: rank
      real, dimension (rank,rank) :: array
      character(*)                 :: name
      print *, " "
      do i = 1, rank, 1
          write ( *,100 ) name, i, array(i,:)
100       format ( 1H , a10, ' row ', i1, ': ', 3f10.5 )
      end do
      end subroutine echo
```

the user would see this prompt-and-response cycle:

```
Enter rank of matrix (2 or 3): 3

Enter matrix in column order: 1 2 3 1 0 7 1 6 1

MATRIX row 1:    1.00000    1.00000    1.00000
MATRIX row 2:    2.00000    0.00000    6.00000
MATRIX row 3:    3.00000    7.00000    1.00000
```

Having retained a copy of the base matrix, the next step is to create values for the mathematical entity called the adjoint:

```
      allocate ( adjoint(rank,rank) )
      call factor ( transpose(matrix), rank, adjoint )
      call echo ( 'ADJOINT', adjoint, rank )
```

It produces this result:

```
ADJOINT row 1:  -42.00000    6.00000    6.00000
ADJOINT row 2:   16.00000   -2.00000   -4.00000
ADJOINT row 3:   14.00000   -4.00000   -2.00000
```

Fortran 90's TRANSPOSE intrinsic rearranges an array so that rows become columns and columns become rows as shown in Figure 2-7. TRANSPOSE works only on two dimensional arrays, but applies to both square (N-by-N) and rectangular (N-by-M) matrices.

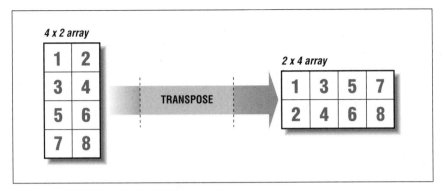

Figure 2-7: TRANSPOSE intrinsic

Creating the adjoint matrix is an exercise in array index manipulation. An entry at row I and column J is based on the determinant of what remains from the original matrix after ignoring row I and column J. Subroutine FACTOR starts this computation by establishing several work arrays:

```
subroutine factor ( matrix, rank, cofactor )
integer                            :: rank
real, dimension (:,:), allocatable :: across
real, dimension (:,:), allocatable :: down
real, dimension (:,:), allocatable :: extract
real, dimension (rank,rank)        :: factored
real, dimension (rank,rank)        :: matrix
real                               :: minor
integer                            :: rankm1
rankm1 = rank - 1
allocate ( across(rankm1,rankm1) )
allocate ( down   (rank,  rank ) )
```

and then rolling through the MATRIX column by column to form the work array DOWN. By careful use of array indices, DOWN becomes a copy of MATRIX without column J:

```
column: do j = 1, rank, 1
     if ( j .ne.    1 )
-        down(:,1:j-1  ) = matrix(:,1:j-1  )
     if ( j .ne. rank )
-        down(:,j:rankm1) = matrix(:,j+1:rank)
```

In turn, DOWN is reduced even further, row by row, to form the work array ACROSS. Using a similar approach of manipulating array indices, ACROSS is created as a copy of DOWN without row I:

```
row: do i = 1, rank, 1
     if ( i .ne.    1 )
```

```
    –      across(1:i-1,   :) = down(1:i-1,   :)
           if ( i .ne. rank )
    –      across(i:rankml,:) = down(i+1:rank,:)
```

Therefore, ACROSS is a copy of the original MATRIX array with row I and column J removed. It is as if a set of cross-hairs were positioned over the array centered on MATRIX(I, J) and that row and column were excised. (See Figure 2-8.)

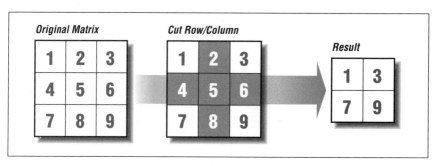

Figure 2-8: Matrix inversion: extracting a submatrix

Taking the determinant of the transpose of ACROSS gives the value of a mathematical entity called the minor. It is required to reverse the sign of the minor for each row and column in which the sum of the row and column index is odd. So, the sign of the minor remains the same at row one and column one, is reversed at row one and column two, remains the same at row one and column three, etc. The result of the FACTOR subroutine is an array, FACTORED, which corresponds to the adjoint of the original matrix:

```
           call determine ( transpose(across), rankml, minor )
           if ( mod (i+j,2) .eq. 1 ) minor = –minor
           factored(i,j) = minor
        end do row
     end do column
     deallocate ( down )
     deallocate ( across )
     end subroutine factor
```

Fortran 90 introduces the feature of DO-loop labels. In this program, labels ROW and COLUMN help clarify the extent of each loop since they appear in both the DO and the END DO statements.

Returning to the main program, the next step computes the determinant of the original matrix:

```
      call determine ( matrix, rank, determinant )
      print 400, determinant
400   format ( / 1H , '    DETERMINANT: ', f10.5 )
```

which results in this display:

```
DETERMINANT:  -12.00000
```

This subroutine computes the value of the determinant:

```
      subroutine determine ( matrix, rank, determinant )
      integer                    :: rank
      real                       :: determinant
      real, dimension(rank,rank) :: matrix
      select case ( rank )
        case ( :0 )
          determinant = 0.0
        case ( 1 )
          determinant =    matrix(1,1)
        case ( 2 )
          determinant = (  matrix(1,1)*matrix(2,2) )
     -                  - (  matrix(1,2)*matrix(2,1) )
        case ( 3 )
          determinant = (  (matrix(1,1)*matrix(2,2)*matrix(3,3))+
     -                     (matrix(1,2)*matrix(2,3)*matrix(3,1))+
     -                     (matrix(1,3)*matrix(2,1)*matrix(3,2))  )
     -                  - (  (matrix(1,3)*matrix(2,2)*matrix(3,1))+
     -                       (matrix(2,3)*matrix(3,2)*matrix(1,1))+
     -                       (matrix(3,3)*matrix(1,2)*matrix(2,1))  )
        case (4:)
          determinant = 0.0
      end select
      end subroutine determine
```

DETERMINE subroutine accepts the number of elements per row as RANK from its caller, and submits it to the SELECT CASE statement. Matrices of rank 1, 2, and 3 can be handled by brute force. Any RANK outside of this range—(:0) or (4:)—is set to zero as a form of error. This subroutine ignores the concerns of numerical accuracy and makes no attempt to present a generalized approach to compute determinants for square matrices of arbitrary size. Many texts on numerical programming cover these subjects in great detail whereas the emphasis here is on Fortran 90 features. Not that these interests cannot co-exist, but in this case, taking all mathematical concerns into account would divert from the principal objective of illustrating array-oriented Fortran 90 concepts.

Returning to the main program, if the determinant is non-zero, then the inverse matrix can be formed in a single assignment statement as follows:

```
if ( determinant .ne. 0.0 ) then
    allocate ( inverse(rank,rank) )
    inverse = ( 1.0 / determinant ) * adjoint
    call echo ( 'INVERSE', inverse, rank )
```

which displays

```
INVERSE row 1:     3.50000  -0.50000  -0.50000
INVERSE row 2:    -1.33333   0.16667   0.33333
INVERSE row 3:    -1.16667   0.33333   0.16667
```

Two tests for correctness are available. One uses the cofactor. The sum, along any row or column, of the product of paired entries from the cofactor matrix and the original matrix must equal the determinant of the original matrix.

These sums of products are illustrated in Figure 2-9. In this specific case, all three row-based and column-based sums do indeed equal-12, which is the value of the determinant.

Although the cofactor can be recognized as the transpose of the adjoint, this program calculates it anew:

```
          allocate ( cofactor(rank,rank) )
          call factor ( matrix, rank, cofactor )
          call echo ( 'COFACTOR', cofactor, rank )
          print *, " "
          do j = 1, rank, 1
              print 500, j, sum ( matrix(:,j) * cofactor(:,j) )
500           format ( 1H , '  CHECK column ', i1, ': ', f10.5 )
          end do
          print *, " "
          do i = 1, rank, 1
              print 600, i, sum ( matrix(i,:) * cofactor(i,:) )
600           format ( 1H , '  CHECK row     ', i1, ': ', f10.5 )
          end do
          deallocate ( cofactor )
```

which displays:

```
COFACTOR row 1:   -42.00000  16.00000  14.00000
COFACTOR row 2:     6.00000  -2.00000  -4.00000
COFACTOR row 3:     6.00000  -4.00000  -2.00000

CHECK column 1:  -12.00000
CHECK column 2:  -12.00000
CHECK column 3:  -12.00000
```

```
CHECK row   1:  -12.00000
CHECK row   2:  -12.00000
CHECK row   3:  -12.00000
```

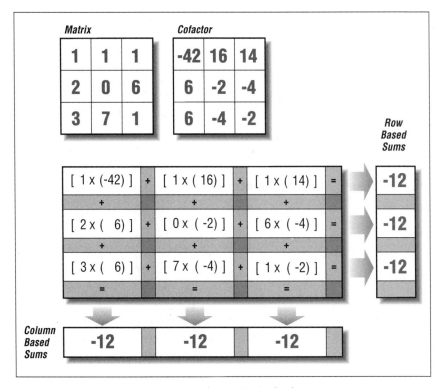

Figure 2-9: Matrix inversion: MATRIX/COFACTOR check

Performing both row and column checks is facilitated by the Fortran 90 intrinsic SUM: it allows a single statement to take the place of the classic Fortran 77 approach of zeroing an accumulator and then, in a pair of nested DO loops, keeping a running total of the multiplication of individual elements of MATRIX and COFACTOR.

A second check is performed by multiplying the original matrix by its inverse and, for completeness, multiplying the inverse by the original matrix. An identity matrix (i.e., ones on the main diagonal with zeros elsewhere) should be the result of both matrix multiplications:

```
allocate ( identity(rank,rank) )
identity = matmul ( matrix, inverse )
call echo ( 'IDENTITYmi', identity, rank )
identity = matmul ( inverse, matrix )
call echo ( 'IDENTITYim', identity, rank )
```

```
deallocate ( identity )
deallocate ( inverse  )
```

which displays:

```
IDENTITYmi row 1:    1.00000   0.00000   0.00000
IDENTITYmi row 2:    0.00000   1.00000   0.00000
IDENTITYmi row 3:    0.00000   0.00000   1.00000

IDENTITYim row 1:    1.00000   0.00000   0.00000
IDENTITYim row 2:    0.00000   1.00000   0.00000
IDENTITYim row 3:    0.00000   0.00000   1.00000
```

Once again, Fortran 90 facilitates matrix manipulations by providing an intrinsic, MATMUL, that results in clear, concise code. MATMUL is applicable to matrices of rank one or two and is fully aware of the conformability rules of matrix multiplication. Finally, if the inverse does not exist, then the user needs to be told before the main program completes.

```
else
    print *, " "
    print *, "INVERSE does not exit."
end if
deallocate ( adjoint )
deallocate ( matrix  )
end program invert
```

This program shows how the complicated movement of data between arrays of different sizes and shapes is facilitated by Fortran 90's methods of treating multiple array elements in a single entity.

Example: Matrix Inversion by Partitions

Matrices larger than 3-by-3 need a different approach from that used in the previous program. An explicit algorithm was used in subroutine DETERMINE in that program, INVERT, to calculate the determinant of a matrix. That algorithm has a strong geometric interpretation that limits its ability to handle matrices larger than 3-by-3.

Larger matrices can be inverted by building on techniques already introduced. Basically, the procedure is inversion by partition, as described on pages 30 through 32 of Ronald E. Miller's *Modern Mathematical Models for Economics and Business* (1972, Holt, Rinehard and Winston, Inc., 488 pages, New York, NY) and pages 86 through 88 of *Numerical Methods for Scientific and Engineering Computations* by Mahinder K. Jain, S. R. K. Iyengard, and Rajendra K. Jain (1985, John Wiley & Sons, 406 pages, New York,

NY). The algorithm is implemented to show more uses of array sections and the MATMUL matrix multiplication intrinsic.

Visually, inversion by partition requires that the original matrix be divided into four quadrants. Here is one partitioning scheme using the 3-by-3 case from the previous example as shown in Figure 2-10.

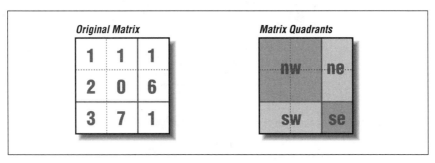

Figure 2-10: Matrix: subdivied into quadrants

Labelling quadrants according to the cardinal directions of the compass makes it easier to reference each submatrix, M, with a subscript. For instance, the Northwest submatix contains:

$$\mathbf{M_{nw}} = \begin{bmatrix} 1 & 1 \\ 2 & 0 \end{bmatrix}$$

Matrix notation is used to show relationships between each submatrix (M), its inverse (I), and its "reciprocal" (R):

$$\mathbf{I_{se}} = (\mathbf{M_{nw}})^{-1}$$

$$\mathbf{R_{nw}} = (\mathbf{M_{nw}} - \mathbf{M_{ne}}\mathbf{I_{se}}\mathbf{M_{sw}})^{-1}$$

$$\mathbf{R_{sw}} = -\mathbf{I_{se}}\mathbf{M_{sw}}\mathbf{R_{nw}}$$

$$\mathbf{R_{ne}} = -\mathbf{R_{nw}}\mathbf{M_{ne}}\mathbf{I_{se}}$$

$$\mathbf{R_{se}} = -\mathbf{I_{se}} - \mathbf{I_{se}}\mathbf{M_{sw}}\mathbf{R_{ne}}$$

As expected, the inverse of the entire original matrix is formed by drawing together all four reciprocals.

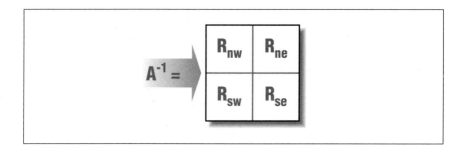

The program PARTS implements this procedure. It begins by declaring various constants and arrays:

```
program parts
integer, parameter      :: m = 2
integer, parameter      :: n = 3
real                    :: determinant
real, dimension (n,n)   :: identity, inverse, matrix
real, dimension (m,  m ) :: nw,      r_nw
real, dimension (m,  n-m) :: ne,      r_ne
real, dimension (n-m,m ) :: sw,      r_sw
real, dimension (n-m,n-m) :: se, i_se, r_se
data matrix / 1, 2, 3, 1, 0, 7, 1, 6, 1 /
```

This original matrix is then drawn-and-quartered into four submatrices through:

```
nw(1:m  ,1:m  ) = matrix(1   :m,1   :m)
sw(1:n-m,1:m  ) = matrix(m+1:n,1   :m)
ne(1:m  ,1:n-m) = matrix(1   :m,m+1:n)
se(1:n-m,1:n-m) = matrix(m+1:n,m+1:n)
```

After forming reciprocals, the procedure to create submatrices is reversed:

```
call invert ( se, n-m, determinant, i_se )
nw   = nw - matmul ( matmul ( ne, i_se ), sw )
call invert ( nw, m, determinant, r_nw )
r_sw = - matmul ( matmul ( i_se, sw ), r_nw )
r_ne = - matmul ( matmul ( r_nw, ne ), i_se )
r_se = i_se - matmul ( matmul ( i_se, sw ), r_ne )
```

All four reciprocals are assembled into the inverse of the original matrix through:

```
inverse(1   :m,1   :m) = r_nw(1:m  ,1:m  )
inverse(m+1:n,1   :m) = r_sw(1:n-m,1:m  )
```

```
inverse(1   :m,m+1:n) = r_ne(1:m  ,1:n-m)
inverse(m+1:n,m+1:n) = r_se(1:n-m,1:n-m)
```

The result is checked by multiplying the original matrix by its inverse to create an identity matrix:

```
call echo ( "MATRIX", matrix, n )
call echo ( "INVERSE", inverse, n )
identity = matmul ( matrix, inverse )
call echo ( "IDENTITY", identity, n )
end program parts
```

which displays:

```
MATRIX row 1:    1.0000  1.0000  1.0000
MATRIX row 2:    2.0000  0.0000  6.0000
MATRIX row 3:    3.0000  7.0000  1.0000

INVERSE row 1:    3.5000 -0.5000 -0.5000
INVERSE row 2:   -1.3333  0.1667  0.3333
INVERSE row 3:   -1.1667  0.3333  0.1667

IDENTITY row 1:    1.0000  0.0000  0.0000
IDENTITY row 2:    0.0000  1.0000  0.0000
IDENTITY row 3:    0.0000  0.0000  1.0000
```

As expected, these results agree exactly with the first, straight-forward inversion program presented earlier. In fact, most of the pieces of INVERT are re-used in the current program. The original main program of INVERT becomes this subroutine:

```
subroutine invert ( matrix, rank, determinant, inverse )
real, dimension (:,:), allocatable :: adjoint
real, dimension (:,:), allocatable :: cofactor
real                               :: determinant
real, dimension (:,:), allocatable :: identity
integer                            :: rank
real, dimension (rank,rank)        :: inverse
real, dimension (rank,rank)        :: matrix
if ( rank .lt. 1 .or. rank .gt. 3 ) then
    print *, "ERROR! matrix rank not 1, 2, or 3 (INVERT)"
    go to 200
end if
```

A special adjustment is to be made to handle 1-by-1 arrays because the technique of inversion by partition can create such small arrays in either the Northwest or Southeast quadrants:

```
if ( rank .eq. 1 ) then
    if ( matrix(1,1) .ne. 0.0 ) then
        determinant = 0.0
```

```
            inverse(1,1) = 1.0 / matrix(1,1)
        else
            print *, "ERROR! 1x1 matrix has no inverse"
        endif
        go to 200
    endif
```

Then, as in the full matrix inversion program, the subroutine forms the adjoint, computes the determinant, performs a sanity check, and deallocates arrays when no longer needed:

```
      allocate ( adjoint(rank,rank) )
      call factor ( transpose(matrix), rank, adjoint )
      call determine ( matrix, rank, determinant )
      if ( determinant .ne. 0.0 ) then
          inverse = ( 1.0 / determinant ) * adjoint
          allocate ( identity(rank,rank) )
          identity = matmul ( matrix, inverse )
          if ( abs ( float ( rank ) -
   -                sum(identity,mask=identity.gt.0.0) )
   -          .gt. 0.05                                    )
   -              print *, "ERROR! sum identity diagonal ",
   -                       "differs from rank (INVERT)"
          deallocate ( identity )
      else
          print *, "ERROR! determinant zero ... no inverse"
      end if
      deallocate ( adjoint )
200   continue
      end subroutine invert
```

Rather than display IDENTITY each time a matrix is inverted, the sanity check adds up all the ones on IDENTITY's main diagonal and makes sure that it is "close"—within 0.05—of the rank of the array.

A final change was made to subroutine ECHO to accommodate 6-by-6 matrices (i.e., change 3F10.5 to 6F8.4):

```
100   format ( 1H , a10, ' row ', i1, ': ', 6f8.4 )
```

Exercising the full capability of inverting a 6-by-6 matrix by adjusting parameters M and N to 3 and 6, respectively, and creating the proper initializing DATA statement, shows that this matrix:

```
MATRIX row 1:   6.0000  2.0000  9.0000  4.0000  2.0000  0.0000
MATRIX row 2:   2.0000  5.0000  2.0000  9.0000  0.0000  4.0000
MATRIX row 3:   4.0000  1.0000  6.0000  0.0000  8.0000  7.0000
MATRIX row 4:   0.0000  2.0000  9.0000  1.0000  1.0000  0.0000
MATRIX row 5:   1.0000  8.0000  0.0000  9.0000  0.0000  7.0000
MATRIX row 6:   2.0000  1.0000  6.0000  1.0000  3.0000  8.0000
```

has this inverse:

```
INVERSE row 1:    0.2360 -0.2073 -0.0536 -0.1859  0.1178  0.0475
INVERSE row 2:    0.0969 -0.3641  0.0127  0.0529  0.3280 -0.1161
INVERSE row 3:    0.0026  0.0236 -0.0309  0.0901 -0.0404  0.0506
INVERSE row 4:   -0.0995  0.3643  0.0344  0.0162 -0.2073 -0.0309
INVERSE row 5:   -0.1176  0.1513  0.2181  0.0666 -0.0850 -0.1920
INVERSE row 6:   -0.0165 -0.0226 -0.0511 -0.0548  0.0177  0.1656
```

3

Derived Types

Until now, Fortran has always required that an array contain information of a single data type. Under this rule, arrays held either numbers or characters and they could not be mixed. When programmers had different kinds of information pertaining to the same object, they had to keep them in separate arrays, increasing the risk of getting out of sync during maintenance. Fortran 90's user-defined derived types provide a mechanism to create bona fide data structures containing elements of any data type mixed freely in any proportion.

Example: Distance Computations

A derived type is such a new concept to many Fortran programmers that it is easier to learn by building slowly towards a full example. Eventually, a program will take shape that can convert a fixed list of distance measures according to both the English and metric standard. It will work with the following input file of "conversion" factors:

```
feet        cubits          0.666667
feet        fathoms         0.166667
feet        furlongs        0.151515e-2
feet        inches          0.120000e+2
feet        kilometers      0.304800e-3
feet        meters          0.304800
feet        miles: nautical 0.164466e-3
feet        miles: statute  0.189394e-3
feet        rods            0.606061e-1
feet        yards           0.333333
```

Four programs will work with this input file. The first, DIST1, manages
conversion factors in traditional Fortran 77 style parallel arrays. The next,
DIST2, introduces a single derived type to bypass the need for parallel
arrays. The third, DIST3, uses a second derived types to manage metric
conversions. Finally, the last version, DIST4, incorporates both English and
metric conversion factors into a single, all encompassing derived type.

DIST1: Parallel Arrays

The first distance program, DIST1, performs a preliminary version of the
task entirely in Fortran 77. It declares a separate vector for each element of
the conversion program:

```
program dist1
real         measure(10)
real         multiplier(10)
character*15 source(10)
character*15 target(10)
data measure / 123,    456,   7890, 123, 4567,
    -               89, 10123, 45678, 901,   23 /
```

Then the input file is opened, read:

```
      open ( unit=5, file='dist.input' )
      do 200 i = 1, 10, 1
          read ( 5,100 ) source(i), target(i), multiplier(i)
100       format ( a15, a15, e11.0 )
200   continue
      print 300
300   format ( 1H , 'From          ', 1x, 'To            ',
    -          1x, '   Multiply'
    -      / 1H , 15('-'), 1x, 15('-'), 1x, 12('-')          )
      do 500 i = 1, 10, 1
          print 400, source(i), target(i), multiplier(i)
400       format ( 1H ,   a15, 1x, a15, 1x, e12.6 )
500   continue
```

and displayed:

```
From             To               Multiply
---------------  ---------------  ------------

feet             cubits           .666667E+00
feet             fathoms          .166667E+00
feet             furlongs         .151515E-02
feet             inches           .120000E+02
```

feet	kilometers	.304800E-03
feet	meters	.304800E+00
feet	miles: nautical	.164466E-03
feet	miles: statute	.189394E-03
feet	rods	.606061E-01
feet	yards	.333333E+00

The factor stored in MULTIPLIER converts each element of MEASURE from SOURCE units to TARGET units:

```
      print *, " "
      do 700 i = 1, 10, 1
          print 600, measure(i),              source(i),
     -              measure(i)*multiplier(i), target(i)
600       format ( 1H , f10.2, 1x, a15, ' = ', f10.2, 1x, a15 )
700   continue
      stop
      end
```

displaying:

```
   123.00 feet      =      82.00 cubits
   456.00 feet      =      76.00 fathoms
  7890.00 feet      =      11.95 furlongs
   123.00 feet      =    1476.00 inches
  4567.00 feet      =       1.39 kilometers
    89.00 feet      =      27.13 meters
 10123.00 feet      =       1.66 miles: nautical
 45678.00 feet      =       8.65 miles: statute
   901.00 feet      =      54.61 rods
    23.00 feet      =       7.67 yards
```

DIST2: A Single Derived Type

Whenever a Fortran 77 program manipulates different arrays using the same index within a loop, as MEASURE and MULTIPLIER do above, the data can be considered as candidates for a derived type. Thus, one natural candidate for a Fortran 90 derived type is the table of conversion factors. The second version of the distance program, DIST2, takes each aspect of this table—SOURCE unit name, TARGET unit name, and the actual conversion MULTIPLIER—and combines them into a new user-defined type called FACTOR. Then, an array called ENGLISH is declared, which contains ten instances of the FACTOR derived type:

```
      program dist2
      real, dimension ( 10 ) :: measure
      type factor
           character*15 source
           character*15 target
```

```
        real            multiplier
     end type factor
     type ( factor ) english(10)
     data measure / 123,   456,   7890, 123, 4567,
        -              89, 10123, 45678, 901,   23 /
```

ENGLISH can be thought of as a 10-by-3 array as in Figure 3-1. The first column contains a character string representing the SOURCE name, the second a character string representing the TARGET name, and the third a real number representing the conversion factor MULTIPLIER. Now, the entire derived type array can be read and displayed by the single mention of the object ENGLISH in the READ and PRINT statement:

```
        open ( unit=5, file='dist.input' )
        read ( 5,100 ) english
100     format ( a15, a15, e11.0 )
        print 200
200     format ( 1H , 'From          ', 1x, 'To            ',
        -              1x, '    Multiply'
        -            / 1H , 15('-'), 1x, 15('-'), 1x, 12('-')          )
        print 300, english
300     format ( 1H ,   a15, 1x, a15, 1x, e12.6 )
```

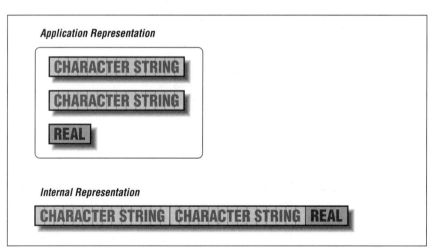

Figure 3-1: ENGLISH derived type

The READ statement above is guaranteed to work on the input shown earlier because Fortran 90 has an implied ordering, just as Fortran 77 traditionally has for arrays and common blocks. When the input file is echoed in this program, DIST2, is appears exactly as it did in the previous program, DIST1.

Each MEASURE is converted from the English to the metric standard by a reference to the proper array element in ENGLISH with the standard "(I)" syntax, and to the proper component of ENGLISH with the "%" separator.

```
        print *, " "
        do i = 1, 10, 1
           print 400, measure(i),
    -                            english(i)%source,
    -                measure(i)*english(i)%multiplier,
    -                            english(i)%target
400        format ( 1H , f10.2, 1x, a15, ' = ', f10.2, 1x, a15 )
        end do
        end program dist2
```

Since the derived type component separator is new in Fortran 90, Table 3-1 is a guide to interpreting a selection of derived type statements.

Table 3-1: Interpretations of Derived Type Statements

```
                type example
                    character*16   unit(10)
                end type example
                type ( example )  derived(5)
```

Construct	Meaning
derived	All components of the whole DERIVED
derived(i)	All components of the I-th element of DERIVED
derived(i)%unit	All elements of the UNIT array within component I of DERIVED
derived%unit(i)	Element I of the UNIT array within all components of DERIVED
derived(i)%unit(j)	Element J of the UNIT array within component I of DERIVED

In general, % separates components of a derived type and a subscript—(I)—affects the component immediately preceding it.

As before, the results of this program, DIST2, are identical to those of the previous program, DIST1. Here, a genuine data structure—ENGLISH—has been created and used in input, output, and computational statements.

DIST3: Two Derived Types

A derived type can also be used to populate another derived type. The third version, DIST3, develops a new object called METRIC that is built from the contents of ENGLISH. Whereas ENGLISH was used to convert certain measurements from the English to the metric standard, METRIC is used to perform the reverse operation.

The program begins by establishing the components of the general derived type FACTOR, declaring both an ENGLISH and METRIC instance, and initializing ENGLISH from the input file.

```
      program dist3
      real, dimension ( 10 ) :: measure
      type factor
           character*15 source
           character*15 target
           real          multiplier
      end type factor
      type ( factor ) english(10)
      type ( factor ) metric(10)
      data measure / 123,    456,   7890, 123, 4567,
     -                89, 10123, 45678, 901,   23 /
      open ( unit=5, file='dist.input' )
      read ( 5,100 ) english
100   format ( a15, a15, e11.0 )
```

Then all ten individual measurements are converted from feet to meters in the single statement:

```
      measure = measure * english(6)%multiplier
```

because ENGLISH(6)%MULTIPLIER holds the factor 0.3048 that converts feet to meters.

METRIC is created to convert from meters to other units. Its SOURCE component needs to be set, it must get the names of the TARGET units, and its MULTIPLIER component has to be converted from the ENGLISH array's feet to meters.

```
      metric%source = 'meters'
      metric%target = english%target
      metric%multiplier = english%multiplier /
     -                   english(6)%multiplier
```

These three statements demonstrate that components in derived types can behave like scalars. Components can be set to a constant, to the component of another object, or to the result of a calculation involving the component of another object and one of its elements.

Upon completing the migration of the data in ENGLISH to METRIC, the name and value of the specific element handling meters to feet needs to be adjusted:

```
metric(6)%target = 'feet'
metric(6)%multiplier = 1.0 / english(6)%multiplier
```

Now, this new conversion table can be displayed:

```
      print 200
200   format ( 1H , 'From           ', 1x, 'To            ',
    -          1x, '    Multiply'
    -          / 1H , 15('-'), 1x, 15('-'), 1x, 12('-')            )
      print 300, metric
300   format ( 1H ,  a15, 1x, a15, 1x, e12.6 )
```

The display looks like:

From	To	Multiply
meters	cubits	0.218723E+01
meters	fathoms	0.546808E+00
meters	furlongs	0.497096E-02
meters	inches	0.393701E+02
meters	kilometers	0.100000E-02
meters	feet	0.328084E+01
meters	miles: nautical	0.539587E-03
meters	miles: statute	0.621371E-03
meters	rods	0.198839E+00
meters	yards	0.109361E+01

Finally, each measure can be converted to the metric standard:

```
      print *, " "
      do i = 1, 10, 1
         print 400, measure(i),
    -                      metric(i)%source,
    -              measure(i)*metric(i)%multiplier,
    -                      metric(i)%target
400      format ( 1H , f10.2, 1x, a15, ' = ', f10.2, 1x, a15 )
      end do
      end program dist3
```

and displayed:

```
     37.49 meters       =       82.00 cubits
    138.99 meters       =       76.00 fathoms
   2404.87 meters       =       11.95 furlongs
     37.49 meters       =     1476.00 inches
   1392.02 meters       =        1.39 kilometers
     27.13 meters       =       89.00 feet
   3085.49 meters       =        1.66 miles: nautical
```

```
13922.65 meters           =        8.65 miles: statute
  274.62 meters           =       54.61 rods
    7.01 meters           =        7.67 yards
```

DIST4: Combined Derived Type

More complicated derived types can be created. Both ENGLISH and METRIC data structures are simple arrays of instances of the same derived type, FACTOR. The final version, DIST4, shows how they can be combined into an overall data structure called BOTH. It begins by declaring each derived type and the associated data structures.

```
program dist4
real, dimension ( 10 ) :: measure
type factor
      character*15 source
      character*15 target
      real          multiplier
end type factor
type either
      type ( factor ) english
      type ( factor ) metric
end type either
type ( either ) both(10)
data measure / 123,    456,   7890, 123, 4567,
    -                   89, 10123, 45678, 901,   23 /
```

The structure of the EITHER data type appears in Figure 3-2.

To clarify the role of each name, it should be noted that EITHER and FACTOR are names for types, and can be used only to declare data and in a few other rare contexts. BOTH contains actual data and appears in executable statements.

Once the English-to-other conversion factors have been read, the corresponding metric-to-other factors can be computed in a manner identical to the previous program.

```
      open ( unit=5, file='dist.input' )
      read ( 5,100 ) both%english
100   format ( a15, a15, e11.0 )
      measure                     = measure *
          -                         both(6)%english%multiplier
      both%metric%source          = 'meters'
      both%metric%target          = both%english%target
      both%metric%multiplier      = both%english%multiplier /
          -                         both(6)%english%multiplier
```

```
both(6)%metric%target    = 'feet'
both(6)%metric%multiplier = 1.0 /
both(6)%english%multiplier
```

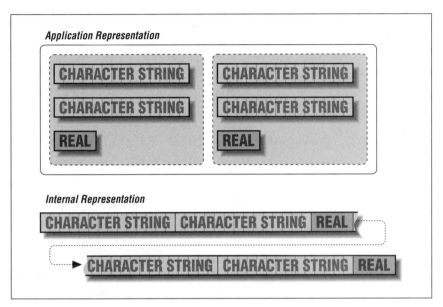

Figure 3-2: BOTH derived type

Now, the combined data structure contains two kinds of conversion factors:

```
      print 200
200   format ( 1H , 'From ',  'To              ','Factor      ',
      -              'From   ','To              ','Factor      '
      -       / 1H , '---- ',  '--------------- ','---------- ',
      -              '------ ','--------------- ','--------- '   )
      print 300, both
300   format ( 1H , a4, 1x, a15, 1x, e10.5,
      -              1x, a6, 1x, a15, 1x, e10.5 )
```

that look like:

From	To	Factor	From	To	Factor
feet	cubits	.66667E+00	meters	cubits	.21872E+01
feet	fathoms	.16667E+00	meters	fathoms	.54681E+00
feet	furlongs	.15151E-02	meters	furlongs	.49710E-02
feet	inches	.12000E+02	meters	inches	.39370E+02
feet	kilometers	.30480E-03	meters	kilometers	.10000E-02
feet	meters	.30480E+00	meters	feet	.32808E+01
feet	miles: nautical	.16447E-03	meters	miles: nautical	.53959E-03

```
feet miles: statute    .18939E-03 meters miles: statute  .62137E-03
feet rods              .60606E-01 meters rods           .19884E+00
feet yards             .33333E+00 meters yards          .10936E+01
```

Finally, each kind of measurement—meters, miscellaneous units, and feet—
can be computed:

```
      print *, " "
      do i = 1, 10, 1
         print 400, measure(i),
    −                          both(i)%metric%source,
    −                measure(i)*both(i)%metric%multiplier,
    −                          both(i)%metric%target,
    −                measure(i)/both(6)%english%multiplier,
    −                          both(6)%english%source
400      format ( 1H , 1x, f10.2, 1x, a6,  ' = ',
    −                       f10.2, 1x, a15, ' = ',
    −                       f10.2, 1x, a4             )
      end do
      end program dist4
```

and displayed:

```
    37.49 meters =      82.00 cubits           =     123.00 feet
   138.99 meters =      76.00 fathoms          =     456.00 feet
  2404.87 meters =      11.95 furlongs         =    7890.00 feet
    37.49 meters =    1476.00 inches           =     123.00 feet
  1392.02 meters =       1.39 kilometers       =    4567.00 feet
    27.13 meters =      89.00 feet             =      89.00 feet
  3085.49 meters =       1.66 miles: nautical  =   10123.00 feet
 13922.65 meters =       8.65 miles: statute   =   45678.00 feet
   274.62 meters =      54.61 rods             =     901.00 feet
     7.01 meters =       7.67 yards            =      23.00 feet
```

These four programs have introduced uses of Fortran 90's derived type in a
step-by-step manner. Since any data type and any data instance—scalar,
vector, array, etc.—can be mixed in a derived type, they may be the most
fruitful area of experimentation with Fortran 90.

Example: The Periodic Table

Derived types, array index manipulation, and vector subscript are drawn
together in a program, PT, that works with information pertaining to the
periodic table of elements. It declares a derived type, MENDELEEV to
define facts about an element:

```
      program pt
      integer, parameter :: elements = 106
      type mendeleev
```

```
        character*12 name
        character* 2 symbol
        integer     number
        real        weight
        integer     year
        character*25 discoverer
        real        radii
    end type mendeleev
```

For display purposes, another derived type, FORMATS, is declared to hold the Fortran formatting convention information for major input/output statements:

```
    type formats
        character*80 input
        character*80 output
        character*80 by_type
        character*80 by_year
        character*80 by_radii
    end type formats
```

Then, two arrays of type MENDELEEV are declared and one single instance of type FORMATS is declared. It is more common to see derived types used to structure arrays:

```
    type ( mendeleev )      periodic(elements)
    type ( mendeleev )      gases(6)
    type ( formats )        layout
```

But, a derived type scalar like LAYOUT is also useful. In this case, it pools input and output FORMATs into one derived type. Other vectors and the LAYOUT structure are initialized:

```
    integer, dimension(6)        :: noble = (/2,10,18,36,54,86/)
    integer, dimension(elements) :: order
    layout%input   = 'a12, 1x, a2, 1x,   i3, 1x, f10.6, ' //
   -                     '1x, i4, 1x, a25, 1x, f5.3 )'
    layout%output  = '( 1H , ' // layout%input
    layout%input   = '( ,'    // layout%input
    layout%by_type ='(1H,                a12,1h[, i3.3, 1h])'
    layout%by_year ='(1H, i4, 1x, a25, 1x, a12,1h[, i3.3, 1h])'
    layout%by_radii='(1H, f5.3,      1x, a12,1h[, i3.3, 1h])'
```

Seven components for all 106 elements of the structure PERIODIC can be read in a single statement. The data include the elements NAME, SYMBOL, atomic NUMBER (i.e., number of protons), atomic WEIGHT in atomic mass units (i.e., 1 amu = 1.660×10^{-24} grams), the YEAR discovered, the name(s) of its DISCOVERER(s), and atomic RADII in angstroms (i.e., 1 angstrom = 1.000×10^{-10} meters). Basic elemental data came from the volume edited by Robert C. Weast for the Chemical Rubber Company, *CRC Handbook of*

Chemistry and Physics: 68th Edition (1987, CRC Press, Inc., Boca Raton, FL). Additional information such as atomic radii from page 43 of Martha J. Gilleland's *Introduction to General, Organic, and Biological Chemistry* (1982, West Publishing Company, 753 pages, St. Paul, MN) and most historical background data from Isaac Asimov's *The Search for the Elements* (1962, Basic Books Publishing Co., Inc., 158 pages, New York, NY).

```
open ( unit=5, file='pt.input' )
read ( 5,layout%input ) periodic
close ( unit=5 )
```

A brief extract from the top and bottom of the input file shows this organization:

```
Hydrogen      H    1   1.00794 1766 Cavendish          0.371
Helium        He   2   4.00260 1895 Ramsay
Lithium       Li   3   6.941   1817 Arfvedson           1.23
  .            .   .    .         .    .
  .            .   .    .         .    .
  .            .   .    .         .    .
Lawrencium    Lr 103 260.       1961 Ghiorso et. al.
Unnilquadium  UQ 104 261.       1964
Unnilpentium  UP 105 262.       1967
Unnilhexium   UH 106 263.       1974
```

Although PERIODIC is declared as an array of 106 instances of type MENDELEEV, its simplest access treats it as an array no more complicated than if were a straightforward list of numbers:

```
print *, " "
print *, "The first few elements in atomic number order ..."
write ( *,layout%output ) ( periodic(i), i = 1, 3 )
```

which display:

```
The first few elements in atomic number order ...
Hydrogen      H    1   1.007940 1766 Cavendish          0.371
Helium        He   2   4.002600 1895 Ramsay             0.000
Lithium       Li   3   6.941000 1817 Arfvedson          1.230
```

A more complicated use extracts all the information about the noble gases. Earlier in this program, a data structure called GASES was declared identical in every respect to PERIODIC except length (i.e., 6 versus 106, respectively). Also, a simple numeric list—NOBLE—was declared containing the atomic number of the half dozen noble gases. This short vector list (i.e., NOBLE was initialized to {2, 10, 18, 36, 54, 86}) is used as a vector subscript into PERIODIC to isolate the noble gases:

```
print *, " "
print *, "The noble gases ..."
```

```
    gases = periodic ( noble )
    do i = 1, size ( noble ), 1
       write ( *,layout%by_type ) gases(i)%name,
    —                             gases(i)%number
    end do
```

It displays:

```
The noble gases ...
Helium      [002]
Neon        [010]
Argon       [018]
Krypton     [036]
Xenon       [054]
Astatine    [085]
```

So far, each example has used a derived type within the confines of a single program unit. To identify those elements discovered in the late 18th century, the YEAR component of PERIODIC is passed to a sorting routine which returns a vector, ORDER, containing array indices in the required sequence.

```
    print *, " "
    print *, "Elements discovered in the late 18th century ..."
    call sort ( order, elements, IARRAY=periodic%year )
    do i = 1, elements, 1
       j = order(i)
       if ( periodic(j)%year .lt. 1750 ) cycle
       if ( periodic(j)%year .gt. 1799 ) exit
       write ( *,layout%by_year ) periodic(j)%year,
    —                             periodic(j)%discoverer,
    —                             periodic(j)%name,
    —                             periodic(j)%number
    end do
```

Both CYCLE and EXIT are new Fortran 90 DO-loop features. CYCLE signals that the DO-loop should begin a new iteration. EXIT stops any further DO-loop iterations and terminates the loop. IARRAY is a keyword in the SORT subroutine call that signifies an optional argument. In this case, SORT is advised that an INTEGER array is being passed. This feature of subroutine calls is discussed in Chapter 4, *Subroutines and Functions Revisited*. The output is:

```
Elements discovered in the late 18th century ...
1751 Cronstedt      Nickel      [028]
1766 Cavendish      Hydrogen    [001]
1772 Rutherford     Nitrogen    [007]
1774 Gahn           Manganese   [025]
1774 Priestley      Oxygen      [008]
1774 Scheele        Chlorine    [017]
```

```
1782 Hjelm                    Molybdenum  [042]
1782 Reichenstein             Tellurium   [052]
1783 de Elhuyar & de Elhuyar  Tungsten    [074]
1789 Klaproth                 Zirconium   [040]
1789 Klaproth                 Uranium     [092]
1791 Gregor                   Titanium    [022]
1794 Gadolin                  Yttrium     [039]
1797 Vauquelin                Chromium    [024]
1798 Vauquelin                Beryllium   [004]
```

Finally, the data is ordered and searched again, keying on atomic radii:

```
    print *," "
    print *,"Five smallest group {IA,IIA,...,VIIA} elements..."
    call sort ( order, elements, RARRAY=periodic%radii )
    do i = 1, elements, 1
       j = order(i)
       if ( periodic(j)%radii .le. 0.0 ) cycle
       write ( *,layout%by_radii ) periodic(j)%radii,
  —                                periodic(j)%name,
  —                                periodic(j)%number
       k = k + 1
       if ( k .eq. 5 ) exit
    end do
    end program pt
```

to report the smallest atoms in certain groups:

```
Five smallest group {IA,IIA,...,VIIA} elements...
0.371 Hydrogen   [001]
0.640 Flourine   [009]
0.660 Oxygen     [008]
0.700 Nitrogen   [007]
0.770 Carbon     [006]
```

Sorting the PERIODIC structure requires a routine that can manage both integers and reals to correspond to the YEAR and RADII components. Fortran 90 can accomplish this with optional keywords in a subroutine call. Chapter 4 will show how to produce even more seamless subprogram integration using Fortran 90's INTERFACE feature, but, for now, the first few lines of PT define the SORT call:

```
    program pt
    interface
      subroutine sort ( indices, n, iarray, rarray )
        integer, dimension(n)           :: indices
        integer                            n
        integer, dimension(n), optional :: iarray
        real,    dimension(n), optional :: rarray
      end subroutine sort
```

```
end interface
integer, parameter :: elements = 106
     .
     .
     .
```

The subprogram is an implementation of a diminishing increment sort as described starting on page 84 of Donald E. Knuth's *The Art of Computer Programming: Volume 3—Sorting and Searching* (1973, Addison-Wesley Publishing Company, 723 pages, Reading, MA). It begins with the following declarations:

```
subroutine sort ( indices, n, iarray, rarray )
integer                                i, im, j, k, l, m, n
integer, dimension(n), optional    :: iarray
integer, dimension(:), allocatable :: icopy
integer, dimension(n)              :: indices
integer                               itemp
real,    dimension(n), optional    :: rarray
real,    dimension(:), allocatable :: rcopy
real                                  rtemp
```

Since the program does not call for an "in place" sort, the input data need to be copied.

```
if ( present(iarray) ) then
     allocate ( icopy(n) )
     icopy = iarray
else
     allocate ( rcopy(n) )
     rcopy = rarray
end if
```

After initializing the array of indices to the sequence {1,2,3,...,N} using Fortran 90's DO-loop array constructor, a stopping rule is set for the sort:

```
      indices = (/ ( i, i = 1, n ) /)
100   continue
      if ( n .le. 1 ) go to 800
```

and the sorting quantum is gradually decremented (whence the "diminish" comes in the phrase "diminishing increment sort"):

```
      m  = 1
200   continue
      m  = m + m
      if ( m .lt. n ) go to 200
      m  = m - 1
300   continue
      m  = m / 2
      if ( m .eq. 0 ) go to 800
```

```
      k = n - m
      j = 1
400   continue
      i = j
500   continue
      im = i + m
```

Depending on the data type, compare elements and exchange as appropriate:

```
      if ( present(iarray) ) then
          if ( icopy(i) .gt. icopy(im) ) go to 700
      else
          if ( rcopy(i) .gt. rcopy(im) ) go to 700
      end if
600   continue
      j = j + 1
      if ( j .gt. k ) go to 300
      go to 400
700   continue
      if ( present(iarray) ) then
          itemp     = icopy(i)
          icopy(i)  = icopy(im)
          icopy(im) = itemp
      else
          rtemp     = rcopy(i)
          rcopy(i)  = rcopy(im)
          rcopy(im) = rtemp
      end if
      l           = indices(i)
      indices(i)  = indices(im)
      indices(im) = l
```

Continue sorting until complete and then deallocate work arrays:

```
      i = i - m
      if ( i .lt .1 ) go to 600
      go to 500
800   continue
      if ( present(iarray) ) then
          deallocate ( icopy )
      else
          deallocate ( rcopy )
      end if
      end subroutine sort
```

Where Fixed Sequence Is Necessary

Normally, Fortran 90 makes no assumptions about the storage of derived types. The processor must always create the illusion that components are being stored and retrieved in the order in which they were declared (for instance, during I/O or TRANSFER statements), but in reality it is free to insert gaps between them to optimize access times. It can theoretically even store them in completely arbitrary locations, such as might happen on a system that supports scatter/gather operations with multiple channels to disk.

Only in two situations does the reality of physical storage have to match the view shown to the programmer. For these situations, Fortran 90 provides a SEQUENCE statement, which appears before any component in the type definition block:

```
type key_facts
    sequence
    character ( len=32 ) :: who
    character ( len=32 ) :: what
    character ( len=32 ) :: where
    character ( len=32 ) :: why
    character ( len=32 ) :: when
end type key_facts
type ( key_facts ) critical_events(100)
common / history / critical_events
```

The first situation is when the derived type appears in a common block. Fortran has always been uncharacteristically strict in calling for sequential storage of data without gaps in the common block. The SEQUENCE statement permits derived types to participate. However, if a program uses the more modern form of global storage endorsed in Fortran 90, the MODULE, then derived types can appear without SEQUENCE.

The second situation is similar to the first: a derived data type that appears in an EQUIVALENCE statement must contain SEQUENCE.

4

Subroutines and Functions Revisited

Programmers avoid modifications to working code. Inheriting a production application puts a programmer in a position of trust, in regard to the robustness and fitness of that code. Being asked to change the code makes that same programmer uncomfortable.

Although program documentation always details input file formats, report layouts, variable names, and their interpretation, it rarely describes the interfaces between subprograms. Somehow, the source code is expected to "speak" and tell the programmer all its intricate structural secrets by inspection.

It doesn't happen that way. Programmers are accustomed to poring over source listings to construct call trees, argument lists, and patterns of COMMON usage. It is tiresome work. Fortran 90 introduces several features that document and clarify program structure:

- INCLUDE statements to share source code fragments

- INTERFACE definitions

- INTENT (IN, OUT, or INOUT) for arguments

- Typeless subprograms

Combining these features with defensive programming practices improves the chances of producing "self documenting" code.

Fortran 90 also introduces additional enhancements to using subprograms. Just like some Fortran statements (i.e., OPEN and WRITE) take position independent keyword parameters, now arguments to user-written subprograms can be declared OPTIONAL. And, finally, a Fortran subprogram can be declared RECURSIVE.

Many of the problems cited in this chapter receive more complete solutions in Chapter 6, *Modules*, which introduces modules. In other words, this chapter offers relatively simple tools for clumping and generalizing program parts, but a truly flexible solution awaits Chapter 6.

Program Structure

One classic program structure organizes the collection as a main program, an initialization routine, a processing driver (responsible for the real work of the program), a reporting routine, some subprogram to finish up, and an error handler. Graphically, this structure can be drawn as shown in Figure 4-1 in which solid lines indicate the call hierarchy, ellipses hold the place of additional, unnamed routines, and dotted lines connect service routines. This classic program structure appears again and again in Fortran programs. It has a rich history reaching back to real memory computers. In that era, each branch in the diagram identified an overlay. Service routines and COMMONs were grouped with the main program in the overlay root. Now, virtual memory systems are ubiquitous and the need for overlays is gone, but this pattern survives.

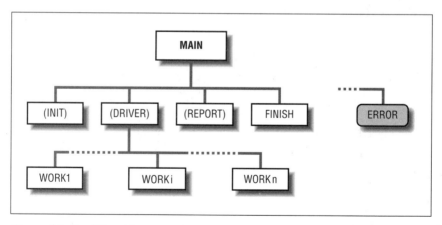

Figure 4-1: Traditional program structure

Example: Kendall's Coefficient of Concordance

A specific example of this classic program structure is the program CONCORD. It computes W, Kendall's coefficient of concordance. W evaluates the consistency in ranking N events by M judges and is well described on pages 229 through 239 in Sydney Siegal's *Nonparametric Statistics for the Behavioral Sciences* (1956, McGraw-Hill Book Company, Inc., 312 pages, New York, NY). One of Kendall's original examples appears in Siegal's text; it concerns the situation of six job applicants being interviewed by three employers who ranked, from 1 to 6, the suitability of each applicant.

Employer	App. 1	App. 2	App. 3	App. 4	App. 5	App. 6
A	1	6	3	2	5	4
B	1	5	6	4	2	3
C	6	3	2	5	4	1

W measures the consistency in the rankings that employers give applicants. If all three employers were in perfect agreement about the applicants' suitability, then W equals one. The more the rankings differ, the closer W becomes to zero. As such, W ranges from 0 to 1: from discord to concordance. In this applicant/employer example, the employers do not present a very consistent view of the applicants suitability, which is supported by a value of W = 0.162.

W is applicable to a variety of settings in which an evaluation occurs. The "applicant" and "employer" labels from the example can be replaced in marketing by six competing products evaluated by three members of a focus group, in archaeology by relative abundance of an artifact type of six different materials found at three sites, or in agriculture by preferences for six feed mixes shown by three individual farm animals. Anywhere that ranked data is the most precise information applicable to an evaluation of N events by M judges, Kendall's coefficient of concordance is an appropriate measure of consistency.

CONCORD is structured in the classic pattern described above. Graphically, it is organized as shown in Figure 4-2.

As usual, details of the implementation will be described as the source code is presented. However, given the focus of this chapter, it makes sense here to kill the suspense and give the output of TELL, input to INPUT, and output from RESULT. In the diagram, execution travels the hierarchy from top to bottom and from left to right. To document that execution flow, CONCORD includes a service routine TELL which, when executed in "debug" mode, displays the call tree.

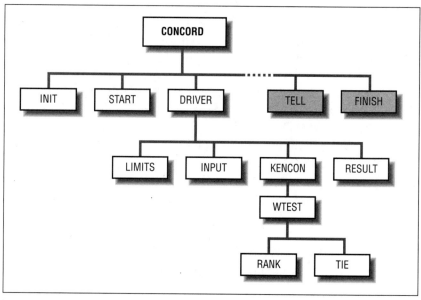

Figure 4-2: CONCORD program structure

```
TELL: .MAIN.
TELL:      start

CONCORD is a classically structured program.

Enter data file name: concord
Input file concord.input open on unit 07
Output file concord.output open on unit 08
TELL: .MAIN.
TELL:      driver
TELL:           limits

Enter number of judges: 3

Enter number of events: 6
TELL:      driver
TELL:           input
INPUT: event 00001 name event1
INPUT: event 00002 name event2
INPUT: event 00003 name event3
INPUT: event 00004 name event4
INPUT: event 00005 name event5
INPUT: event 00006 name event6
INPUT: judge 00001 name JUDGEA
INPUT: judge 00002 name JUDGEB
INPUT: judge 00003 name JUDGEC
```

```
INPUT: scores   1.0  6.0  3.0  2.0  5.0  4.0
INPUT: scores   1.0  5.0  6.0  4.0  2.0  3.0
INPUT: scores   6.0  3.0  2.0  5.0  4.0  1.0
TELL:      driver
TELL:              kencon
TELL:                      wtest
TELL:                              rank
TELL:                      wtest
TELL:                              tie
TELL:                      wtest
TELL:                              rank
TELL:                      wtest
TELL:                              tie
TELL:                      wtest
TELL:                              rank
TELL:                      wtest
TELL:                              tie
TELL:                      wtest
TELL:              kencon
TELL:      driver
TELL:              result
TELL:      driver
TELL: .MAIN.
TELL:      finish

Closing files ...
UNIT=07 NAME=concord.input
UNIT=08 NAME=concord.output

CONCORD is finished.
TELL: .MAIN.
TELL:      error

No errors detected.

TELL: .MAIN.
```

Given an input file with the following data:

```
event1
event2
event3
event4
event5
event6
JUDGEA  1.0  6.0  3.0  2.0  5.0  4.0
JUDGEB  1.0  5.0  6.0  4.0  2.0  3.0
JUDGEC  6.0  3.0  2.0  5.0  4.0  1.0
```

the program prints the following results:

```
              KENDALL'S COEFFICIENT OF CONCORDANCE

          event1 event2 event3 event4 event5 event6

JUDGEA    1.0     6.0     3.0     2.0     5.0     4.0
JUDGEB    1.0     5.0     6.0     4.0     2.0     3.0
JUDGEC    6.0     3.0     2.0     5.0     4.0     1.0

        0.162 Kendall's Coefficient
        0.000 Chi-squared [if number of events, 06, exceeds 7]
            0 Degrees of Freedom
```

The main program of CONCORD is short, but introduces two Fortran 90 features. INCLUDE statements allow programmers to consolidate code that is shared across the whole program, and INTERFACEs provide a subprogram prototype for strong error-checking. Each subprogram INTERFACE is defined in the file CONCORD.INT and all COMMON variables are declared in the file CONCORD.INS.

```
program concord
INCLUDE 'concord.int'
INCLUDE 'concord.ins'
name = '.MAIN.'
call init
call tell ( name, push )
call start
call tell ( name, pass )
call driver
call tell ( name, pass )
call finish
call tell ( name, pass )
call error
call tell ( name, pass )
call tell ( name, pop )
end program concord
```

INCLUDE Files

In CONCORD, two definition files are brought into play by Fortran 90's INCLUDE feature. Many Fortran implementations have extended Fortran 77 to incorporate a feature such as INCLUDE. Fortran 90 has standardized it as a convenience, but, as seen in Chapter 6, supersedes it with the idea of a MODULE and the USE statement that brings a MODULE into play.

Fairly common restrictions apply to the source in the INCLUDE file: it must not begin with a continuation line, it may contain other INCLUDE lines nested to whatever depth the processor allows, and it must never incorporate source files in a circular, deadly embrace (i.e., INCLUDE A contains INCLUDE B which in turn contains INCLUDE A). Also, the INCLUDE line itself cannot carry a statement label. However, one area not standardized is the syntax indicating the name of the included file. Here, the filename is enclosed in single quotation marks, but that is processor dependent. Other processor-dependent issues that reduce the portability of the preFortran 90 INCLUDE lines may exist (e.g., searching standard "include" directories). Chapter 1, *Compatibility*, contains recommendations for coding style in INCLUDEd files.

Subprogram INTERFACE Blocks

The CONCORD.INT file contains definitions of the INTERFACE for all thirteen subprograms. Some are quite simple because the subprogram has no arguments and is serviced entirely through COMMON.

```
interface
   subroutine driver
      end subroutine driver
   .
   .
   .
```

Others are more complex because the subprogram requires several arguments:

```
   .
   .
   .
   subroutine tie ( ranked_scores, mevents, ties )
      integer,                       intent(in ) :: mevents
      real,    dimension (mevents), intent(in ) :: ranked_scores
      real,                          intent(out) :: ties
      end subroutine tie
   .
   .
   .
end interface
```

Declaring the INTENT to Use a Argument

It is optional, but very valuable, to declare the INTENT of each argument as input to the subprogram (IN), output from the subprogram (OUT), or either (INOUT). An argument declared with INTENT(IN) cannot be defined or redefined in the subprogram. An argument declared with INTENT(OUT) must be defined before it is referenced. Arguments I and J are treated incorrectly in the following program, and a Fortran 90 complier should flag the problem, thus showing the value of INTENT for rudimentary errorchecking.

```
program wrong
interface
  subroutine way ( i, j )
    integer, intent(IN ) :: i
    integer, intent(OUT) :: j
  end subroutine way
end interface
integer :: m = 123
integer :: n = 0
call way ( m, n )
end program wrong

subroutine way ( i, j )
integer, intent(IN ) :: i
integer, intent(OUT) :: j
integer          :: k
i = 456 ! ERROR: INTENT(IN) ARGUMENT RE-DEFINED
k = j   ! ERROR: INTENT(OUT) ARGUMENT UNDEFINED
end subroutine way
```

The example includes two blatant errors: INTENT(IN) argument I is redefined during execution and INTENT(OUT) argument J is referenced before being assigned a value. The intended use of an argument—IN, OUT, or INOUT—is similar in concept to the new ACTION keyword in the OPEN statement where file usage is declared to be READ, WRITE, or READWRITE (see Chapter 8, *File Handling*).

Variable and COMMON Definitions in INCLUDE Files

Consistent definitions of COMMON facilitates rapid program development. Managing COMMON definitions without a feature like INCLUDE is a very tall order. It is time consuming and error prone to edit all occurrences where COMMON is declared when a change needs to be made. But INCLUDE keeps the source for COMMON declarations in one or more related files where change can be managed. Here, a parameter is set, global and local variables are declared, and COMMON /AREA/ is established in the CONCORD.INS file.

```
integer                    MAXUNT
parameter                  ( MAXUNT=10 )
```

```
real                                              chisqr
integer                                           crtin
integer                                           crtout
logical                                           debug
integer                                           degfre
character* 6, dimension(:  ), pointer :: ename
integer                                           events
integer                                      :: i = 0
character*14                                       ifile
integer                                           io
integer                                           iunit
integer                                      :: j = 0
character* 6, dimension(:  ), pointer :: jname
integer                                           judges
real                                              kendal
logical                                           mistak
character* 6                                 :: name = ' '
character*14                                       ofile
integer                                           ounit
integer                                           pass
integer                                           pop
integer                                           push
real,          dimension(:,:), pointer :: scores
logical                                           units(MAXUNT)
common / area /  chisqr, crtin,   crtout, debug,  degfre,
    –                events, io,      iunit,   judges, kendal,
    –                mistak, ounit,   pass,    pop,    push,
    –                scores, units,
    –                ename,  ifile,   jname,   ofile
```

Some variables—I, J, and NAME—are declared because they will be used in nearly every routine and, not appearing in a COMMON statement, are thereby local to each routine. I and J are generic indices and are likely to appear almost anywhere. NAME ties directly into the hierarchy diagram of the CONCORD program shown earlier. Each time control arrives in and returns to a subprogram, its NAME is passed to the TELL routine to display the call tree.

Three arrays—ENAME, JNAME, and SCORES—are dynamic. They are initialized to the null state in INIT and their size will be established in the LIMITS routine. As covered in the previous chapter, dynamic arrays have some terrific advantages over static arrays. But ALLOCATABLE arrays can not be placed in COMMON. This seems to severely restrict all the advantages of run time allocation. However, if these arrays are declared with the POINTER attribute (see Chapter 7, *Dynamic Memory Management*), then they can be carried in COMMON.

Note that both numeric and character variables appear in COMMON. Fortran 77 required that if a COMMON block contained any character variable or array then all entities in that COMMON block had to be of type character. Many implementations of Fortran 77 relaxed this requirement and Fortran 90 follows that lead.

Variables and arrays in both COMMON areas are initialized and the three pointer arrays are nullified in the INIT routine that appears in Appendix D, *Selected Source Code Listings*.

Tracing Execution Flow

Earlier, output from the service routine TELL was shown. It traces the execution flow of the entire CONCORD program.

```
      subroutine tell ( what, where )
      INCLUDE 'concord.ins'
      character*6,              intent(in ) :: what
      integer,                  intent(in ) :: where
      integer                              :: depth
      save depth
      if ( where .ne. pop ) then
            if ( where .eq. push ) depth = depth + 1
            if ( debug ) then
                  write ( crtout,100,advance="NO" )
100               format ( 1H , "TELL: " )
                  do i = 2, depth, 1
                     write ( crtout,200,advance="NO" )
200                  format ( 6x )
                  end do
                  write ( crtout,300 ) what
300               format ( a6 )
            end if
      end if
      if ( where .eq. pop ) depth = depth - 1
      end subroutine tell
```

Each time a subprogram begins, it calls TELL with two arguments: the subprogram's name and an indicator of "level change" in the hierarchy of CONCORD. The indicator informs TELL whether control has gone down a level (PUSH), up a level (POP), or stayed the same (PASS). TELL then displays that subprogram's name indented corresponding to that subprogram's level in the hierarchy of CONCORD. Furthermore, each time control returns to a subprogram, it calls TELL again to document the course of execution. This mechanism is a convenient method to record the structure of a program.

Preparation for Calculating Kendall's W

Four subprograms are used to complete preparation for calculating Kendall's W. START is responsible for getting the name of the input file, verifying its existence, and opening the output file. At this stage, DRIVER is invoked by CONCORD and calls LIMITS and INPUT. LIMITS solicits the number of judges and events for this run of CONCORD and allocates the data arrays:

```
        .
        .
        .
    allocate (  ename(events) )
    allocate (  jname(judges) )
    allocate ( scores(judges,events) )
        .
        .
        .
```

which will remain allocated until the end of the program. Note that if a fatal error occurs, CONCORD calls ERROR, which will clear these dynamic arrays. INPUT reads the input file and checks for any out-of-line values. Because these subprograms contain no particularly new features promoting Fortran 90, the source code for them appear in Appendix D.

Incorporating Pre-existing Code

Having finally acquired all the data, routine KENCON makes the call to compute W, Kendall's coefficient of concordance, and checks its computation for validity.

```
        subroutine kencon
        INCLUDE 'concord.ins'
        real, dimension(:), allocatable :: a
        name  = 'kencon'
        call tell ( name, push )
        allocate ( a(events*judges) )
        a  = pack ( scores, MASK=scores.ne.0.0 )
        call wtest ( a, judges, events, kendal, chisqr, degfre )
        call tell ( name, pass )
        if ( kendal .lt. 0.0 .or. kendal .gt. 1.0 ) then
            write ( crtout,100 ) kendal
100         format ( 1H , 'Coefficient negative or exceeds one!' )
            mistak = .TRUE.
            call error
        end if
        deallocate ( a  )
```

```
call tell ( name, pop )
end subroutine kencon
```

The algorithm to compute the coefficient of concordance expects the table of raw scores to be expressed as a vector. Consequently, KENCON creates the vector in A and uses Fortran 90's PACK intrinsic to collapse the scores table into one dimension.

Computing the coefficient is the province of the WTEST routine. At execution time, WTEST declares arguments and local variables:

```
subroutine wtest ( raw, njudges,     mevents,
  —                    w,    chi_square, ndf        )
  INCLUDE 'concord.ins'
  real                                        :: avr_rank
  real,                        intent(out):: chi_square
  integer,                     intent(in ):: mevents
  integer,                     intent(out):: ndf
  integer,                     intent(in ):: njudges
  integer                                     :: nm
  real,   dimension(njudges*mevents)          :: ranked
  real,   dimension(njudges*mevents),intent(in) :: raw
  real                                        :: rm
  real                                        :: rn
  real                                        :: t
  real                                        :: ties
  real,                        intent(out):: w
  real,   dimension(mevents)                  :: work
```

and initializes the latter.

```
name  = 'wtest'
call tell ( name, push )
nm = njudges * mevents
rm = real(mevents)
rn = real(njudges)
t  = 0.0
```

It then ranks the scores on the M events for each of N judges by working with one judge at a time. Scores for all events for an individual judge are passed to RANK using Fortran 90's concept of a "stride," since the selection of every Nth element of RAW_SCORES reconstructs a row of the original SCORES array.

```
do i = 1, njudges, 1
   call rank ( raw(i:nm:njudges),
   —                ranked(i:nm:njudges),
   —                mevents                 )
   call tell ( name, pass )
```

This is very compact code. Without Fortran 90's array syntax, each "row" of the original scores would have had to have been extracted from RAW_SCORES in a complicated series of DO loops and stored in a temporary work vector. That work vector would have then been passed to RANK along with another temporary work vector to receive the results of RANK. Fortran 90's array syntax avoids both work vectors. The source code for the RANK subprogram appears in Appendix D.

If a judge assigns the same score to two events, then that affects the value computed for W. So, a correction factor for ties is maintained.

```
call tie  ( ranked(i:nm:njudges), mevents, ties )
call tell ( name, pass )
t = t + ties
```

The source code for the TIE subprogram appears in Appendix D.

Computing Kendall's Coefficient of Concordance

Kendall's coefficient of concordance is defined by equation 9.16 on page 234 from Siegal's 1956 text:

$$w = \frac{s}{\frac{1}{12}n^2(m^3 - m) - n\sum_{i=1}^{n} t_i}$$

where S is the sum of squares of deviations from the mean rank, N is the number of judges, M is the number of events, and T_i is the tie correction factor for the Ith judge. S is formed by summing the ranks for each of M events given by all N judges, getting the average rank (SM), computing the sum of squared deviations using Fortran 90's DOT_PRODUCT intrinsic, and then calculating the value for W.

```
work = 0.0
do j = 1, mevents, 1
    work(j) = sum ( ranked(1+(njudges*(j-1)):njudges*j) )
end do
avr_rank = sum ( work ) / rm
s = dot_product ( work-avr_rank, work-avr_rank )
w   = s / ( ( ( rn*rn ) * ( rm*rm*rm - rm ) / 12.0 ) - rn*t)
```

The complicated index scheme for RANKED in the SUM intrinsic extracts N-length segments from RANKED (i.e., 1 to N, N+1 to 2N, 2N+1 to 3N, 3N+1 to 4N, etc.). If the number of events, M, is more than seven, then the statistic N(M-1)W is approximately distributed as chi square with N-1 degrees of freedom.

```
      if ( mevents .gt. 7 ) then
          chi_square = rn * ( rm - 1.0 ) * w
          ndf        = mevents - 1
      else
          chi_square = 0.0
          ndf        = 0
      end if
      call tell ( name, pop )
      end subroutine wtest
```

If the number of events, M, is seven or less, the significance of the value computed for W can be evaluated based on the value of the sum of squared deviations, S, using Table R on page 286 of the Siegal text. When the results for this particular example are produced by REPORT, the value computed for W of 0.162 is not significant. The source code for REPORT appears in Appendix D.

Clean Exits

Two final housekeeping tasks remain: closing files and deallocating arrays. FINISH examines the UNITS vector to close open files and its source appears in Appendix D. ERROR takes care of the dynamic arrays ENAME, JNAME, and SCORES.

```
      subroutine error
      INCLUDE 'concord.ins'
      name = 'error'
      call tell ( name, push )
      if ( mistak ) then
          write ( crtout,100 )
100       format ( / 1H , 'ERROR! Fatal mistake!' / )
          stop
      else
          write ( crtout,200 )
200       format ( / 1H , 'No errors detected.' / )
      end if
      if ( associated ( ename ) ) deallocate ( ename )
      if ( associated ( jname ) ) deallocate ( jname )
      if ( associated ( scores ) ) deallocate ( scores )
      call tell ( name, pop )
      end subroutine error
```

Since this routine might be called by START before these three dynamic arrays have been allocated in LIMITS, they are DEALLOCATEd only if the ASSOCIATED intrinsic indicates that they have been created. But even before START, all three pointer arrays were nullified in the INIT routine. If that had not been done, then their associated status would have been undefined, leading to an inappropriate use of the ASSOCIATED intrinsic.

Classic Program Structure

CONCORD is an example of classic program structure. Files must be opened, tracked, and closed. Problem size (i.e., here, events and judges) must be determined and arrays and vectors declared, initialized, and populated. Input file must be read with great care to trap and report format and data errors. Computations must be performed and diligently checked (i.e., $0 \leq W \leq 1$). Reports must be created. And all the while, the user—and, optionally, the developer—has to be reassured that processing is going forward through prompts and displays. CONCORD is no different from an untold number of Fortran programs in terms of form and basic division of labor. Fortran 90 can improve programs through rigorous adherence to clear and clean subroutine INTERFACEs, dynamic array management, and powerful intrinsic functions.

Generic Subprograms

It has always been a marvel that many Fortran intrinsic functions can accept arguments of a variety of types. Fortran permits the generic intrinsic ABS to accept complex, double precision, and integer arguments even though specific intrinsics CABS, DABS, and IABS exist. But until Fortran 90, Fortran programmers had no mechanism to create user-defined generic subprograms.

Defining a single name that can be invoked on data of different types is just a form of documentation, superficially speaking. But its true meaning is deeper: it allows the programmer to conceive of a "method" that applies to data of different types. In other words, to define a single subprogram name on different data types announces that they share some attribute that permits a common activity to be performed on them.

The program GENERIC declares the interface to a generic routine INCREMENT that will accept either an integer or a real argument.

```
program generic
interface increment
  subroutine i_increment ( value )
    integer, intent ( inout ) :: value
    end subroutine i_increment
```

```
      subroutine r_increment ( value )
         real,    intent ( inout ) :: value
         end subroutine r_increment
   end interface
```

Note that names of the subroutines are arbitrarily chosen. I_INCREMENT and R_INCREMENT are named to remind the programer of their data type and the INTERFACE they represent. They could just as well have been named FRED and TED. Once defined, calls can be made to INCREMENT— not I_INCREMENT or R_INCREMENT—with either an INTEGER or REAL argument.

```
      integer :: i = 123
      real    :: r = 456.0
      print *, " "
      print *, "Incrementing", i
      call increment ( i )
      print *, " "
      print *, "Incrementing", r
      call increment ( r )
      print *, " "
      end program generic
```

The INTEGER and REAL code that implements the two INCREMENT routines follow:

```
      subroutine i_increment ( value )
      integer, intent ( inout ) :: value
      value  = value + 1
      print *, "      yields", value
      end subroutine i_increment

      subroutine r_increment ( value )
      real,    intent ( inout ) :: value
      value  = value + 1.0
      print *, "      yields", value
      end subroutine r_increment
```

When executed, this display results:

```
Incrementing 123
      yields 124

Incrementing    4.5600000E+02
      yields    4.5700000E+02
```

Programmers can use a single name to reference a routine for any of several data types: both the intrinsic types—INTEGER, REAL, etc.—and newly invented derived types. For example, the program GEOMETRY has a

generic interface, COMPUTE_AREA, for routines to calculate the area of
selected geometric shapes.

```
type rectangle
      sequence
      real base
      real height
end  type rectangle
type circle
      sequence
      real radius
end  type circle
```

One generic INTERFACE can be declared that references subprograms to
compute the area of rectangles and circles.

```
program geometry
interface compute_area
  subroutine rectangle_area ( some_rectangle, area )
    include 'geometry.inc'
    type ( rectangle ) some_rectangle
    real area
    end subroutine rectangle_area
  subroutine circle_area ( some_circle, area )
    include 'geometry.inc'
    type ( circle ) some_circle
    real area
    end subroutine circle_area
end interface
```

Declare instances of both derived types.

```
include 'geometry.inc'
type ( rectangle ) four_sides
type ( circle   ) round
real :: area = 0.0
```

Compute the area of either geometric shape by calling the generic
COMPUTE_AREA routine.

```
      four_sides = rectangle ( 2.3, 4.5 )
      call compute_area ( four_sides, area )
      write ( 6,100 ) four_sides, area
100   format ( / 1H , "Area of ", f3.1, " by ", f3.1,
      -                " rectangle is ", f5.2 )
      round = circle ( 6.7 )
      call compute_area ( round, area )
      write ( 6,200 ) round, area
200   format ( 1H , "Area of circle with ", f3.1,
      -               " radius is ", f9.5 )
```

```
      print *, " "
      end program geometry
```

The program displays the following lines:

```
      Area of 2.3 by 4.5 rectangle is 10.35
      Area of circle with 6.7 radius is 141.02611
```

The area computations for each specific geometric shape is accomplished in the following routines:

```
      subroutine rectangle_area ( some_rectangle, area )
      include 'geometry.inc'
      type ( rectangle ) some_rectangle
      real area
      area = some_rectangle%base * some_rectangle%height
      end subroutine rectangle_area

      subroutine circle_area ( some_circle, area )
      include 'geometry.inc'
      type ( circle ) some_circle
      real area
      area = 3.141593 * ( some_circle%radius * some_circle%radius )
      end subroutine circle_area
```

For default types, generic routines simplify using user-written mathematical and statistical libraries. It doesn't eliminate the need to maintain separate single and double precision subprograms. Even if they are called through the same interface, such subprograms would still require their own set of constants, formats, and (perhaps) algorithms to handle different precision. However, using such routines is easier because the applications programmer needs only to recall one procedure name.

For user-defined types, generic routines simplify the adaptation of routines to multiple data types. It just makes sense to have one procedure name represent one algorithm or functional area of a program regardless of the data structure inside a user-defined type.

Optional Arguments

Just like Fortran's multitype intrinsics, it also is enviable that certain Fortran statements—CLOSE, OPEN, INQUIRE, READ, WRITE—accept keywords that signal the presence of optional arguments. Fortran 90 extends that capability to the programmer. The program PANIC exercises a general error handler, ERROR, that accepts four different optional arguments.

```
      program panic
      interface
```

```
subroutine error ( wrong, alpha, float, whole, logic )
  character(*), optional :: alpha
  real,         optional :: float
  integer,      optional :: whole
  logical,      optional :: logic
  integer                   wrong
 end subroutine error
end interface
```

The OPTIONAL qualifier establishes that any or all of the arguments ALPHA, FLOAT, WHOLE, or LOGIC may occur in any combination. On the other hand, WRONG is a required argument that is positional. Fixed, positional arguments must appear before any OPTIONAL arguments, but the caller can give OPTIONAL arguments in any order.

```
call error ( 0 )
call error ( 1, alpha = 'mistake' )
call error ( 1, float = 1.2 )
call error ( 1, whole = 345 )
call error ( 1, logic = .TRUE. )
call error ( 1, logic = .FALSE.,  float = 6.7,
-              alpha = 'failure',whole = 890  )
end program panic
```

Here, the routine that accepts these OPTIONAL arguments displays its own name.

```
subroutine error ( wrong, alpha, float, whole, logic )
character(*), optional :: alpha
real,         optional :: float
integer,      optional :: whole
logical,      optional :: logic
integer                   wrong
write ( 6,100,advance='NO' )
100  format ( / 1H , 'ERROR: ' )
```

Then, if the WRONG error indicator is set, Fortran 90's PRESENT intrinsic checks to see if an OPTIONAL argument has been given. If so, its value is displayed:

```
if ( wrong .ne. 0 ) then
    if ( present ( a ) ) write ( 6,200,advance='NO' ) alpha
    if ( present ( f ) ) write ( 6,200,advance='NO' ) float
    if ( present ( i ) ) write ( 6,200,advance='NO' ) whole
    if ( present ( l ) ) write ( 6,200,advance='NO' ) logic
200     format ( g10.5, 1x )
```

Otherwise, the user is reassured that no error has occurred:

```
    else
        write ( 6,300,advance='NO' )
300     format ( 'everything''s fine!' )
    end if
    end subroutine error
```

On execution, the following display results.

```
    ERROR: everything's fine!
    ERROR:    mistake
    ERROR: 1.2000
    ERROR:         345
    ERROR:          T
    ERROR:    failure 6.7000              890            F
```

Optional arguments have applicability throughout the domain of Fortran programs. However, as demonstrated in the PANIC example, one area in which they are very useful is error handling. Another area is in porting programs between platforms. Fortran vendors commonly offer extensions in the form of keywords to vendor-specific library routines. Fortran 90's OPTIONAL arguments allow the migration programmer to develop replacements for such extensions without having to change the original interface.

Recursion

Many Fortran implementations have offered recursion as an extension. Now the Fortran 90 standard provides a guaranteed, portable way to write recursive subprograms. The program APPROX implements a series approximation to the arcsin function. It is based on the equation given on page 351 of the *C. R. C. Standard Mathematical Tables* (Eleventh Edition), edited by Charles D. Hodgman (1957, Chemical Rubber Publishing Company, 480 pages, Cleveland, OH) and is appropriate for any angle Y as measured in radians in the range of $-1 < y < 1$.

$$
\begin{aligned}
\sin^{-1}(y) = \ & y \\
& + y^3 \times \tfrac{1}{6} \\
& + y^5 \times (\tfrac{1}{2} \times \tfrac{3}{4} \times \tfrac{1}{5}) \\
& + y^7 \times (\tfrac{1}{2} \times \tfrac{3}{4} \times \tfrac{5}{6} \times \tfrac{1}{7}) \\
& + y^9 \times (\tfrac{1}{2} \times \tfrac{3}{4} \times \tfrac{5}{6} \times \tfrac{7}{8} \times \tfrac{1}{9}) \\
& + y^{11} \times (\tfrac{1}{2} \times \tfrac{3}{4} \times \tfrac{5}{6} \times \tfrac{7}{8} \times \tfrac{9}{10} \times \tfrac{1}{11}) \\
& + \ldots
\end{aligned}
$$

The program defines the interface to the function ARCSIN as RECURSIVE.

```
program approx
interface
  recursive function arcsin ( angle, terms ) result ( value )
    double precision angle
    integer           terms
    double precision value
    end function arcsin
end interface
double precision :: y
integer          :: parts
```

The FUNCTION declaration has a different syntax from Fortran 77, and contains two new keywords: RECURSIVE and RESULT. RECURSIVE, which precedes the word FUNCTION, is required so that the compiler can prepare the function properly for self-calling (for instance, to use the stack for local variables). RESULT denotes a local variable to contain the value that the function will return.

RESULT is required because the name of a recursive function appears within the function, and must not be confused with the return value. A RESULT statement can be convenient for nonrecursive functions too, but it is not required for them.

A subroutine can also be recursive. Again, the word RECURSIVE must appear first. But there is no need for a RESULT variable.

Since the type of the RESULT variable is declared within the function, the type is no longer required in the FUNCTION statement itself. However, it is permitted to declare the type; it can go either before the RECURSIVE keyword:

```
double precision recursive function arcsin ( angle, terms ) &
                                     result ( value )
```

or after it:

```
recursive double precision function arcsin ( angle, terms ) &
                                     result ( value )
```

The program prompts the user for an angle:

```
100   continue
      print *, " "
      write ( 6,200,advance='NO' )
200   format ( 1H , 'Enter angle (in radians): ' )
      read ( 5,*,err=100 ) y
      if ( ( y * y ) .ge. 1.0d0 ) go to 400
      parts = 0
```

```
         print *, " "
         write ( 6,300 ) y, arcsin ( y, parts ), parts-1
300      format ( 1H , "ARCSIN(", f5.2, ') = ', f10.6,
     -                  ' computed in ', i4.4, ' terms.' )
         go to 100
400      continue
         print *, " "
         end program approx
```

and reports the result and the number of terms required to compute the result. APPROX stops when an angle in entered outside of the range $Y^2 > 1$.

```
Enter angle (in radians):  .5

ARCSIN( 0.50) =   0.523599 computed in 0058 terms.

Enter angle (in radians): 99
```

A stopping rule is a very important part of any recursive code. Here, ARCSIN stops when the number of terms exceeds 100 or the absolute VALUE of the double precision function is less than the smallest REAL the processor can represent.

```
         recursive function arcsin ( angle, terms ) result ( value )
         double precision angle
         double precision factors
         integer          terms
         double precision value
         terms = terms + 1
         select case ( terms )
           case ( 1 )
             factors = 1.0d0
           case ( 2 )
             factors = 1.0d0 / 6.0d0
           case ( 3: )
             factors = 1.0d0
             do i = 1, ((2*terms)-2), 2
                factors = factors * ( dble(i) / dble(i+1) )
             end do
             factors = factors * ( 1.0d0 / ((2*terms)-1) )
         end select
         value = ( angle ** ((2*terms)-1) ) * factors
         if ( abs(value) .ge. TINY(0.0) .and.
     -        terms        .le. 100                )
     -        value = value + arcsin ( angle, terms )
         end function arcsin
```

Recall that the graph of the arcsine function (see Figure 4-3) is fairly smooth between -0.6 and 0.6 and turns sharply towards its endpoints. When APPROX runs, the TERMS part of the stopping rule seems to apply when ANGLE is bigger than ±0.674. Otherwise, the TINY(0.0) part of the stopping rule is effective.

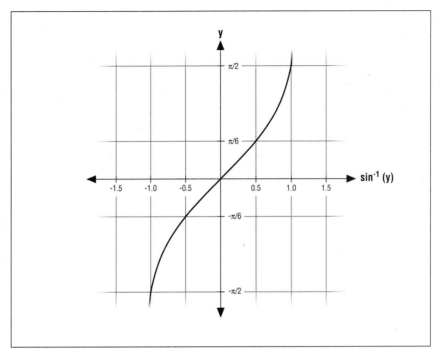

Figure 4-3: Arcsine

5

Overloaded Operators

Fortran 90 revises an old standby, operators, to help meet the challenge of data independence. For nearly forty years, Fortran has defined the basic operators (+, -, *, and /) to correspond as closely as possible to their symbolic counterparts in arithmetic. Relational operators—.LT., .LE., .EQ., .NE., .GE., and .GT.—represent the fundamental comparisons from mathematics. Now, these operators can be extended and new operators created.

If a program has defined two derived data types, POINT_INTERCEPT_LINE and CIRCLE, a function can be invoked in the following manner:

```
touch = point_intercept_line + circle
```

instead of the traditional syntax of a function call:

```
touch = intersect ( point_intercept_line, circle )
```

User-defined operators are an alternate syntax for the invocation of a function. Their use for standard data types is a matter of personal choice. If a function call ends up looking too much like an array reference, then the syntax of a user-defined operator would be the better choice. A programmer's preference for one syntax is the deciding factor in invoking a function directly or via a user-defined operator.

Fortran 90's INTERFACE statement is used to define the interaction between a subprogram and its caller. A syntax of INTERFACE OPERATOR introduces the name or symbol for a new or extended operator. It allows functions to be invoked in the form of binary (infix) and unary (prefix) operators.

A syntax of INTERFACE ASSIGNMENT gives additional meaning to the assignment operator =. It provides an alternate syntax for certain subroutine calls.

In both situations, the INTERFACE statement is followed by a prototype of the function or subroutine that will be executed when the operator is put in service. The scope of the new operator is the same as any other definition: if the interface is defined in a subprogram, the operator is used in that fashion within that subprogram; if the operator is defined in the global portion of a MODULE, it can be recognized wherever the MODULE is USEd (MODULEs are discussed in Chapter 6, *Modules*).

Extending Existing Operators

All standard unary and binary operators can be extended in Fortran 90. For example, the + and - unary operators normally appear in statements such as:

```
i = +57
j = -46
```

with the traditional result that I is 57 and J is -46. But both of these operators can be extended to take on an additional meaning. The program OPERATE uses both of these operators to change the case of a character string: + translates a string to all upper case and - translates a string to all lower case. The program begins by joining the + operator with the UPPER_CASE function and—with LOWER_CASE.

```
program operate
interface operator ( + )
    function upper_case ( old ) result ( new )
      character*20                 :: new
      character*20, intent(in ) :: old
      end function upper_case
end interface
interface operator ( - )
    function lower_case ( old ) result ( new )
      character*20                 :: new
      character*20, intent(in ) :: old
      end function lower_case
end interface
```

Only functions can be used to redefine an operator. To define a unary operator, let the function take one argument. To defined a binary operator, use

two arguments: the first represents the expression that precedes the operator, while the second represents the expression that follows. In this
example, the character string is initialized and then displayed as is,
converted to uppercase, and changed to lowercase:

```
character*20  :: string = 'This uses MIXED case'
print *, " "
print *, "Base string .. ",   string
print *, "Upper case ... ", + string
print *, "Lower case ... ", - string
print *, " "
end program operate
```

showing the following strings:

```
Base string .. This uses MIXED case
Upper case ... THIS USES MIXED CASE
Lower case ... this uses mixed case
```

The real work is done by functions UPPER_CASE and LOWER_CASE. They
are very similar and quite simple: each checks the string character by character to find out whether it lies in the range of letters requiring conversion,
and adds or subtracts the ASCII code value required to change the letter's
case. Note that the IACHAR intrinsic is new in Fortran 90. It returns the position of the character argument in the ASCII collating sequence.

```
function upper_case ( old ) result ( new )
character*20              :: new
character*20, intent(in ) :: old
new = old
do i = 1, len_trim(old), 1
   if ( lge ( old(i:i), 'a' ) .and. &
        lle ( old(i:i), 'z' )        ) &
        new(i:i) = achar ( iachar(old(i:i)) - 32 )
end do
end function upper_case


function lower_case ( old ) result ( new )
character*20              :: new
character*20, intent(in ) :: old
new = old
do i = 1, len_trim(old), 1
   if ( lge ( old(i:i), 'A' ) .and. &
        lle ( old(i:i), 'Z' )        ) &
        new(i:i) = achar ( iachar(old(i:i)) + 32 )
end do
end function lower_case
```

Extending the unary arithmetic operators to apply to character strings might prove useful in handling prompts. A fairly standard code sequence is:

```
          write ( 6,100,advance='NO' )
100       format ( 1H , 'Continue execution (yes or no): ' )
          read *, string
          if ( answer .eq. 'Y' .or. &
               answer .eq. 'y'      ) then
```

in which ANSWER is compared to both Y and y. Revising this fragment to

```
          write ( 6,100,advance='NO' )
100       format ( 1H , 'Continue execution (yes or no): ' )
          read *, answer
          if ( + answer .eq. 'Y' ) then
```

condenses the code without a great sacrifice in clarity.

In general, it does not make a lot of sense to extend an existing operator. Unless the new circumstance closely parallels the normal meaning of the operator, the resulting code will probably be confusing. In the example, + and - have some relation to upper and lower case, so they were fair candidates for extension. The only real benefit for extending an existing operator is to define how they should apply to derived types. Since Fortran 90 permits virtually any data structure to be devised, it is helpful to enlist the standard operators to compare instances of derived types.

Any existing operator can be extended to apply in novel situations, but it cannot be used to completely redefine its normal role. For example, the character concatenation operator can be trained to manipulate two REAL arrays, but cannot be extended to handle character variables in a new way. Three further restrictions govern operator definition:

- An existing operator cannot be changed to operate on a different number of arguments (i.e., * cannot be redefined as a unary operator nor can .NOT. be redefined to be a binary operator).

- Arguments to functions invoked by an operator must be declared INTENT(IN).

- Arguments to functions involved by an operator cannot be declared OPTIONAL.

Relational operators have two forms in Fortran 90: the traditional word form like .LT. and the new symbol such as <. The compiler treats them as identical, so if .LT. acquires a new meaning, so does the < symbol.

Table 5-1 shows which data types can be used as the object of an extended standard operator.

Table 5-1: Standard Operators Available for Extension

Symbol	Description	Can Operator be Extended for This Data Type?[1]					
		A	I	R	C	L	Derived
+	identity	yes	no	no	no	no	yes
-	negation	yes	no	no	no	no	yes
+	addition	yes	no	no	no	no	yes
-	subtraction	yes	no	no	no	no	yes
*	multiplication	yes	no	no	no	no	yes
/	division	yes	no	no	no	no	yes
**	exponentiation	yes	no	no	no	no	yes
//	concatenation	no	yes	yes	yes	yes	yes
.EQ. ==	equal to	no	no	no	no	no	yes
.NE. /=	not equal to	no	no	no	no	no	yes
.GT. >	greater than	no	no	no	yes	yes	yes
.GE. >=	greater or equal	no	no	no	yes	yes	yes
.LT. <	less than	no	no	no	yes	yes	yes
.LE. <=	less or equal	no	no	no	yes	yes	yes
.NOT.	negation	yes	yes	yes	yes	no	yes
.AND.	conjunction	yes	yes	yes	yes	no	yes
.OR.	disjunction	yes	yes	yes	yes	no	yes
.NEQV.	nonequivalence	yes	yes	yes	yes	no	yes
.EQV.	equivalence	yes	yes	yes	yes	no	yes

[1] The data types are: A for character, I for integer, R for real, C for complex, L for logical, and DERIVED for a user-defined type.

Finally, precedence rules demand that defined unary operators have a higher precedence than any intrinsic operator and defined binary operators have a lower precedence than any intrinsic operator.

Creating New Operators

Brand new operators, both unary and binary, can be devised. Like extending intrinsic operators, the process involves coding a function that accepts INTENT(IN) arguments, and writing an interface block that maps the function to the desired name. The first argument for a new binary operator maps to the left operand and the second maps to the right operand.

Names for new operators take the form .X. where X can be from 1 to 31 alphanumeric characters. The name must not conflict with any intrinsic operator or the .TRUE. and .FALSE. literal constants.

For example, the program MOVING implements a moving average operator called .RUNNING_AVERAGE. It associates the SERIES function with the new operator:

```
program moving
interface operator ( .running_average. )
    function series ( rough, run ) result ( smooth )
        real,     dimension ( : ), intent(in) :: rough
        integer,                   intent(in) :: run
        real,     dimension ( size(rough) )   :: smooth
        end function series
end interface
```

defines a vector of random numbers ranging from 0.0 to 10.0:

```
      real, dimension ( 15 ) :: raw
      call random_number ( raw )
      raw = raw * 10.0
      print *, " "
      print 100, "Raw    ", raw
100   format ( 1H , a, 15f4.1 )
      print *, " "
```

and applies the .RUNNING_AVERAGE. operator successively with a run length ranging from 0 to 8.

```
      do i = 0, 8, 1
         print 100, "Smooth", raw .running_average. i
      end do
      print *, " "
      end program moving
```

As the run length gets larger, the "smoothed" values converge towards 5.0: the expected value of the series.

```
Raw     4.1 1.5 6.7 4.3 1.5 5.7 1.1 6.4 2.3 6.3 5.3 0.6 9.9 8.5 8.7

Smooth 4.1 1.5 6.7 4.3 1.5 5.7 1.1 6.4 2.3 6.3 5.3 0.6 9.9 8.5 8.7
Smooth 4.9 4.1 4.2 4.2 3.8 2.8 4.4 3.3 5.0 4.6 4.1 5.3 6.4 9.0 4.9
Smooth 4.9 4.9 3.6 3.9 3.9 3.8 3.4 4.4 4.3 4.2 4.9 6.1 6.6 4.9 4.9
Smooth 4.9 4.9 4.9 3.6 3.9 4.0 3.9 4.1 4.0 4.6 5.6 5.9 4.9 4.9 4.9
Smooth 4.9 4.9 4.9 4.9 3.7 4.0 4.4 3.7 4.4 5.1 5.5 4.9 4.9 4.9 4.9
Smooth 4.9 4.9 4.9 4.9 4.9 4.1 3.8 4.6 4.7 5.1 4.9 4.9 4.9 4.9 4.9
Smooth 4.9 4.9 4.9 4.9 4.9 4.9 4.3 4.6 5.2 4.9 4.9 4.9 4.9 4.9 4.9
Smooth 4.9 4.9 4.9 4.9 4.9 4.9 4.9 4.9 4.9 4.9 4.9 4.9 4.9 4.9 4.9
Smooth 4.9 4.9 4.9 4.9 4.9 4.9 4.9 4.9 4.9 4.9 4.9 4.9 4.9 4.9 4.9
```

Many forms of a moving average algorithm exist. Here, each element of the SMOOTH series equals the average of itself and its RUNth nearest neighbors. Near the ends of the vector, some elements will lack a neighbor; these elements are simply set to the average of all the input values in the vector.

```
function series ( rough, run ) result ( smooth )
real,     dimension ( : ), intent(in) :: rough
integer,                   intent(in) :: run
real,     dimension ( size(rough) )   :: smooth
n = size ( rough )
m = run + 1 + run
if ( n .lt. m ) then
     smooth = sum ( rough ) / n
else
     smooth = sum ( rough ) / n
     j = lbound(rough,DIM=1) + run
     k = ubound(rough,DIM=1) - run
     do i = j, k, 1
         smooth(i) = sum ( rough(i-run:i+run) ) / m
     end do
end if
end function series
```

Extending the Assignment Operator

Fortran 90 permits the assignment operator, =, to be extended. The INTERFACE ASSIGNMENT statement associates a SUBROUTINE with the assignment operator. This SUBROUTINE takes exactly two nonOPTIONAL arguments. The first must have an INTENT of OUT or INOUT and corresponds to the left hand side of the assignment. The second must have an INTENT of IN and corresponds to the right hand side of the assignment. The extension is executed every time both sides of the assignment operator match the type and rank of the subroutine, otherwise the standard assignment operator is invoked.

For example, the program DEFINE extends the assignment operator to a subroutine that will extract the main diagonal of a matrix. It begins by defining the prototype of the CENTER subroutine:

```
program define
interface assignment ( = )
   subroutine center ( line, matrix )
      integer, dimension( : ), intent(out) :: line
      integer, dimension(:,:), intent(in ) :: matrix
```

```
          end subroutine center
      end interface
```

and then declares, populates:

```
      integer, dimension(4,4) :: array
      integer, dimension( 4 ) :: diagonal
      array = reshape ( (/ (i,i=1,16) /), (/ 4,4 /) )
      print *, " "
      i = 1
      print 100, "Array row ", i, array(i,:)
100   format ( 1H , a, i1, ' : ', 4i3 )
      do i = 2, 4, 1
         print 100, "      row ", i, array(i,:)
      end do
```

and displays the ARRAY of numbers:

```
Array row 1 :   1  5  9 13
      row 2 :   2  6 10 14
      row 3 :   3  7 11 15
      row 4 :   4  8 12 16
```

The redefinition of = means that an assignment statement will extract the main diagonal of a matrix, whenever the lefthand side is an INTEGER vector and the righthand side is a two-dimension INTEGER array. Furthermore, an expression producing such an array will also invoke the special meaning. Under any other circumstances, an assignment statement behaves in the standard manner. Thus, the standard meaning would apply if the base array were being transformed in a statement such as ARRAY = 2 * ARRAY, or a single variable were being set such as I = 123, or some new REAL vector was being extracted from a REAL array such as VECTOR = TABLE (:,1).

The next line of code presents the assignment operator with arguments that exactly match its extension. The first line below is equivalent to CALL CENTER (DIAGONAL, ARRAY):

```
      diagonal = array
      print *, " "
      print 200, "Main diagonal ", diagonal
200   format ( 1H , a, 4i3 )
      print *, " "
      end program define
```

which displays:

```
      Main diagonal   1  6 11 16
```

Getting the main diagonal relies on Fortran 90's PACK intrinsic to "deflate" an array into a one-dimensional vector and then picking out the on-diagonal values using Fortran 90's stride syntax.

```
subroutine center ( line, matrix )
integer, dimension( : ), intent(out) :: line
integer, dimension(:,:), intent(in ) :: matrix
integer, dimension( : ), allocatable :: vector
allocate ( vector(size(matrix)) )
vector = pack ( matrix, .TRUE. )
line = vector (1:size(matrix):size(matrix,DIM=1)+1)
deallocate ( vector )
end subroutine center
```

Extending the assignment operator benefits the handling of user defined types. The program DISCOVER manages a list of geographical adventurers both alphabetically in a structure called EXPLORER and chronologically in a structure called TIMELINE. Both are objects of a derived type called DISCOVERY, defined in a file called *discover.inc*:

```
type discovery
      sequence
      character (len=21) :: name
      character (len=21) :: event
      character (len=10) :: nationality
      integer            :: when
end  type discovery
```

and brought into the program's source code when required with Fortran 90's INCLUDE statement. The program begins by associating a sort routine, BUBBLE, with the assignment operator:

```
program discover
interface assignment ( = )
  subroutine bubble ( sorted, unsorted )
    INCLUDE 'discover.inc'
    type ( discovery ), intent (out) :: sorted(:)
    type ( discovery ), intent (in ) :: unsorted(:)
  end subroutine bubble
end interface
```

Then, objects of type DISCOVERY are declared and the base information about the EXPLORERs is set:

```
INCLUDE 'discover.inc'
type ( discovery ) :: explorer(5)
type ( discovery ) :: timeline(5)
explorer(1) = discovery ( 'Amudsen, Roald', &
               'reach South Pole', 'Norwegian', 1911 )
```

```
explorer(2) = discovery ( 'Cook, James', &
                'map New Zealand', 'English', 1770 )
explorer(3) = discovery ( 'Lewis, M. & W. Clark', &
                'explore NW USA', 'American', 1805 )
explorer(4) = discovery ( 'Magellan, Ferdinand', &
                'circumnavigate world', 'Portugese', 1521 )
explorer(5) = discovery ( 'Polo, Marco', &
                'overland to China', 'Venetian', 1275 )
print *, " "
do i = 1, size(explorer), 1
   print *, "EXPLORER: ", explorer(i)
end do
```

and displayed:

```
EXPLORER: Amudsen, Roald         reach South Pole     Norwegian  1911
EXPLORER: Cook, James            map New Zealand      English    1770
EXPLORER: Lewis, M. & W. Clark explore NW USA         American   1805
EXPLORER: Magellan, Ferdinand  circumnavigate world Portugese   1521
EXPLORER: Polo, Marco            overland to China    Venetian   1275
```

Then a single statement populates the object TIMELINE with data in the proper chronological order. All the elements from EXPLORER are automatically sorted on the WHEN component before being stored in TIMELINE:

```
timeline = explorer
print *, " "
do i = 1, size(timeline), 1
   print *, "TIMELINE: ", timeline(i)
end do
print *, " "
end program discover
```

as seen in this display:

```
TIMELINE: Polo, Marco            overland to China    Venetian   1275
TIMELINE: Magellan, Ferdinand  circumnavigate world Portugese   1521
TIMELINE: Cook, James            map New Zealand      English    1770
TIMELINE: Lewis, M. & W. Clark explore NW USA         American   1805
TIMELINE: Amudsen, Roald         reach South Pole     Norwegian  1911
```

Sorting the derived type into chronological order is done by the BUBBLE routine. An INTERFACE block extends the .GT. operator to have a special meaning whenever it appears between two variables or expressions of the type DISCOVERY. It that context it invokes the function CHRONOLOGY, which establishes their chronological position.

```
subroutine bubble ( sorted, unsorted )
interface operator ( .gt. )
  logical function chronology ( event, other_event )
    INCLUDE 'discover.inc'
```

```
      type ( discovery ), intent (in) :: event
      type ( discovery ), intent (in) :: other_event
   end function chronology
end interface
INCLUDE 'discover.inc'
integer                          :: n
type ( discovery )               :: temporary
type ( discovery ), intent (out) :: sorted(:)
type ( discovery ), intent (in ) :: unsorted(:)
```

The bubble sort has significant drawbacks in terms of performance on large data sets (particularly when the order is widely skewed), but it is very simple to implement.

```
sorted = unsorted
n = size(sorted)
do i = 1, n-1, 1
   do j = i+1, n, 1
      if ( sorted(i) .gt. sorted(j) ) then
            temporary = sorted(j)
            sorted(j) = sorted(i)
            sorted(i) = temporary
      end if
   end do
end do
end subroutine bubble
```

The CHRONOLOGY function, which runs when the .GT. operator is reached, looks at the WHEN component of the arguments to determine what order they should be in. The CHRONOLOGY function specifically identifies which component of a DISCOVERY type must be compared to establish order.

```
logical function chronology ( event, other_event )
INCLUDE 'discover.inc'
type ( discovery ), intent (in) :: event
type ( discovery ), intent (in) :: other_event
if ( event%when .gt. other_event%when) then
     chronology = .true.
else
     chronology = .false.
end if
end function chronology
```

The scopes of the two extended operators = and .GT. are established by the placement of their respective INTERFACE definition. BUBBLE is a selected replacement for the assignment operator only in the main program because that is where it is named in an INTERFACE ASSIGNMENT block. That is why the statement involving the assignment of two DISCOVERY type objects can appear in BUBBLE, and the normal definition for assignment applies:

```
sorted = unsorted
```

CHRONOLOGY is a selected replacement for the greater than relational operator only in SUBROUTINE BUBBLE because that is where it is named in an INTERFACE OPERATOR block. The scope of an extension to either the assignment or intrinsic operators can be tailored with Fortran 90's MODULE and USE statements.

One more subtlety must be mentioned in relation to interface assignment. If one derived type is nested within another.

```
type conference
    sequence
    type ( discovery ) :: expedition
    character (len=20) :: location
end type
```

The assignments from one CONFERENCE to another use the standard assignment operator. The special assignment from one DISCOVERY type to another is not involved, because it is nested within the larger type.

6

Modules

Professional software developers are responding to a driving need to consolidate code in easily maintained packages. Computer-aided software engineering tools are readily available on the market to track the structure and interdependencies of code modules. Object oriented programming methods, languages, and data base management systems can be employed to cleanly divide functional parts of a program. Building on these modern approaches, Fortran 90's MODULEs provide a simple but highly adaptable method to compartmentalize code.

Modules can replace all uses of INCLUDE statements, COMMON blocks, and statement functions. They have taken the basic concept represented by each of these original Fortran features—shared declarations, globally accessible data, and inline code expansion—and generalized it in the powerful and flexible concept of a module. In a simple case, a module can be used to hold the specifications for a data type and related constants. As such, it builds a "fire wall" between data specification and use.

The program CONSTANTS keeps track of two different sets of values for PI and E in individual modules.

```
module single
  integer, parameter :: float = selected_real_kind ( 6, 37 )
  real ( float ) :: pi = 3.1415927_float
  real ( float ) :: e  = 2.7182818_float
end module single

module double
  integer, parameter :: float = selected_real_kind ( 15, 307 )
  real ( float ) :: pi = 3.141592653589793_float
```

```
    real ( float ) :: e = 2.718281828459045_float
end module double
```

When normal precision is satisfactory, the program can USE the module called SINGLE.

```
program constants
use single
print *, " "
print *, "Constants: pi", pi, "and e", e
call more_precision
print *, " "
end program constants
```

When extra precision is desired, say in a subprogram, the other module called DOUBLE can be in USE.

```
subroutine more_precision
use double
print *, " "
print *, "Constants: pi", pi, "and e", e
end subroutine more_precision
```

Executing this program reports both precisions for the two constants.

```
Constants: pi    3.1415927 and e    2.7182817

Constants: pi    3.1415926535897931 and e    2.7182818284590451
```

This trivial example begins to show the benefits that result from modules. Pieces of programs like MORE_PRECISION can be written without explicit reference to the size, shape, and structure of key variables. If a full application was written with normal precision through the USE of SINGLE, it would be trivial to substitute DOUBLE to get that extra precision. Later examples in this chapter, using PRIVATE variables and functions, show increasingly sophisticated ways to hide implementation details from high-level program units.

Fortran 90 compilers in all likelihood will support separate compilation of MODULE files. All specifications and subprograms placed in a module can be compiled independently of the programs in which they are employed. Then, they would be "linked" to the program as object or binary files. This means that an application programmer need not have access to the source code of major data type specifications or service subprograms. This supports good programming team discipline because it helps resist the temptation to "adjust" standard code to suit a particular purpose.

Also, separate compilation makes it very easy to deliver new versions of common user-written libraries. Upgrading an application from Version 1.00 to Version 2.00 or releasing a development version of a library to production may mean only relinking with the new MODULEs' object files. Now, installing a new version of a library can introduce new data, new functions, and/or change the algorithms used in existing functions. With MODULEs, installing a new version of a library can allow necessary changes to data structures and functions together, and still the calling program units do not have to be recompiled.

Module Contents and Syntax

Formally, Fortran 90 defines a module as a collection of declarations and subprograms. Each module has one or two components. The specification component declares variable types, defines derived types, and marks what is visible to or hidden from calling programs and subprogram interfaces. The subprogram part actually provides the code for subroutines and functions involved in a module.

As seen in the CONSTANTS example, a module begins with the MODULE statement and concludes with an END statement. A name is required on the MODULE statement. The module can be finished off with the more complete END MODULE or the full END MODULE NAME where NAME is the same name given on the opening MODULE statement.

Specification Part in MODULE

The first MODULE part—specification—can incorporate variable declarations in all of their complexity: INTERFACE blocks, and IMPLICIT, PARAMETER, and TYPE statements. The CONSTANTS example is the simplest case, with a single parameter and the definition of two variables. In effect, MODULEs make objects shared among programs that use that module. Naming an object in a module is like putting it in COMMON, but has several advantages. Access is restricted to those subprograms that USE the module. None of the old storage-order restrictions on COMMON blocks apply, which frees the programmer to include ALLOCATABLE arrays and derived types without SEQUENCE statements.

Three other statements—PRIVATE, PUBLIC, and USE—can also appear. More will be said later about PRIVATE and PUBLIC. In this context, a USE statement, covered in detail below, allows all or part of another module to be used in the current module. For example, MODULE A can contain the line USE B to incorporate whatever is defined in MODULE B.

A few elements of Fortran cannot appear in the specification part of a module: statement functions, ENTRY statements, and FORMAT statements.

Subprogram Part in MODULE

The second MODULE part—subprogram—actually lists the code for subroutines and functions. It is separated from the module specification part with the CONTAINS statement.

The program HISTORY starts with a module that declares a data structure to record information about U. S. presidents and CONTAINS the source code for a subroutine to display that data.

```
      module facts
         integer, parameter :: WIDTH=32
         type key_facts
           character (len=WIDTH) :: who
           character (len=WIDTH) :: what
           character (len=WIDTH) :: where
           character (len=WIDTH) :: when
         end type key_facts
         contains
           subroutine show_facts ( fact_set, number )
             type ( key_facts ) fact_set
             integer number
             print 100, number
100          format ( / 1H , 'Number ', i2.2 / )
             print 200, fact_set
200          format (   1H , 10x, a )
           end subroutine show_facts
      end module facts
```

Using MODULEs in a Program

When it comes time to write the main program, all the detailed code about a data structure and display mechanism are brought in through the single USE statement.

```
      program history
      use facts
      type ( key_facts ) presidents(42)
      presidents(1)%who   = "George Washington"
      presidents(1)%what  = "Engineer, General"
      presidents(1)%where = "Mount Vernon, VA"
```

```
presidents(1)%when  = "1789-1797"
presidents(42) = key_facts ( "Bill Clinton", "Governor", &
                             "Little Rock, AK", "1993-?" )
call show_facts ( presidents( 1),  1 )
call show_facts ( presidents(42), 42 )
print *, " "
end program history
```

Note that there is no allowance for conditionals surrounding the USE statement. It might be convenient to USE a particular MODULE under one circumstance and another MODULE at that same place when other conditions prevail. That is not possible in Fortran 90: a USE statement appears before executable statements so it can not appear in any form of conditional construct.

Figure 6-1 shows the dual use of FACTS data, both by direct assignment and by invocation of the SHOW_FACTS subroutine. At execution, HISTORY shows key facts about the first and the 42nd U. S. presidents.

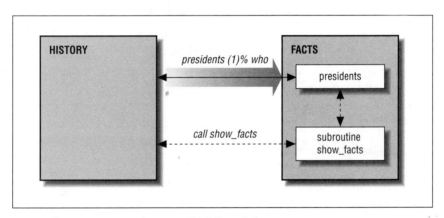

Figure 6-1: Data manipulation in FACTS module

```
Number 01

        George Washington
        Engineer, General
        Mount Vernon, VA
        1789-1797

Number 42

        Bill Clinton
        Governor
        Little Rock, AK
        1993-?
```

Modules need not contain both parts. A specification part without a subprogram part can act like a BLOCK DATA subprogram, but with broader features because it can store INTERFACE blocks as well as global data definitions. A subprogram part without a specification part is just a convenient way to group related subprograms. But modules are most powerful when both parts work together, as shown in the MODULE FACTS from the previous example. It is a classic case of encapsulation, where a data type is declared along with a method to manipulate specific instances of such a data type. The power of modules is magnified by hiding the work arrays and operations that are not needed outside the module.

Accessibility

The accessibility of specifications and subprograms in a module can be controlled with PUBLIC and PRIVATE qualifiers and with options on the USE statement. Both mechanisms allow a programmer to choose which elements in a module are available to code outside the module.

Controlling the accessibility of module elements has parallels in the familiar Fortran concepts of local variables, COMMON areas, and one reason for using EQUIVALENCE statements. A local variable in a subprogram has meaning only in that subprogram just like a variable marked PRIVATE has meaning only in the module in which it is declared. Conversely, variables in a COMMON area are globally available throughout the program as are PUBLIC variables from a module. Finally, a statement like

```
use my_module, new_variable => old_variable_name
```

allows the old variable name from MY_MODULE to be known as NEW_VARIABLE in the program unit in which such a USE statement appears. This parallels one use of EQUIVALENCE statements: renaming variables to correct spelling, conform to new coding convention, etc. The same idea is extended to subroutine and function names because this technique of establishing a local name also applies to subprograms:

```
use my_module, new_subroutine => old_subroutine_name
use my_module, new_function  => old_function_name
```

But these parallels have limits. An issue always surrounds the retention of values for local variables between execution of a subprogram. PRIVATE variables in a module always retain their value between USE statements.

COMMON is the traditional method of centralizing storage and preserving values of key variables throughout a program. However, it is restricted to variables, whereas the new Fortran 90 accessibility mechanisms are extended to subprograms, derived types, parameters, or namelist groups.

An EQUIVALENCE statement establishes a synonym for a variable. Both the original and the new name can be used interchangeably. In Fortran 90, when NEW_VARIABLE is established as an alias for the old variable name, it becomes the only name for that variable in the scope of the USE statement. OLD_VARIABLE_NAME can no longer be used—in fact, the subprogram is free to define a new and completely different entity called OLD_VARIABLE_NAME having nothing to do with its original meaning.

PUBLIC Versus PRIVATE Elements of a MODULE

By default, everything in a module has PUBLIC accessibility. If no accessibility statement appears, then nothing is PRIVATE and everything is PUBLIC.

The ATMOSPHERE program displays the name of the atmospheric zone at a given altitude:

```
Troposphere is the zone surrounding an altitude of   1.2 miles.
 Mesosphere is the zone surrounding an altitude of  45.6 miles.
  Exosphere is the zone surrounding an altitude of 789.0 miles.
```

But the number of zones, their names, and the altitude of the boundary between each zone are things that the main program does not need to know. All of that information can be PRIVATE and unavailable outside of the module that determines the zone's name. In this example, that information is drawn from Louise B. Young's *Earth's Aura* (1977, Alfred A. Knopf, Publisher, 305 pages, New York, NY). SKY is such a module with only one PUBLIC element: the naming function.

```
module sky
   private
   public  :: sphere
   real,         dimension(5) :: bottom
   character*6, dimension(5) :: layer
   data bottom /     0.0,     5.0,    30.0,    50.0,   300.0 /
   data layer  / ' Tropo','Strato',' Meso',' Iono',' Exo'/
   contains
      character*6 function sphere ( miles ) result ( zone )
         real, intent(IN) :: miles
         do i = 1, size(bottom), 1
            if ( miles .ge. bottom(i) ) zone = layer(i)
         end do
      end function sphere
   end module sky
```

When the main program is coded, it has access to the SPHERE function and nothing else. Figure 6-2 shows how data is manipulated indirectly through the SPHERE function.

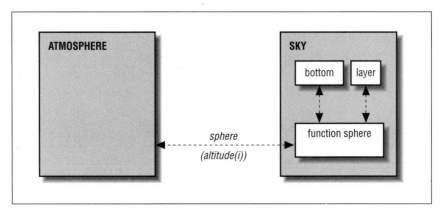

Figure 6-2: Data manipulation in SKY module

```
        program atmosphere
        use sky
        real, dimension(3) :: altitude = (/ 1.2, 45.6, 789.0 /)
        print *, " "
        do i = 1, size(altitude), 1
            print 100, sphere ( altitude(i) ), altitude(i)
100         format ( 1H , a, 'sphere is the zone ', &
                            'surrounding an altitude of ', &
                            f5.1, ' miles.' )
        end do
        print *, " "
        end program atmosphere
```

Since everything is PRIVATE in module SKY except the function SPHERE, the main program knows nothing about the size, structure, or the exact contents of BOTTOM and LAYER, or even that they exist. ATMOSPHERE might not have to change one whit if, later, SPHERE was modified to consider other determinants of the altitude of atmospheric zone boundaries (i.e., latitude, time of day, season of the year, barometric pressure, etc.). Such modifications might be in the form of new, PRIVATE data structures and subprograms added to the module SKY.

Selecting Elements of a MODULE by the USE Statement

By default, everything in a given module is available to subprograms that reference it. Although the PRIVATE statement might shield some things, the unqualified USE statement brings in all PUBLIC elements from a module.

But this can change. This ATMOSPHERE example could be reworked with a USE statement to achieve a similar result. If the accessibility statements in SKY are commented out, then everything defaults to PUBLIC accessibility.

```
      module sky
!        private
!        public  :: sphere
         :
      end module sky
```

A corresponding change in the main program achieves the original effect of hiding all names but SPHERE. The old USE statement is reduced to a comment, while a new one introduces the ONLY clause to restrict access.

```
      program atmosphere
!     use sky
      use sky, ONLY : sphere
         :
      end program atmosphere
```

Functionally, this approach is equivalent to the original: ATMOSPHERE can only access SPHERE from the SKY module. This could be relaxed to allow ATMOSPHERE more access. Extending the new USE statement to read as:

```
      use sky, ONLY: sphere, xpause=>bottom
```

would allow the altitude of the boundaries between each zone carried in BOTTOM to be available in the main program under the name XPAUSE. Then, the atmospheric boundary of the tropopause would be at an altitude of XPAUSE(2) miles, the stratopause at XPAUSE(3) miles, the mesopause at XPAUSE(4) miles, etc. Conversely, the names of all the zones could be made available.

```
      use sky, ONLY: sphere, layer
```

The way a program will use data is the decisive issue in managing accessibility. The approach selected depends on the richness of the module. If the module is fairly single purpose—as SKY is—then the PUBLIC/PRIVATE accessibility statements seem to make the most sense. If a module is a collection of less closely linked elements, then qualified USE statements would suffice. An exception arises if it is desired to cloak certain processing details from user-written programs. Then, PUBLIC/PRIVATE accessibility statements and separately compiled MODULEs is more secure.

Independent Compilation

It is very likely, but not required, that all Fortran 90 compilers will support separate compilation of MODULE files. The expected ability to independently compile MODULE files is no different from the ability of just about every production Fortran 77 compiler to allow subprograms to be placed in individual files and compiled independent from each other. That facility is likely to be extended to files comprised entirely of MODULEs.

CONCORD Example Program with a MODULE

Subprogram and data declarations for the major example in Chapter 4, *Subroutines and Functions Revisited*, CONCORD, can be placed in modules to produce a new version called CONCORD2. Six steps were followed to effect this conversion.

First, relegate general system data to its own module. In this program, only the unit numbers for the terminal and keyboard are candidates.

```
MODULE global_data
integer                              :: crtin  =  5
integer                              :: crtout =  6
end module global_data
```

Second, declare truly local variables in each subprogram. In this case, the variables I, J, and NAME appear in most, if not all, subprograms. They could be placed in INCLUDE file if that style is acceptable. They could be placed in a MODULE, but they would need to be reinitialized in each subprogram because their values would then persist between subprogram invocations.

Third, isolate program specific data and trivial subprogram interfaces in another module. Since the major program variables appear in a module, there is no need for the COMMON space declared in the first version of this program.

```
MODULE program_data
integer                              MAXUNT
parameter                            ( MAXUNT=10 )
real                                 chisqr
integer                              degfre
character* 6, dimension(:  ), pointer :: ename
```

```
integer                                        events
character*14                                    ifile
integer                                        iunit
integer                                        io
character* 6, dimension(:  ), pointer :: jname
integer                                        judges
real                                           kendal
logical                                        mistak
character*14                                    ofile
integer                                        ounit
real,          dimension(:,:), pointer :: scores
logical                                        units(MAXUNT)
end module program_data

MODULE program_interface
interface
  subroutine driver
    end subroutine driver
  subroutine error
    end subroutine error
  subroutine finish
    end subroutine finish
  subroutine init
    end subroutine init
  subroutine input
    end subroutine input
  subroutine kencon
    end subroutine kencon
  subroutine limits
    end subroutine limits
  subroutine result
    end subroutine result
  subroutine start
    end subroutine
end interface
end module program_interface
```

Fourth, the service routine, TELL, that tracks the progress of execution ends up in another module.

```
MODULE tracking
logical                                 debug
integer                          :: pass   =  0
integer                          :: push   =  1
integer                          :: pop    = -1
contains
SUBROUTINE tell ( what, where )
use global_data
```

```
         .
         .
         .
    end subroutine tell
    end module tracking
```

Fifth, place the computational portion of the program in the last module defined.

```
    MODULE compute
    private
    public  :: wtest
    contains
    SUBROUTINE wtest ( raw, njudges,    mevents, &
                        w,   chi_square, ndf      )
    use global_data
         .
         .
         .
    use tracking
    end subroutine wtest
    SUBROUTINE rank ( raw_scores, ranked_scores, mevents )
    use global_data
    use tracking
         .
         .
         .
    end subroutine rank
    SUBROUTINE tie ( ranked_scores, mevents, ties )
    use global_data
    use tracking
         .
         .
         .
    end subroutine tie
    end module compute
```

Both RANK and TIE are declared PRIVATE since they are called only by WTEST.

Sixth, USE statements need to be inserted into the program file where the two original INCLUDE lines appeared. The original version of the program began as follows:

```
    program concord
    INCLUDE 'concord.int'
    INCLUDE 'concord.ins'
         .
         .
         .
```

The new version begins:

```
program concord2
use global_data
use program_data
use tracking
use program_interface
.
.
.
```

and the first three USE statements replace "INCLUDE 'concord.int'" throughout the source code file. Also, the routine KENCON is modified to reference the MODULE called COMPUTE:

```
subroutine kencon
use global_data
use program_data
use tracking
use compute
.
.
.
```

Finally, the new CONCORD2 executable is created with these separate compile and link steps:

1. Compile the file containing the source code for all the MODULEs to produce the first object file.

2. Compile the program source code file to produce the second object file

3. Link both object files to produce an executable file.

If the module file or the program file has to be changed later, then that is the only file that needs to be compiled (i.e., Step 1 or Step 2) before relinking (i.e., Step 3).

This expected ability to compile modules independent from the program files in which they are employed adds another layer of complexity to software development. In medium- to large-scale programming projects, a staggering amount of discipline and effort are needed to implement source code change control across programming teams, computer platforms, and networks. One more element of change in the form of independently compiled modules will not be a crushing blow, but it will need to be managed.

At the same time, independent compilation contributes a measure of flexibility to the software development process. Modules can be used as a quick means to switch between alternative algorithms. One MODULE can implement one processing rule and another MODULE can implement an alternative. The program can then switch between the alternatives by selecting a different MODULE to USE.

Module Procedures

If a subprogram is truly general purpose and can be encapsulated in an operator, then it makes sense to place it in a MODULE. The upper- and lowercase routines from the OPERATE program in Chapter 5, *Overloaded Operators*, qualify. Fortran 90 requires that the connection between an extended or new operator and the subprogram that implements it be specified in a MODULE PROCEDURE statement.

```
module casing
   interface operator ( + )
     module procedure upper_case
   end interface
   interface operator ( - )
     module procedure lower_case
   end interface
contains
   function upper_case ( old ) result ( new )
     .
     .
     .
   end function upper_case

   function lower_case ( old ) result ( new )
     .
     .
     .
   end function lower_case
end module casing
```

Once these operators are declared in the MODULE called CASING, a new program version, OPERATE2, is constructed as follows:

```
program operate2
use casing
character*20  :: string = 'This uses MIXED case'
print *, " "
print *, "Base string .. ",    string
print *, "Upper case ... ", + string
print *, "Lower case ... ", - string
print *, " "
end program operate2
```

The decision to place an operator's definition in a MODULE versus inline in the program is a matter of personal choice. The only design decision hinges on whether the procedure that implements the operator can be called by name

```
print *, "Lower case ... ", lower_case ( string )
```

as well as by the operator:

```
print *, "Lower case ... ", - string
```

As written, both OPERATE and OPERATE2 can invoke the case functions directly as well as through their respective operators. If it is desirable to force access to the case functions to their respective operators and disallow direct invocation, then they can be declared PRIVATE.

```
module casing
    private :: upper_case, lower_case
    interface operator ( + )
    .
    .
    .
```

7

Dynamic Memory Management

Many traditional Fortran programming techniques were developed to conserve memory. Intricate COMMON arrangements, EQUIVALENCEs between variables of different data types, subprograms that receive arrays into vectors declared with unit length, and reading/writing arrays from direct access files were all strategies to minimize the memory requirements of a Fortran program. Often, tactics used to implement these strategies grew so complex that the problem solving objective of individual programs became obscured. Fortran 90 provides tools for dynamic memory management that directly address the goal of memory conservation.

Allocatable arrays allow the total size of an array to be specified when the program executes. They take away the waste and uncertainty inherent in the old practice of giving arrays the largest conceivable size that users might need. Fortran 90 allows the programmer to ask the user to specify the length of arrays.

```
      program query_array_size
      integer, dimension ( : ), allocatable :: array
      integer                               :: array_length
      write ( *,100,advance='NO' )
100   format ( 1H , 'Enter length of array: ' )
      read ( *,* ) array_length
      allocate ( array(array_length) )
      .
      .
      .
      deallocate ( array )
      end program query_array_size
```

Each invocation of this program could create, use, and release an array of different size. Allocatable arrays are particularly elegant for creation of internal work arrays within subprograms.

Until now, Fortran programmers expect a one-to-one relationship between the name of a variable and the data storage it represents. But Fortran 90 allows the name of a new class of variable, POINTER, to become associated with variables of another new class of variable, TARGET, at execution time. Pointers and targets allow the size of a data structure to change during the execution of a program.

```
         program switch
         integer, target  :: a(2,2)
         integer, target  :: b(3,3)
         integer, pointer :: p(:,:)
         character        :: choice = ' '
         a = reshape ( (/1,2,3,4/), (/2,2/) )
         b = reshape ( (/5,6,7,8,9,10,11,12,13/), (/3,3/) )
         write ( *,100,advance='NO' )
100      format ( / 1H , 'Select A(2,2) or B(3,3) ...',
        -                ' (enter A or B): ' )
         read *, choice
         if ( choice .eq. 'A' ) p => a
         if ( choice .eq. 'B' ) p => b
         print *, "Pointer set to array ", choice, " ..."
         print *, "P ", p
         .
         .
         .
         nullify ( p )
         end program switch
```

Depending on the user's response to the query, P might be assigned to the first array:

```
         Pointer set to array A ...
         P  1 2 3 4
```

or refer to the second array:

```
         Pointer set to array B ...
         P  5 6 7 8 9 10 11 12 13
```

Any operation that refers to P (except one that reassigns it to another location) now acts upon the array chosen by the user, A or B. Pointers and targets enable Fortran 90 to deal directly with such modern programming constructs as dynamic array sections, adjustable data structures, true linked lists, and functions returning pointers.

Memory Models

The Fortran 90 standard makes no demands on the physical properties or implementation technique of a processor's memory. Historically, Fortran does assume two features: sequential storage, and the relationship between a variable name and the memory location of the data to which it refers. Allocatable arrays and pointers disrupt these assumptions, which is why they must be examined here.

Both COMMON and EQUIVALENCE rely on sequential storage. Elements held in COMMON by different subprograms must align: intrinsic type to intrinsic type, derived type to derived type, POINTERs to POINTERs, etc. Fortran has traditionally required variables to be stored sequentially, without gaps, in the order specified in the COMMON statement. Both requirements—alignment and fixed storage order—reveal the assumption Fortran makes about an appearance of linear memory.

EQUIVALENCE arranges for two variable names to reference the same memory in some precise, fixed, one-to-one pairing. A fundamental constraint of EQUIVALENCE is that the pairing must not disrupt the assumption of consecutive storage: elements cannot appear twice nor can a pairing create gaps (i.e., pair A(1) with B(1) and A(2) with B(100)).

In regard to Fortran's second historical assumption, a normal variable has a fixed association with a certain data space. The relationship between the variable name and the memory location of the data to which it refers is permanent throughout the life and scope of the variable. When a programmer mentions a variable name, it is an implied reference to some clearly delimited area of memory. That same area of memory is referenced every time the variable name appears in a program. Furthermore, sufficient memory is allocated when normal variables are declared to contain a fixed number of values for that variable.

Both allocatable arrays and pointers dissolve the powerful one-to-one relationship between a variable and its memory space. When these new kinds of variables are declared, they exist simply as "dope vectors," lists of dimensions with no attached space for data.

At run time, when the space for arrays is allocated, it comes from an arbitrary place in memory, thus making sequential storage of variables impossible.

Pointers can dynamically change their association among different data spaces. Each time a pointer is mentioned, it might refer to dissimilar memory. Ample evidence was seen in the example above where P could point to A or B's data depending on the user's choice. Thus, storage for data is neither sequential nor fixed when pointers are involved.

These two assumptions—sequential storage and the variable name/data space relationship—will reappear several times in this chapter to explain when to use and when to avoid Fortran 90's dynamic memory management features.

Allocatable Arrays

An allocatable array is an array that is declared with a defined number of dimensions but undefined bounds. It is best used when the shape of an array is known but the limits of any given dimension are established at each invocation of the program.

There is no way to declare a location for data without indicating the number of dimensions. Amid all the flexibility afforded by Fortran 90, the one restriction that the standard consistently imposes is the need to declare the rank (number of dimensions) of each variable at compile time. A few loopholes in this restriction are discussed in Chapter 2, *Array Operations*.

For example, temperature can be measured on three different scales: Fahrenheit, Centigrade, or Kelvin. If a program needs a single array to hold counts of particular readings, it must contend with the different sizes of Fahrenheit degrees and Centigrade degrees, and the different numbering scales for Centigrade and Kelvin degrees. A solution is to declare a DEGREES array as ALLOCATABLE.

```
program temperature
integer, dimension(:), allocatable :: degrees
integer                            :: error
integer, dimension(3,2)            :: limits
integer                            :: scale = 0
logical                            :: true_false
data limits / -460, -274, 0, 212, 100, 374 /
print *, " "
print *, "Fahrenheit, Centigrade, or Kelvin? (1,2,3)"
read ( *,* ) scale
```

No space has been set aside for storing any values in DEGREES. It is just a place holder. It is known to have a single dimension, but the extent of that dimension is unspecified. Once the user has selected a scale, the array can be allocated with limits. Here, the limits represent absolute zero and the boiling point of water in units appropriate to the scale.

```
allocate ( degrees(limits(scale,1):limits(scale,2)),
-           stat = error )
if ( error .ne. 0 ) then
    print *, "Allocation error!"
    go to 100                              ! TERMINATE
else
    print *, "DEGREES allocated from", limits(scale,1),
-                          "to", limits(scale,2)
end if
```

If memory could not be allocated, the status would be set to some processor dependent positive integer. Similarly, it is an error to ALLOCATE an array that is already allocated. Success appears as follows:

```
Fahrenheit, Centigrade, or Kelvin? (1,2,3)
1
DEGREES allocated from -460 to 212
```

The program is free to perform whatever computations are required, dealing with DEGREES as if the array had been fully specified at its declaration.

During processing, it might be important to recheck the allocation status of the array. The intrinsic function, ALLOCATED, can determine whether an allocatable array has been allocated or not:

```
true_false = allocated ( degrees )
if ( true_false ) then
    print *, "ALLOCATED reports DEGREES is allocated"
else
    print *, "ALLOCATED reports DEGREES is NOT allocated"
end if
```

It displays:

```
ALLOCATED reports DEGREES is allocated
```

In a real application, ALLOCATED would probably be used in two places: detecting the first call to a subprogram, and error handling. The first time a subprogram is called, ALLOCATED would detect that required arrays are not allocated and then branch to code to allocate them. On subsequent calls, ALLOCATED would detect that the arrays are allocated and bypass the code to allocate them. In an error routine, ALLOCATED would be used to check if global arrays were allocated before the error occurred. Then, only those arrays that had been successfully allocated would be deallocated (see the ERROR routine in CONCORD in Chapter 4, *Subroutines and Functions Revisited*).

Finally, the memory set aside for DEGREES needs to be released.

```
        deallocate ( degrees, stat = error )
        if ( error .ne. 0 ) then
            print *, "Deallocation error!"
            go to 100
        else
            print *, "DEGREES deallocated"
        end if
100     continue
        print *, " "
        end program temperature
```

The DEALLOCATE statement releases the allocated memory. As with the ALLOCATE statement, a zero-valued STAT variable signals success while a processor dependent, positive integer would be returned on failure. For example, it is an error to DEALLOCATE an array that is not allocated.

When a program exits, it is very likely that the host computer will have safeguards in place to reclaim any memory allocated on the fly. However, it is good practice for each program to manage its own deallocation of allocated memory. This is no more unreasonable a chore of housekeeping than the common practice of each program closing files at the end of a run.

Formal Restrictions on ALLOCATABLE Arrays

Two restrictions apply to the use of ALLOCATABLE arrays. First, they cannot appear in COMMON. That is perfectly consistent with the sequential memory model described earlier in this chapter. At the point when a compiler designs the layout of COMMON storage, it couldn't possibly have any idea about how much space to set aside for an ALLOCATABLE array since only its rank is known, not the extent of each individual dimension.

This restriction is not problematic because Fortran 90's MODULE provides a solution. If it were necessary to make the example's DEGREES array available to subprograms, it could be placed in a MODULE, which would then be included through the a USE statement:

```
        module global
            integer, dimension(:), allocatable :: degrees
        end module global
```

Second, the RESULT of a function cannot be an ALLOCATABLE array. This restriction can be overcome using Fortran 90's POINTERs and TARGETs. If it were necessary for the example's DEGREES array to be "returned" by a function, its declaration could be augmented with the TARGET attribute, a POINTER assigned to it, and the POINTER manipulated by the function. Functions returning pointers will be discussed later in this chapter.

Pointers and Targets

Since pointers represent a new level of abstraction in Fortran, and since it is easy to be led astray by comparisons to other languages for extensions to Fortran, a discussion of variables and their values is a useful starting point. Fortran's variables are convenient names for the memory address at which their values are stored. An assignment to an INTEGER variable means a change to memory at the address to which this variable refers.

A pointer contains a memory address instead of an integer or floating-point value. Thus, to alter the pointer is to make it point to a different memory address.

Pointers can be assigned to locations, but in order to be useful of course they must also allow references directly to data. Here lies the reason for the new pointer assignment operator, =>, and a distinction between it and the traditional = assignment operator. A traditional assignment statement refers to the data at the ultimate destination of the pointer. Thus, if pointer P points to target A, the statement:

```
p = c
```

has exactly the same effect (and probably without any significant execution overhead) as:

```
a = c
```

Both cases assume that C exists as another variable of the same shape as A. The contents of C are copied into A.

By contrast, pointer assignment merely changes where a pointer points to. So, the example below:

```
p => c
```

means that P now points to C, not to A. Neither the contents of A nor of C are changed in any way.

It is indirect. But it is no more complicated a concept than the distinction between a variable and its value.

Fortran does not support "pointer arithmetic," where a new memory location can be reached by incrementing the pointer or adding an offset. In this respect, Fortran 90 is comparable to Pascal, not C or Cray Fortran.

Most modern programming languages support pointers: Ada, C, C++, Pascal, and PL/1. Now, Fortran 90 introduces pointers to the language. Pointers are reputed to be difficult to work with, hard to control, and the first step in the long road to unmaintainable code. But Fortran 90 offers some protection in the form of two caveats: the data type and rank of each POINTER must be declared, and pointers can point only to other pointers or to objects specifically declared with the TARGET attribute. Therefore, on encountering a POINTER in a source code listing, the programmer can quickly determine its data type, its dimensions, and the small set of variables that it can point to.

These constraints do not debase the value of pointers. Fortran 90 POINTERs can be employed to provide a shorthand reference to a complicated array section, to embed variable arrays in derived types, to build and manage true linked lists, and to implement functions returning pointers. In the long run, it is conceivable that the pointer type might improve Fortran's ability to interact with libraries written in other programming languages. That is not assured by the Fortran 90 standard, but it seems reasonable to expect.

Pointers and Housekeeping

A pointer must be declared with its data type and rank. This declaration can appear on a single line of source code or spread over several lines.

```
integer, dimension(:), pointer :: a_pointer
integer, dimension(:)           :: b_pointer
pointer                         :: b_pointer
integer                         :: c_pointer
pointer                         :: c_pointer(:)
```

Similar options are available when declaring a TARGET.

```
integer, dimension(3), target :: x_target
integer, dimension(3)         :: y_target
target                        :: y_target
integer                       :: z_target
target                        :: z_target(3)
```

During the execution of a program, the status of a pointer can be detected with the ASSOCIATED intrinsic to see if it is in use at all or in use with a particular TARGET. The state of A_POINTER and Z_TARGET are modeled in Figure 7-1.

```
integer, dimension(:), pointer :: a_pointer
integer, dimension(3), target  :: z_target
logical                        :: true_false
.
.
.
nullify ( a_pointer )
true_false = associated ( a_pointer )
.
.
.
a_pointer => z_target
true_false = associated ( a_pointer )
true_false = associated ( a_pointer, TARGET = z_target )
.
.
.
```

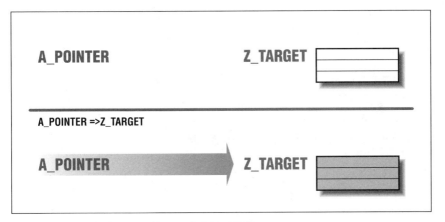

Figure 7-1: State of A_POINTER and Z_TARGET

In the code fragment above, the association status of A_POINTER is initially undefined. NULLIFY sets it to disassociated, so the first use of ASSOCI-ATED returns false. Then A_POINTER is associated with Z_TARGET, so the next two calls to ASSOCIATED return true.

Pointers and Array Sections

POINTERs provide a convenient means to refer to an array section and reduce storage. The more complex the array section, the more POINTERs help streamline code. Furthermore, pointers point to other locations; they aren't copies of data, so their use can help eliminate redundant data storage.

The PARTS matrix inversion program from Chapter 2 (in the section entitled "Example: Matrix Inversion By Partitions"), can be recast to use pointers and thus save nearly one-third of the required memory storage. For comparative purposes, the original main program for PARTS follows:

```
program parts
integer, parameter        :: m = 2
integer, parameter        :: n = 3
real                      :: determinant
real, dimension (n,n)     :: identity, inverse, matrix
real, dimension (m,  m )  :: nw,        i_nw
real, dimension (m,  n-m) :: ne,        i_ne
real, dimension (n-m,m )  :: sw,        i_sw
real, dimension (n-m,n-m) :: se,        i_se
data matrix / 1, 2, 3, 1, 0, 7, 1,  6, 1 /
nw(1:m  ,1:m  ) = matrix(1   :m,1   :m)
sw(1:n-m,1:m  ) = matrix(m+1:n,1   :m)
ne(1:m  ,1:n-m) = matrix(1   :m,m+1:n)
se(1:n-m,1:n-m) = matrix(m+1:n,m+1:n)
call invert ( se, n-m, determinant, i_se )
nw   = nw - matmul ( matmul ( ne, i_se ), sw )
call invert ( nw, m, determinant, i_nw )
i_sw = - matmul ( matmul ( i_se, sw ), i_nw )
i_ne = - matmul ( matmul ( i_nw, ne ), i_se )
i_se = i_se - matmul ( matmul ( i_se, sw ), i_ne )
inverse(1   :m,1   :m) = i_nw(1:m  ,1:m  )
inverse(m+1:n,1   :m) = i_sw(1:n-m,1:m  )
inverse(1   :m,m+1:n) = i_ne(1:m  ,1:n-m)
inverse(m+1:n,m+1:n) = i_se(1:n-m,1:n-m)
call echo ( "MATRIX", matrix, n )
call echo ( "INVERSE", inverse, n )
identity = matmul ( matrix, inverse )
call echo ( "IDENTITY", identity, n )
end program parts
```

There is no separate need for most of the individual matrix quadrants or any of the individual sections of the INVERSE matrix. Consequently, they can be declared as POINTERS.

```
program part2
integer, parameter         :: m = 2
integer, parameter         :: n = 3
real                       :: determinant
real, dimension (n,n)      :: identity
real, dimension (n,n), target :: inverse
real, dimension (n,n), target :: matrix
real, dimension (m,m)      :: t_nw
```

```
real, dimension (:,:), pointer :: i_nw, i_ne, i_sw, i_se
real, dimension (:,:), pointer ::  nw,   ne,   sw,   se
data matrix / 1, 2, 3, 1, 0, 7, 1, 6, 1 /
```

The individual matrix quadrants are initialized by making them point to sections of the input matrix:

```
nw => matrix(1    :m,1   :m)
sw => matrix(m+1:n,1   :m)
ne => matrix(1    :m,m+1:n)
se => matrix(m+1:n,m+1:n)
```

then, the individual quadrants of the INVERSE matrix are ranged:

```
i_nw => inverse(1    :m,1   :m)
i_sw => inverse(m+1:n,1   :m)
i_ne => inverse(1    :m,m+1:n)
i_se => inverse(m+1:n,m+1:n)
call invert ( se, n-m, determinant, i_se )
```

and computed in a similar way to the original program. A change is needed to handle the northwest quadrant. A temporary copy is required as an intermediate result. If the pointer NW was used in place of a copy of that portion of the original data in the next line of code, then the original MATRIX would be modified. Since MATRIX has to be left intact throughout the program, the intermediate result is stored in T_NW. Since no pointer ever references T_NW, it does not have to be declared with the TARGET attribute, although no harm would have come of doing so.

```
t_nw = nw - matmul ( matmul ( ne, i_se ), sw )
call invert ( t_nw, m, determinant, i_nw )
i_sw = - matmul ( matmul ( i_se, sw ), i_nw )
i_ne = - matmul ( matmul ( i_nw, ne ), i_se )
i_se = i_se - matmul ( matmul ( i_se, sw ), i_ne )
```

Finally, the results can be displayed as in the original version.

```
call echo ( "MATRIX", matrix, n )
call echo ( "INVERSE", inverse, n )
identity = matmul ( matrix, inverse )
call echo ( "IDENTITY", identity, n )
end program part2
```

The use of pointers has made the program easier to understand. The main programs of both versions are the same length. However, PART2 does not have to repeat the complicated array section specifications to transfer data between the full MATRIX and INVERSE arrays and their individual quadrants. Furthermore, the memory requirements for arrays and vectors in PARTS is $5n^2$ units, whereas PART2 requires $3n^2+m^2$ units, saving over 30% of the storage burden.

Pointers and Derived Types

Pointers can hold the place of allocated arrays in a derived type. This is a very powerful combination. Derived types provide logical grouping of data, and pointer components provide a means to reference a varying amount of memory per instance of a derived type. Together, they can manage data structures whose total size is not known until the moment that part of the program executes.

As an example, each atomic element has a varying number of isotopes. Although exactly 106 elements are known, nearly 1500 isotopes exist: hydrogen has three isotopes, helium has five, neon has nine, etc. A derived type can be constructed that allocates only as much memory per element as is needed to contain the weights of that element's isotopes.

The program ISOWEIGHT is a variation on the PT program from Chapter 3, *Derived Types*. It begins by declaring a derived type including a pointer, WEIGHT, standing for the isotopic weights for that element.

```
program isoweight
integer, parameter                          :: elements = 106
type mendeleev
      character (len=12)                    :: name
      character (len=2 )                    :: symbol
      integer                               :: atomic_number
      double precision                      :: mass
      integer                               :: isotopes
      double precision, dimension(:),pointer :: weight
end  type mendeleev
type ( mendeleev ) periodic(elements)
```

The input file contains identifying information about each element on one line and then as many lines as necessary follow to record the weights of all of the element's isotopes. These data are from the volume edited by Robert C. Weast for the Chemical Rubber Company, *CRC Handbook of Chemistry and Physics*: 68th Edition (1987, CRC Press, Inc., Boca Raton, FL). Part of the input file appears below.

```
Hydrogen      H    1    1.00794    3
  1.007825  2.014000  3.016050
Helium       He    2    4.00260    5
  3.016030  4.002600  5.012220  6.018886  8.033920
  .
  .
  .
```

```
Neon            Ne  10  20.179      9
 17.017690 18.005710 19.001879 19.992435 20.993843 21.991383
 22.994465 23.993613 24.997690
 .
 .
 .
```

For each element, a loop reads an initial line in a straightforward fashion directly into the fixed components of the PERIODIC derived type.

```
open ( unit=5, file='isoweight.input' )
rewind 5
do i = 1, elements, 1
    read ( 5,100 ) periodic(i)%name,           &
                   periodic(i)%symbol,          &
                   periodic(i)%atomic_number,  &
                   periodic(i)%mass,            &
                   periodic(i)%isotopes
100     format ( a12, 1x, a2, 1x, i3, 1x, f9.5, 1x, i3 )
```

But before the loop can read the weights, it must allocate sufficient memory for each isotopic weight. The "size" of the required memory pool is carried in PERIODIC(I)%ISOTOPES and the address of this memory is stored in PERIODIC(I)%WEIGHT. Thus the following ALLOCATE statement uses the ISOTOPES component as the subscript to WEIGHT, which is the component being dimensioned:

```
allocate ( periodic(i)%weight(periodic(i)%isotopes) )
```

Then the individual weights are read into the allocated memory:

```
    read ( 5,  * ) periodic(i)%weight
end do
close ( unit=5 )
```

The first pass sets aside three elements at PERIODIC(1)%WEIGHT for hydrogen; the second pass, five elements at PERIODIC(2)%WEIGHT for helium, etc. The actual weight data is stored in the memory referenced by these pointers. Figure 7-2 shows the progressive allocation of memory during the loop.

Identifying information for the element and weights for each of that element's isotopes is then displayed.

```
    print 200
200   format ( 1H , 'Name              Symbol Number       Mass ', &
                    'Isotope    Weights',                          &
                 / 1H , '------------ ------ ------ ---------- ',   &
                    '-------- ---------'                        )
    do i = 1, elements, 1
```

```
            m = nint ( periodic(i)%weight(1) )
            print 300, periodic(i)%name,            &
                       periodic(i)%symbol,          &
                       periodic(i)%atomic_number, &
                       periodic(i)%mass,            &
                       m,                           &
                       periodic(i)%weight(1)
300         format ( 1H , a12, 1x, a2, 5x, i6, 1x, &
                      f9.6, 1x, i7, 1x, f9.6       )
            do j = 2, periodic(i)%isotopes, 1
              m = nint ( periodic(i)%weight(j) )
              print 400, m, periodic(i)%weight(j)
400           format ( 1H , 37x, i7, 1x, f9.6 )
            end do
            deallocate ( periodic(i)%weight )
            print *, " "
          end do
        end program isoweight
```

Part of the output file appears as:

Name	Symbol	Number	Mass	Isotope	Weights
Hydrogen	H	1	1.007940	1	1.007825
				2	2.014000
				3	3.016050
Helium	He	2	4.002600	3	3.016030
				4	4.002600
				5	5.012220
				6	6.018886
				8	8.033920

.
.
.

Name	Symbol	Number	Mass	Isotope	Weights
Neon	Ne	10	20.179000	17	17.017690
				18	18.005710
				19	19.001879
				20	19.992435
				21	20.993843
				22	21.991383
				23	22.994465
				24	23.993613
				25	24.997690

.
.
.

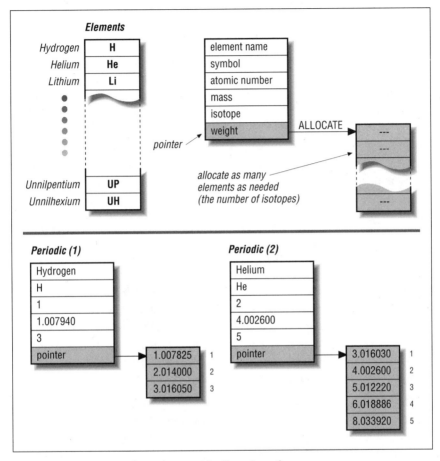

Figure 7-2: PERIODIC derived type with allocation of memory

This example also contains an illustration of one restriction on pointers. Since each instance of PERIODIC contains the WEIGHT pointer, certain expressions involving the derived type cannot appear in an input or output list. It is not possible to write the entire array in a statement like PRINT *, PERIODIC. It is not possible to write an entire element of the array in a statement like PRINT *, PERIODIC(I). Both statements would require writing the value of the pointer WEIGHT. However, as shown in the program just mentioned, the constructs PERIODIC(I)%WEIGHT and PERIODIC(I)%WEIGHT(J) can appear in input or output lists because they explicitly mention the pointer that references data.

Pointers and Linked Lists

Pointers are the mechanism to manage linked lists. These are extraordinarily flexible data structures because their size can grow or shrink during the execution of a program. The basic technique is to create a derived type that consists of one or more data elements and at least one pointer. Memory is allocated to contain the data and a pointer is set to reference the next occurrence of data. If one pointer is present, the list is a singly linked list and can only be traversed in one direction: head to tail, or vice versa. Its two pointers are present: the list is a doubly linked list and can be traversed in either direction. Linked lists allow the data of interest to be scattered all over memory and uses pointers to weave through memory gathering data as required.

Example: Surveying Traverse as a Singly Linked List

When a surveyor determines the exact perimeter of a building or plot of land, critical measurements are taken at each angle. If the perimeter has N sides, the surveyor measures the length of each side and the interior angle each side forms with the next. Regardless of how careful the surveyor is, errors are invariably introduced during the measurement process. However, the error in angle measurements can be bounded.

Geometrically, lines can be drawn leading from each corner of the perimeter to one single corner selected at random (see Figure 7-3). Together with the perimeter line, these lines define triangles. In fact, for a perimeter of N sides, there will be N-2 triangles. Since the sum of the interior angles of any triangle is 180 degrees, then the sum of the interior angles of the perimeter must be N-2 times 180 degrees. If the sum of the surveyor's measurements for the interior angles of the building or plot's perimeter isn't 180(N-2), then the difference must be distributed equally among the angle.

The program SURVEY implements the recording and correcting of angles in a survey traversed as a singly linked list. A linked list was chosen because the programmer has no idea how many sides the perimeter has, and linked lists can grow arbitrarily. Because of the linked list's ability to absorb a short or long data stream, the user does not have to be asked to count the number of legs in the traverse. The program begins by declaring a derived type, MARK, that contains one angle measurement and a pointer to the next measurement.

```
program survey
type mark
    real                   :: angle
    type (mark), pointer :: next_mark
end  type mark
```

Three instances of this derived type are declared as are various local variables:

```
type ( mark ), pointer    :: begin
type ( mark ), pointer    :: temp
type ( mark ), pointer    :: traverse
real                      :: adjustment     = 0.0
real                      :: angle_input
integer                   :: legs           = 0
logical                   :: need_adjustment = .false.
real                      :: total_angles   = 0.0
```

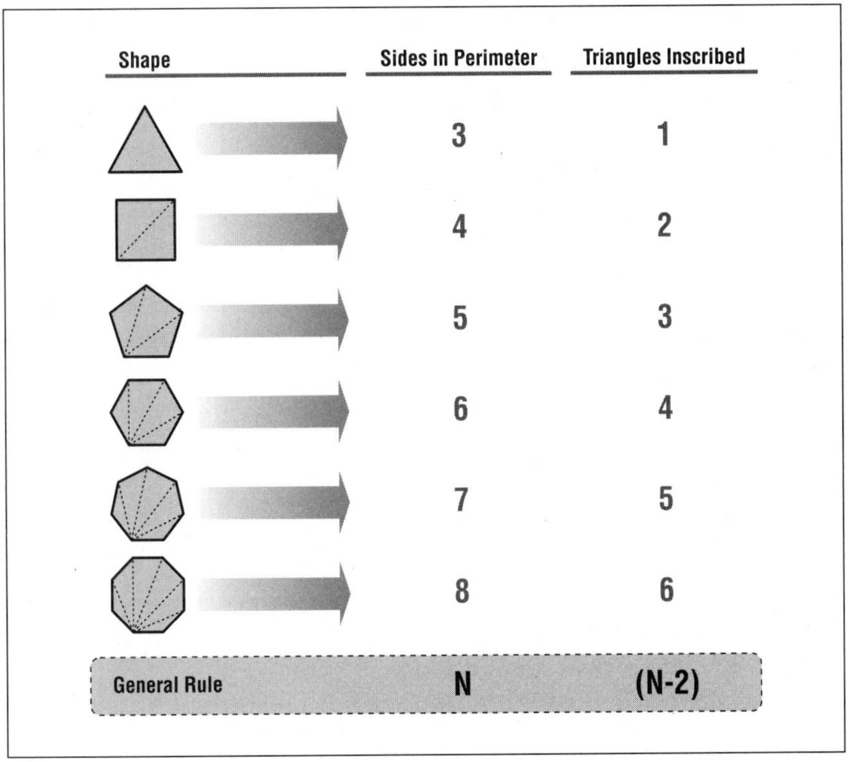

Shape	Sides in Perimeter	Triangles Inscribed
(triangle)	3	1
(square)	4	2
(pentagon)	5	3
(hexagon)	6	4
(heptagon)	7	5
(octagon)	8	6
General Rule	N	(N-2)

Figure 7-3: Triangles in a closed convex polygon

A linked list has to begin and end somewhere. Memory is allocated at the pointer BEGIN and the surveyor's TRAVERSE is initialized by pointing to that allocated memory for the beginning of the list.

```
allocate ( begin )
traverse => begin
```

By convention, programs generally use a null pointer to mark the end of the list. Since no data has been read yet, the forward pointer can be nullified immediately. Fortran 90 provides a NULLIFY statement for the purpose of disassociating a pointer.

```
nullify ( traverse%next_mark )
```

It is not necessary to NULLIFY a POINTER before its first use. The Fortran 90 standard says that pointers are created in the null state, although the association status of a new pointer is undefined. This is just a safety measure. It is similar to the practice of REWINDing a file before its first use even though the vast majority of Fortran implementations connect a file and position its first use at the beginning of file.

Now all the angles can be read, provided any individual angle is less that 180 degrees.

```
        print *, " "
        print *, "Enter angles (0 to finish) ..."
        do
100     continue
        read ( *,*,err=100,end=200 ) angle_input
        if ( angle_input .le. 0.0 ) then
            exit
        else if ( angle_input .ge. 180.0 ) then
            print *, "Angles must be less than 180 degrees!"
            go to 100
        end if
```

For each angle read, the value is stored in the data element of TRAVERSE, memory is allocated to hold the next angle, and linked list is advanced to the next element.

```
        traverse%angle = angle_input
        allocate ( traverse%next_mark )
        traverse => traverse%next_mark
```

A count is kept of the number of legs in this traverse and the forward pointer for the last angle read is cleared to signal the end of list.

```
        legs = legs + 1
     end do
200  continue
     nullify ( traverse%next_mark )
```

If fewer than three legs were read, then it wasn't much of a traverse and the program aborts.

```
print *, " "
print *, "All", legs, "angles have been read ..."
if ( legs .lt. 3 ) then
    print *, " "
    print *, "ERROR! Fewer than 3 angles read!"
    go to 600
end if
```

The entire list of angles is reviewed to get the total of the measurements. This starts by revisiting the head of the list and adding together all the angle measurements until a null pointer is encountered, signalling the end of list.

```
traverse => begin
do
   total_angles = total_angles + traverse%angle
   traverse => traverse%next_mark
   if ( .not. associated ( traverse%next_mark ) ) exit
end do
```

Then the error can be computed and distributed equally among the legs of the traverse.

```
adjustment = ( ( ( legs - 2 ) * 180 ) - total_angles ) / legs
print *, " "
print *, "Measurement adjustment is", adjustment, "degrees."
if ( abs ( adjustment ) .gt. 0.0 ) need_adjustment = .true.
print *, " "
traverse => begin
i = 0
do
   i = i + 1
   write ( *,300,advance="NO" ) i, traverse%angle
300   format ( 1H , 'Angle ', i2.2, ' is ', f10.5 )
   if ( need_adjustment ) then
        traverse%angle = traverse%angle + adjustment
        write ( *,400,advance="NO" ) traverse%angle
400        format ( ' adjusted to ', f10.5 )
   end if
   write ( *,500 )
500   format ( ' degrees.' )
```

```
» traverse => traverse%next_mark
  if ( .not. associated ( traverse%next_mark ) ) exit
end do
```

In the simplest case of a building perimeter that is a perfect square, this program makes no adjustment.

```
Enter angles (0 to finish) ...
90
90
90
90
0

All 4 angles have been read ...

Measurement adjustment is   0.0000000E+00 degrees.

Angle 01 is   90.00000 degrees.
Angle 02 is   90.00000 degrees.
Angle 03 is   90.00000 degrees.
Angle 04 is   90.00000 degrees.
```

Of course, even "square" structures are not perfect, but may have off-setting angles so that no adjustment is needed. The Great Pyramid at Giza in Egypt is such an example where no individual corner diverges from a perfect right angle by more than ±0.066%, and what differences there are cancel each other out. Entering the corner angles reported in Barbara Mertz's *Red Land, Black Land: The World of the Ancient Egyptians* (1966, Coward-McCann Inc., 380 pages, New York, NY) lets the program compute a null adjustment.

```
Enter angles (0 to finish) ...
90.05006
89.99944
89.94083
90.00917
0

All 4 angles have been read ...

Measurement adjustment is   0.0000000E+00 degrees.

Angle 01 is   90.05056 degrees.
Angle 02 is   89.99944 degrees.
Angle 03 is   89.94083 degrees.
Angle 04 is   90.00917 degrees.
```

In a more complex case of the perimeter of a theoretical plot of land, the program does make adjustments. The plot is shown in Figure 7-4. The six angles total 719.83891 degrees, leaving a pool of 0.16109 degrees to be distributed among the six angles. The per angle adjustment of 0.02685 degrees is small—only 1' 36.67"—and represents no more than 0.3% of any individual angle.

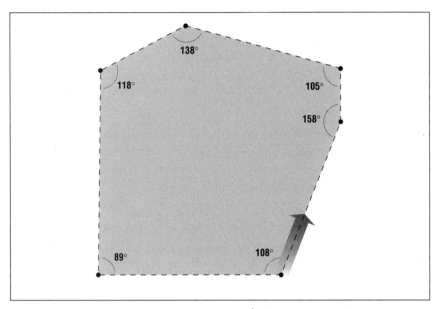

Figure 7-4: Surveying traverse

```
Enter angles (0 to finish) ...
108.89444
158.43333
105.64583
138.28612
118.71250
89.86667
0

All 6 angles have been read ...

Measurement adjustment is   2.6855469E-02 degrees.

Angle 01 is  108.89444 adjusted to  108.92130 degrees.
Angle 02 is  158.43333 adjusted to  158.46019 degrees.
Angle 03 is  105.64583 adjusted to  105.67268 degrees.
Angle 04 is  138.28612 adjusted to  138.31297 degrees.
Angle 05 is  118.71250 adjusted to  118.73936 degrees.
Angle 06 is   89.86667 adjusted to   89.89352 degrees.
```

At the conclusion of the program, the list is scanned one more time and all the reserved memory is DEALLOCATEd.

```
        traverse => begin
        do
            temp => traverse%next_mark
            deallocate ( traverse )
            if ( .not. associated ( temp%next_mark ) ) exit
            traverse => temp
        end do
        nullify ( begin )
        nullify ( temp  )
600     continue
        print *, " "
        end program survey
```

It is likely that any given implementation of Fortran 90 will release allocated memory at the conclusion of a program. However, it is good programming practice to do so within the program.

At first it might seem hard to distinguish DEALLOCATE from NULLIFY. Both leave the pointer disassociated, where an ASSOCIATED intrinsic would return a false result. The difference is that DEALLOCATE destroys data, reducing the amount of memory used by the program, while NULLIFY leaves the data intact.

Thus, DEALLOCATE is used when a program is finished with the data. NULLIFY is useful to free a pointer, when other pointers are still pointing to the data and it must be left intact for them. As shown in the program above, NULLIFY is also useful to disassociate a pointer when its associated target has already been deallocated by reference to a different pointer.

Example: Mississippi River Tour as a Doubly Linked List

Doubly linked lists carry a forward and backward pointer in each link. Whereas a singly linked list can be scanned in one direction, the contents of a doubly linked lists can be examined from head to tail and vice versa. They also provide a more interesting case for replacing, inserting, and deleting elements from the list.

The program TOUR implements a trip along the Mississippi River as a doubly linked list. It begins by declaring a derived type, RIVER, and embedding its definition in a MODULE called CITY_LIST.

```
module city_list
type river
      type (river), pointer :: upstream
      character (len=25)    :: city
      type (river), pointer :: downstream
end  type river
type ( river ), pointer    :: finish
type ( river ), pointer    :: start
type ( river ), pointer    :: travel
end module city_list
```

Several instances of the derived type are declared to clarify list creation and manipulation.

```
program tour
use city_list
character (len=25)         :: city_input
type ( river ), pointer    :: hannibal
type ( river ), pointer    :: memphis
type ( river ), pointer    :: natchez
type ( river ), pointer    :: rock_island
type ( river ), pointer    :: st_louis
type ( river ), pointer    :: temp
type ( river ), pointer    :: vicksburg
```

The first list element is initialized at both ends of the list: both backward, START%UPSTREAM, and forward pointer, START%DOWNSTREAM, are NULLIFY-ied.

```
allocate ( start )
nullify ( start%upstream  )
start%city = ' '
nullify ( start%downstream )
travel => start
```

These selected cities and place names form the initial list.

```
Lake Itaska, Minnesota
Minneapolis, Minnesota
La Crosse, Wisconsin
Davenport, Iowa
Rock Island, Illinois
St. Louis, Missouri
Wickliffe, Kentucky
Osceola, Arkansas
Memphis, Tennessee
Vicksburg, Mississippi
```

```
Natchez, Mississippi
New Orleans, Louisiana
Gulf of Mexico
```

The program reads each city name, one at a time, into a static variable, CITY_INPUT, and then threads it onto the linked list.

```
      print *, " "
      print *, "Enter cities ..."
      do
          read ( *,100,end=200 ) city_input
100       format ( a25 )
          temp => travel
          travel%city = city_input
          allocate ( travel%downstream )
          travel => travel%downstream
          travel%upstream => temp
      end do
200   continue
```

After all cities have been read, a pointer to the end of the list is retained and the last pointer is NULLIFY-ied to signal the end of list.

```
      print *, " "
      print *, "All city names have been read ..."
      finish => temp
      nullify ( travel%downstream )
```

The process so far has created the list illustrated by Figure 7-5. The original tour is listed by traversing the list using the forward pointers

```
      print *, " "
      print *, "LIST the original tour"
      print *, "======================="
      call droute
```

in a subroutine called DROUTE. Here, the tour begins at the head of the list and city names are printed until a null downstream pointer is encountered.

```
      subroutine droute
      use city_list
      print *, " "
      print *, "    Cities passed going downstream ..."
      travel => start
      do
         print *, "      ", travel%city
         travel => travel%downstream
         if ( .not. associated ( travel%downstream ) ) exit
      end do
      end subroutine droute
```

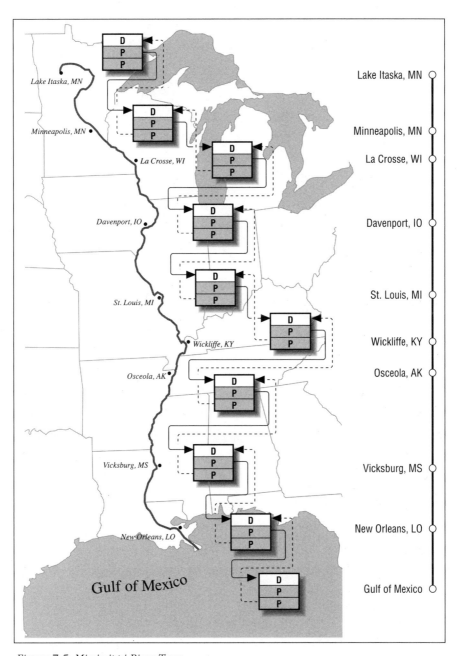

Figure 7-5: Mississippi River Tour

The list displayed is:

```
LIST the original tour
========================


        Cities passed going downstream ...
        Lake Itaska, Minnesota
        Minneapolis, Minnesota
        La Crosse, Wisconsin
        Davenport, Iowa
        Rock Island, Illinois
        St. Louis, Missouri
        Wickliffe, Kentucky
        Osceola, Arkansas
        Memphis, Tennessee
        Vicksburg, Mississippi
        Natchez, Mississippi
        New Orleans, Louisiana
        Gulf of Mexico
```

An individual link can be replaced simply by changing the TRAVEL%CITY component. In Iowa, Davenport is replaced by Dubuque.

```
print *, " "
print *, "REPLACE Davenport with Dubuque"
print *, "===============================" 
travel => start
do
    if ( travel%city(1:4) .eq. 'Dave' ) then
        travel%city = 'Dubuque, Iowa'
        exit
    else
        travel => travel%downstream
        if ( .not. associated ( travel%downstream ) ) exit
    end if
end do
call uroute
```

The resulting list is displayed in reverse order—upstream—by the UROUTE subroutine.

```
subroutine uroute
use city_list
print *, " "
print *, "    Cities passed going upstream ..."
travel => finish
do
    print *, "    ", travel%city
    if ( .not. associated ( travel%upstream ) ) exit
    travel => travel%upstream
```

```
end do
end subroutine uroute
```

Here, the list is scanned from the tail towards the head. Each place name is displayed until a null upstream pointer is encountered.

```
REPLACE Davenport with Dubuque
==================================

          Cities passed going upstream ...
          Gulf of Mexico
          New Orleans, Louisiana
          Natchez, Mississippi
          Vicksburg, Mississippi
          Memphis, Tennessee
          Osceola, Arkansas
          Wickliffe, Kentucky
          St. Louis, Missouri
          Rock Island, Illinois
          Dubuque, Iowa
          La Crosse, Wisconsin
          Minneapolis, Minnesota
          Lake Itaska, Minnesota
```

Inserting a link means that both the downstream and upstream pointers of the surrounding cities need adjustment. Hannibal, MO, is between Rock Island and St. Louis, so the list is searched until Rock Island is encountered.

```
print *, " "
print *, "INSERT Hannibal between Rock Island and St. Louis"
print *, "==================================================="
travel => start
do
    if ( travel%city(1:11) .eq. 'Rock Island' ) then
```

Then the existing links for Rock Island and St. Louis are retained, memory for Hannibal is allocated, pointers upstream and downstream for Hannibal are set, and the forward pointer for Rock Island and the backward pointer for St. Louis are adjusted to point to Hannibal.

```
          rock_island => travel
          st_louis => rock_island%downstream
          allocate ( hannibal )
          hannibal%upstream => rock_island
          hannibal%city = 'Hannibal, Missouri'
          hannibal%downstream => st_louis
          rock_island%downstream => hannibal
          st_louis%upstream => hannibal
          exit
    else
          travel => travel%downstream
```

```
            if ( .not. associated ( travel%downstream ) ) exit
    end if
end do
call droute
```

It was not necessary to use place-specific POINTER names like ROCK_ISLAND, ST_LOUIS, and HANNIBAL. The generalized subroutine below accomplishes this general, repeatable insertion. It is incorporated into a separate version of the TOUR program, called DETOUR, that appears in Appendix D, *Selected Source Code Listings.*

As an internal subroutine, it is able to use the variables already declared in the main program. It is called with the name of the new city, and assumes that this new city should be inserted just downstream of the one to which TRAVEL is pointing. Insertion requires operations on two downstream pointers and two upstream pointers.

First, two temporary pointers store information. Corresponding to the example, DOWN points to the old downstream city (St. Louis) and TEMP holds information about the new city.

```
subroutine city_insert (city_input)
use city_list
type ( river ), pointer    :: down, temp
down => travel%downstream
allocate ( temp )
temp%city = city_input
```

The new stop on the journey (Hannibal) can now be integrated with its neighbors. TRAVEL is upstream (Rock Island), while the city that followed TRAVEL is downstream (St. Louis).

```
temp%upstream => travel
temp%downstream => travel%downstream
```

The city at TRAVEL (Rock Island) should update its downstream pointer to link in the new city (Hannibal).

```
travel%downstream => temp
```

The upstream pointer at TEMP%DOWNSTREAM should also point back to TEMP (i.e., Hannibal is upstream from St. Louis). However, it is illegal to refer to that upstream pointer indirectly. In other words, the following construct does not work:

```
travel%downstream%upstream ! Will NOT compile
```

However, DOWN still points to the original downstream city (St. Louis). So, its upstream pointer can be adjusted to link in the new city (Hannibal).

```
down%upstream => temp
```

All four pointers now refer to their new targets, so the temporary pointers are no longer needed.

```
nullify ( down, temp )
end subroutine city_insert
```

Deleting a link also implies repairing pointers in adjoining links. For instance, the following code searches for Vicksburg in the list and deletes it.

```
print *, " "
print *, "DELETE Vicksburg from between Memphis and Natchez"
print *, "=============================================="
travel => start
do
    if ( travel%city(1:9) .eq. 'Vicksburg' ) then
```

A pointer to the Vicksburg link is retained, pointers for Memphis and Natchez are retrieved from the Vicksburg link, the forward pointer for Memphis and the backward pointer for Natchez are reset, and the memory reserved for Vicksburg is DEALLOCATEd.

```
        vicksburg => travel
        memphis => vicksburg%upstream
        natchez => vicksburg%downstream
        memphis%downstream => natchez
        natchez%upstream => memphis
        deallocate ( vicksburg )
        exit
    else
        travel => travel%downstream
        if ( .not. associated ( travel%downstream ) ) exit
    end if
end do
call uroute
```

Reallocating a data structure that contains a pointer will leave allocated, but unaccessible, memory where the pointer originally pointed. This useless memory (often called a memory leak) can increase paging overhead for a program and, over time, cause it to run out of memory.

It was not necessary to use place-specific POINTER names like VICKS-BURG, MEMPHIS, and NATCHEZ. More generalized code shown below accomplishes this same deletion. It is incorporated into a separate version of the TOUR program, called DETOUR, that appears in Appendix D.

A temporary pointer stores the rest of the list so that it remains when the current item is deleted.

```
temp => travel%downstream
```

Now the current item can be safely deleted. The journey retraces back one step to the previous stop.

```
travel => travel%upstream
deallocate ( travel%downstream )
```

The pointer is now updated to find the rest of the list, which was stored at TEMP.

```
travel%downstream => temp
```

Finally, the next city downstream repairs its pointer so that it no longer points to the deleted data.

```
temp%upstream => travel      nullify ( temp )
```

Good programming practice demands that all memory reserved for the doubly linked list should be released.

```
print *, " "
print *, "DEALLOCATE the linked list"
print *, "═══════════════════════"
print *, " "
print *, "    Cities deallocated going downstream ..."
travel => start
do
    print *, "     ", travel%city
    temp => travel%downstream
    deallocate ( travel )
    if ( .not. associated ( temp%downstream ) ) exit
    travel => temp
end do
```

Finally, each remaining pointer is disassociated in a final flurry of housekeeping chores.

```
nullify ( finish      )
nullify ( hannibal    )
nullify ( memphis     )
nullify ( natchez     )
nullify ( rock_island )
nullify ( st_louis    )
nullify ( start       )
nullify ( temp        )
nullify ( vicksburg   )
print *, " "
end program tour
```

Pointers and Functions

The simplicity of giving a name to an array section is extended by Fortran 90, allowing functions to return pointers. This is beneficial because the rules to select one array section over another can be embedded in a separate subprogram, thereby enhancing the source code's maintainability.

For example, in the Gauss-Jordan elimination technique of solving a set of linear equations, there is a requirement to repeatedly select and manipulate the row in a matrix that contains the largest element. This is a key ingredient of the process of pivoting. Pivoting is discussed and a full Gauss-Jordan program is presented on pages 24 through 29 of *Numerical Recipes* by William H. Press et. al. (1986, Cambridge University Press, 818 pages, Cambridge, England). The program PIVOT addresses just the pivot selection process. It begins by declaring the INTERFACE to the function returning a pointer as well as the key variables in the main program.

```
program pivot
interface
  function pivot_row ( a )
     real,     dimension ( :,: ), target  :: a
     real,     dimension ( :   ), pointer :: pivot_row
  end function pivot_row
end interface
real, dimension (3,3), target  :: a
integer                        :: i, m, n
real, dimension ( : ), pointer :: p
```

The data array, A, is initialized:

```
n = size ( a, dim=1 )
m = n * n
a = reshape ( (/ (i,i=1,m) /), (/ n,n /) )
print *, " "
print *, "Array ... row 1 : ", a(1,:)
do i = 2, n, 1
   print *, "      ... row", i, ": ", a(i,:)
end do
```

and displayed as:

```
Array ... row 1 :   1.0000000   4.0000000   7.0000000
      ... row 2 :   2.0000000   5.0000000   8.0000000
      ... row 3 :   3.0000000   6.0000000   9.0000000
```

Then, the function that returns a pointer, PIVOT_ROW, is invoked to select some row-wise array section from the data array, A.

```
p => pivot_row ( a )
```

Following the usual heuristic for selecting a pivot row, the function uses the Fortran 90 intrinsic MAXLOC to get the array indices of the largest element in the array. The row index is then used to specify the array section that will be the pointer to the pivot row.

```
function pivot_row ( a )
real,    dimension ( :,: ), target  :: a
real,    dimension (  :  ), pointer :: pivot_row
integer, dimension (  2  )          :: location
location = maxloc ( a )
pivot_row => a(location(1),:)
end function pivot_row
```

After returning to the main program, the values of the entire pivot row and the largest value in that row are displayed through the pointer, P:

```
print *, " "
print *, "Pivot row       : ", p
print *, " "
print *, "Pivot element   : ", maxval ( p )
nullify ( p )
print *, " "
end program pivot
```

and appear as follows:

```
Pivot row      :    3.0000000   6.0000000   9.0000000

Pivot element  :    9.0000000
```

Fortran 90 permits functions to return pointers. There is a distinction between functions returning pointers and pointers to functions. Fortran 90 supports the former but not the latter.

There are practices in other programming languages to allow a function to be invoked by referencing a pointer to its executable code. Pointers to functions are convenient, and Fortran comes close with its abilities to pass a function as a subprogram name, to build generic functions with one name accepting multiple data types, and to create aliases for operators. But none of these three features offer quite the algorithmic possibilities of pointers to functions.

Dynamic Memory and Pointer Management

Formal restrictions on ALLOCATABLE arrays, pointer arrays, and POINTERs and TARGETs appear throughout this chapter. However, both programming constructs can be managed by a few simple common sense rules:

- Always allocate and deallocate an ALLOCATABLE array in the same subprogram.

- Always perform ALLOCATE and DEALLOCATE of memory at a local pointer array in the same subprogram.

- Always perform pointer assignment and NULLIFY of local POINTERs in the same subprogram.

- If data must be left intact when the pointer is freed (for example, to leave it for use by other pointers), use NULLIFY; otherwise use DEALLOCATE.

If these rules are not followed, the ALLOCATABLE array, pointer array, or POINTER may enter an "undefined" state which renders it useless. Undefined means just what it says. Who knows what data remains? Who knows where the POINTER points? Who knows what is safe to use anymore?

There is no inherent danger in using Fortran 90 pointers and they do confer some terrific benefits, but, being such a powerful tool, they need to be carefully managed. Common errors include:

- Calling a subprogram that allocates memory, but fails to deallocate it before returning. If this subprogram is called often enough, it can have a significant effect on program performance because it builds up useless memory (a memory leak).

- Using ALLOCATE to allocate memory at a pointer, and NULLIFY to free the pointer. Unless some other pointer currently points to the data, it continues to exist in program memory, but is unaccessible. This, too, is a dangerous memory leak.

Restrictions on POINTER and TARGET Attributes

Most Fortran data type attributes can coexist with the POINTER or TARGET attribute. The few exceptions are listed in Table 7-1.

Table 7-1: Exceptions to POINTER and TARGET Declarations

POINTERs Cannot Be	TARGETs Cannot Be
ALLOCATABLE	
EXTERNAL	EXTERNAL
INTENT	
INTRINSIC	INTRINSIC
PARAMETER	PARAMETER
TARGET	POINTER

Restricting EXTERNAL or INTRINSIC functions from being pointers or targets surely reflects a desire to simplify compiler development. INTENT is disallowed for a POINTER argument because it would be ambiguous with respect to its association status or its value.

PARAMETERs perform a special role in Fortran as a named constant. Given the rules surrounding the placement and statement order when declaring a PARAMETER, it is not surprising that they cannot be POINTERs or TARGETs.

It is easy to see why TARGETs cannot also be declared as POINTERs. If an array is a TARGET, then its dimensions are fully declared. If an array is a POINTER, then its dimensions are partially declared (i.e., its rank is given, but not the bounds along any dimension). TARGET and POINTER attributes are mutually exclusive.

But pointers can point at other pointers. In the following code fragment:

```
integer, dimension(:), pointer :: a_pointer
integer, dimension(:), pointer :: b_pointer
integer, dimension(3), target  :: z_target
logical                        :: true_false
a_pointer => z_target
b_pointer => a_pointer
true_false = associated ( b_pointer, TARGET = a_pointer )
true_false = associated ( a_pointer, TARGET = z_target  )
nullify ( b_pointer )
nullify ( a_pointer )
```

both uses of the ASSOCIATED intrinsic report true because B_POINTER points at A_POINTER, which in turn points at Z_TARGET (see Figure 7-6).

So, when this kind of indirection occurs, a pointer like A_POINTER acts like a "target" for B_POINTER. The trickiness of this restriction is that although a POINTER might perform in the role normally fulfilled by a TARGET, it can never be declared with the TARGET attribute.

At first it might be confusing to be introduced to the => operator. But the difference between => and = is soon grasped after a little practice. Essentially, = transfers data to the target of the pointer, while => makes the pointer point to something new. For example, if A_POINTER and B_POINTER are both pointers associated with some target:

```
a_pointer => z_target
b_pointer => y_target
```

then the regular assignment statement

```
b_pointer = a_pointer
```

has exactly the same effect as

```
y_target = z_target
```

But the pointer assignment statement

```
b_pointer => a_pointer
```

makes B_POINTER point to Z_TARGET.

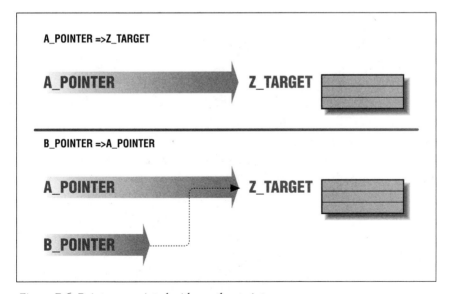

Figure 7-6: Pointer associated with another pointer

An array cannot be declared with both the ALLOCATABLE and POINTER attributes. Although both types of arrays are declared with the same deferred shape syntax, their memory requirements are totally different. Memory for an ALLOCATABLE array is set aside at the ALLOCATE statement and is located at the address of the array. Once allocated, the memory needs for such an array are fixed and do not change until the array is reallocated or deallocated. The essential reason that a POINTER cannot be ALLOCATABLE is that a POINTER is free to change and point to a new location. An ALLOCATABLE array cannot.

But POINTER arrays can also appear in an ALLOCATE statement. This is the essence of how linked lists are supported. In the following code fragment:

```
integer, dimension(:), allocatable :: i_allocatable
logical                             :: true_false
allocate ( i_allocatable(3) )
a_allocatable = (/ 123, 456, 789 /)
true_false    = allocated ( i_allocatable )
deallocate ( i_allocatable )
```

the three elements in the list {123,456,789} are stored at the beginning of the allocatable array I_ALLOCATABLE. Conversely, in this fragment:

```
integer, dimension(:), pointer     :: a_pointer
integer, dimension(:), pointer     :: b_pointer
logical                            :: true_false
allocate ( a_pointer(3) )
a_pointer  = (/ 123, 456, 789 /)
b_pointer  => a_pointer
true_false = associated ( b_pointer, TARGET = a_pointer )
nullify ( b_pointer )
deallocate ( a_pointer )
```

the effect appears to be about the same as the previous example; three elements are allocated, the variable A_POINTER can be used to refer to them, and the elements are assigned the three values {123,456,789}. But a memory address is stored at the location of the pointer A_POINTER. See Figure 7-7 for an illustration of the creation of unnamed memory and its assignment to the pointer.

The distinction raises the question of why one kind of an array would be used in favor of another. ALLOCATABLE arrays provide the basic features of dynamic memory management: array sizes can change with each execution of a program. Pointer arrays do the same thing and more. Pointer arrays can appear in COMMON whereas ALLOCATABLE arrays cannot. Pointer arrays can appear in user-defined derived types but ALLOCATABLE

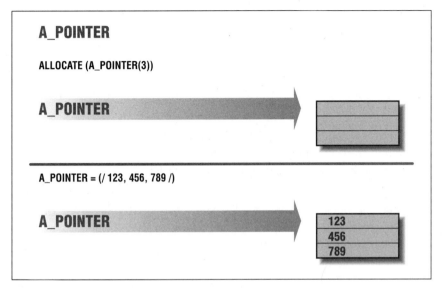

Figure 7-7: Pointer allocation and assignment

arrays cannot. Finally, pointers are absolutely necessary for applications that manipulate relationships between variables (i.e., linked list).

Restrictions on POINTERs

Once associated with a TARGET, a POINTER can appear almost anywhere that a nonpointer can. Some restrictions limit the appearance of POINTERs:

- POINTERs cannot point to a constant (i.e., pointer => 5 is not permitted).

- POINTERs cannot point to an array section with vector subscripts. The statement pointer => array(list) where although array is a proper target, list is a vector subscript, is not permitted.

- Arrays appearing with an explicit shape list in a COMMON statement cannot be declared with the POINTER attribute. If array appears in the COMMON statement as COMMON / AREA / ARRAY(5,5) then it is not permitted to be declared with the POINTER attribute.

- In a subprogram, if a dummy argument is a POINTER, then the corresponding actual argument must be a POINTER. Conversely, if the actual argument is a POINTER, then the corresponding dummy argument may be a POINTER.

- POINTERs cannot be EQUIVALENCEd to any other data type.

- POINTERs cannot be read or written unless currently associated with a TARGET.

- If a derived type contains a pointer component at any level, the derived type cannot be named in an input/output list.

- POINTERs cannot appear in the dummy argument list for the ENTRY statement in a FUNCTION subprogram, unless the ENTRY argument list is identical to the FUNCTION argument list.

- Pointers should not point to a literal constant. No application would benefit from pointing to a constant, and the practice would fail given the ways in which some compilers store constants.

- Pointers can point to whole arrays, array sections, and individual array elements, but cannot point to vector subscripted arrays. Without this restriction, there could be situations of many-to-one array section mappings that would vastly complicate the resolution of pointer references.

- Explicitly dimensioned pointer arrays do not belong in COMMON. This is consistent with Fortran's sequential memory model. Note that a pointer to a multidimensional TARGET array or a pointer array that subsequently appears in an ALLOCATE statement can appear in COMMON. This is allowed because the POINTER itself occupies a fixed amount of memory regardless of the extent of the dimensions of its TARGET.

- There needs to be a precise mapping between actual and dummy POINTER arguments, because if a subprogram declares that a variable to be a POINTER, presumably it will be assigned to something.

- In general, EQUIVALENCE is restricted to pairing like data types. Forcing POINTERs to be EQUIVALENCEd only to other POINTERs makes sense given the distinction between a variable and its value. Fortran POINTERs contain a memory address, which cannot be mapped onto the data values contained in any other data type.

- Reading or writing unassociated POINTERs would imply an ability to read or write the actual value that represents a memory location. As there is no processor-independent representation of such a data element, this is not permitted. Reading or writing associated POINTERs is fine because data is transmitted to or from the TARGET referenced by the POINTER.

- Permitting input or output of a pointer-derived type would imply an ability to read or write the value representing a memory location. That cannot be done. If a derived type structure included several variables, arrays, and a pointer, then its individual components could appear in an input or output list, but the name of the entire structure could not. The ISOWEIGHT program appearing earlier in this chapter is an example.

- Keeping a FUNCTION's ENTRY argument list POINTER-free reflects the association of the two argument lists. If the FUNCTION and ENTRY arguments do not match, then they are associated only by mutual storage, and a POINTER would disrupt that mapping.

8

File Handling

An old saw declares that only 20% of a Fortran program involves computation, while the remainder marshals input data and formats output reports. Compared to the "formula translation" role of Fortran to implement algorithms, input/output housekeeping chores are not glamourous. However, careful, meticulous file handling leads to robust and flexible programs. Robust programs can identify, log, and (possibly) recover from input/output errors. Flexible programs can accept and generate data in a variety of patterns.

Fortran 90 liberalizes file handling. A few things that were hard to do in Fortran 77 are directly supported by Fortran 90. Facilities now available to the Fortran programmer include:

- Read- and write-only files
- Concatenation of sequential files
- Replacing files
- Computing record lengths of direct access files
- Detecting file position
- Genuine prompt/response formatting with nonadvancing input/output
- Error detection down to the byte in sequential files
- NAMELIST
- Binary/hexadecimal/octal input/output
- Generalized editing

Changes to files and input/output handling are scattered in Fortran 90; therefore, this chapter is less cohesive than the others. Many topics are conveniences, mentioned only briefly.

Short shrift is given here to any file handling feature that is the same in Fortran 77 and Fortran 90. Thus, CLOSE syntax is not repeated, E edit rules regarding exponents are ignored, no attention is given to which OPEN keywords group with which other keywords depending on file type, etc.

On the other hand, any change introduced to file handling by Fortran 90, however subtle, will be covered here. Subtle changes are few: G edit now uses E rather than D to prefix the exponent when writing double precision numbers, the new line edit, /, is now repeatable, etc. None of these subtle changes seem destined to "break" existing Fortran 77 code. Profound changes are extensively reviewed in the text along with a complete example programs.

Expanded File Options

Aside from the user's monitor and keyboard, Fortran programs source data from files. Fundamentally, a file type is defined by access method—sequential or direct—and whether it is formatted or unformatted, but additional file attributes mold the file to a program's design. Fortran 90 can set a dozen file attributes in the OPEN statement and query two dozen in the INQUIRE statement.

All Fortran 77 file attributes are preserved in Fortran 90. Some have changed a little and this chapter will point out those differences in detail. Some are new and appear in Table 8-1.

Table 8-1: New Fortran 90 File Attributes

Attribute	Description
ACTION	Sets allowable actions for a file (i.e., READ, READWRITE, or WRITE) at file OPEN and reports setting at file INQUIRE
DELIM	Sets APOSTROPHE, QUOTE, or NONE as the signal to delimit character strings in list-directed or namelist input/output at file OPEN and reports setting at file INQUIRE

Table 8-1: New Fortran 90 File Attributes (Continued)

Attribute	Description
PAD	Determines whether a program can attempt to read more characters from a formatted input record that it contains (YES to permit, NO to deny) and reports setting at file INQUIRE
POSITION	Sets file position for SEQUENTIAL access files to APPEND, ASIS, or REWIND at file OPEN
READ	INQUIRE reports NO, UNKNOWN, or YES if allowable actions for a file include the ability to read the file
READWRITE	INQUIRE reports NO, UNKNOWN, or YES if program can read and write to the file
RECL	New use to set record length for FORMATTED files at file OPEN and reports setting at FORMATTED file INQUIRE
STATUS	New option (REPLACE) to overwrite existing file, otherwise creates new file
WRITE	INQUIRE reports NO, UNKNOWN, or YES if allowable actions for a file include the ability to write to the file

The program F90OPEN displays every one of the two dozen Fortran 90 file attributes. The full source of the program appears in Appendix D, *Selected Source Code Listings*, but its results are given here. It opens a file taking all the default OPEN statement options and reports their value:

```
Fortran 90 OPEN keyword values ...
access                  action
blank                   delim
file        FOPEN.SF    form
iostat      00000       pad
position                recl        00000
status                  unit        00007
```

Then the program INQUIREs about the file and reports the value of every file option:

```
Fortran 90 INQUIRE keyword values ...
access      SEQUENTIAL  action      READWRITE
blank       NULL        delim       NONE
direct      NO          exist       T
file        FOPEN.SF    form        FORMATTED
formatted   YES         iostat      00000
name        FOPEN.SF    named       T
nextrec     00001       number      00007
opened      T           pad         YES
position    ASIS        read        YES
```

```
readwrite   YES           recl          01024
sequential  YES           unformatted   NO
unit        00007         write         YES
```

Read-only Files

Programs need to protect sensitive input files. The ACTION specifier can restrict file access to reading or to writing. READ action means it cannot be the target of ENDFILE or WRITE statements. WRITE action dedicates a file for output, because no READ statement can refer to the file. Input and output can be done on files connected for READWRITE action.

Note that these file access permissions are in effect only when the program executes and only affect this program's behavior. This new Fortran 90 feature does not affect operating system permissions.

File protection offered by the ACTION keyword helps programs when many different files must be processed. There are times when an application demands that programs transfer data among ten, twenty, thirty, etc., files open all at once. But operating systems limit the number of simultaneously open files, and this limit may be too small for a program to open all files at the beginning and leave them open throughout the run. Programmers have long answered this challenge by "file unit number gymnastics:" closing file A on one unit, opening file B on same unit only for as long as it is needed, closing file B, and reopening file A again. Of course, if A is an input file and B an output file, this can get confusing. Rigorously setting a file ACTION for each file eases initial design and subsequent maintenance.

List-directed Input/Output of Character Strings

List-directed input/output is a convenience. Entering numbers is a snap with list-directed input. Strings are another story. Fortran 77 required character data to be contained within apostrophes on input, but couldn't easily write apostrophes around character data on output. This meant strings in list-directed output files could not be read as list-directed input without human intervention. Users had to "preprocess" files with an editor to insert apostrophes.

Fortran 90 solves this problem. The program DELIMIT demonstrates that Fortran 90 allows the programmer to choose the familiar APOSTROPHE, substitute a QUOTE mark, or chose NONE as the character string delimiter in list-directed input and output.

After setting local variables, the DELIMIT program exercises all three string delimiting modes:

```
program delimit
integer       :: crtin  = 5
integer       :: crtout = 6
character*21 :: string = 'When in doubt, don''t!'
character*21 :: blanks = '                     '
print *, "Same string in NONE, APOSTROPHE, and QUOTE mode"
call screen ( crtout, 'NONE      ', string )
call screen ( crtout, 'APOSTROPHE', string )
call screen ( crtout, 'QUOTE     ', string )
call screen ( crtout, 'NONE      ', blanks )
```

and displays the result:

```
Same string in NONE, APOSTROPHE, and QUOTE mode
When in doubt, don't!
'When in doubt, don''t!'
"When in doubt, don't!"
```

In order to change the behavior of the screen display, the subprogram SCREEN must re-OPEN the screen afresh each time the delimiter is changed:

```
subroutine screen ( crtout, edging, string )
integer        crtout
character*10 edging
character*21 string
open ( unit=crtout,  delim=edging,
       status='NEW', action='WRITE' )
write ( crtout,* ) string
end subroutine screen
```

After displaying the static string, the user is asked to enter a string in each mode. Now that Fortran 90 programs can select one of three different delimiters, it is important to tell the user which delimiter is in effect:

```
print *, "Enter string in NONE, APOSTROPHE, and QUOTE mode"
call keyboard ( crtin, 'NONE      ', string )
call keyboard ( crtin, 'APOSTROPHE', string )
call keyboard ( crtin, 'QUOTE     ', string )
end program delimit
```

with the appropriate delimiters:

```
Enter string in NONE, APOSTROPHE, and QUOTE mode
When in doubt, don't!
When
'When in doubt, don''t!'
When in doubt, don't!
"When in doubt, don't!"
When in doubt, don't!
```

Interestingly, in order to change the delimiter associated with the keyboard, it must be re-OPENed each time as an existing device. Since this is not explicitly required in the Fortran 90 standard, it may be system specific:

```
      subroutine keyboard ( crtin, edging, string )
      integer       crtin
      character*10 edging
      character*21 string
      open ( unit=crtin,   delim=edging,
    -        status='OLD', action='READ' )
100   continue
          read ( crtin,*,err=200 ) string
          go to 300
200      continue
          print *, "ERROR! Can NOT read string as entered!"
          go to 100
300   continue
      print *, string
      end subroutine keyboard
```

The DELIMIT program demonstrates how preconnected units can have file attributes reset. Fortran 77 allowed BLANK interpretation to be reset for preconnected units. Fortran 90 allows BLANK and two new attributes, DELIM—as shown in subroutines SCREEN and KEYBOARD—and PAD to be reset for preconnected units.

Blank Padding Records in Sequential Files

The PAD keyword solves a problem that is not common, but is hard to deal with when it does occur: an input record of insufficient length. To a READ statement, records in sequential formatted files seem endless. Reading three variables from a record that only contains two values usually means that the rest of the record would be read as if it were blank-filled: the third variable would be "read" as zero. For example, if a record contained the values

```
    1234
```

then reading that record as

```
      read ( 7,100 ) a, b, c
100   format ( 3f2.0 )
```

would establish values of 1.2, 3.4, and 0.0 for the three variables. And that is exactly what will happen if Fortran 90's PAD file attribute is left at its default value of YES. However, if PAD is set to NO, the READ in the short example would force an error because it attempted to bring in six bytes from a record that only contained four.

The PADDING program demonstrates the effect of this enabling and disabling the PAD file attribute. First, a file is written with PAD='YES':

```
      program padding
      integer         iostat
      real            number
      character*50    string
      integer    :: unit = 7
      open ( unit=unit, file='pad.file', pad='YES' )
      write ( unit,100 )
100   format ( '1234.56'
     -          / 'This is a 40 byte long character string.' )
```

then rewound, and read in its entirety:

```
      rewind unit
      print *, "Reading with PAD=YES ..."
      read ( unit,200 ) number
200   format ( f10.0 )
      read ( unit,300 ) string
300   format ( a50 )
      print 400, number, string
400   format ( 1H , '... read [', f7.2, '] and [', a40, ']' )
```

It then displays:

```
Reading with PAD=YES ...
... read [1234.56] and [This is a 40 byte long character string.]
```

Resetting the PAD option to turn off padding causes errors reading this file:

```
      open ( unit=unit, file='pad.file', pad='NO' )
      rewind unit
      print *, " "
      print *, "Reading with PAD=NO ..."
      read ( unit,200,iostat=iostat ) number
      if ( iostat .ne. 0 )
     -    print *, "... error reading number with PAD=NO"
      read ( unit,300,iostat=iostat ) string
      if ( iostat .ne. 0 )
     -    print *, "... error reading string with PAD=NO"
```

which displays:

```
Reading with PAD=NO ...
... error reading number with PAD=NO
... error reading string with PAD=NO
```

because the edit descriptor F10.0 is too wide for the seven characters it finds in the first record, and A50 is too long for the forty-byte string it finds in the second record.

Turning padding back on means that the file can be processed correctly as before:

```
open ( unit=unit, file='pad.file', pad='YES' )
rewind unit
print *, " "
print *, "Re-reading with PAD=YES ..."
read ( unit,200 ) number
read ( unit,300 ) string
print 400, number, string
close ( unit=unit, status='DELETE' )
end program padding
```

which displays:

```
Rereading with PAD=YES ...
... read [1234.56] and [This is a 40 byte long character string]
```

Strictly enforcing a format increases the probability that a program will accept properly prepared data and otherwise reject records. Programs that must process data files created "by hand" benefit from setting PAD='NO' because data files created or modified by system editors are prone to blank or under-filled fields as a result of the whims of the data entry person. Even "automatically" created files produced by one version of a preprocessing program might differ from those produced by that program's successor with the net effect of tripping up the exact format expected by the ultimate analysis program.

Concatenating Output in Sequential Files

Augmenting a sequential file has always meant opening the file, reading to the end, and then writing to the file. Fortran 90 allows a file to be opened directly at the end-of-file. The APPEND program adds records to an existing file by using the value of APPEND for the new Fortran 90 POSITION keyword. It builds a file containing three lines:

```
      program append
      integer        i
      character*32   line
      integer     :: unit = 7
      open ( unit=unit, file='append.file', status='NEW' )
      write ( unit,100 )
100   format ('First line.'/'2nd line.'/'Initial EOF (line 3).')
      rewind unit
```

```
       print *, "... file initially contains these lines"
       do i = 1, HUGE(i), 1
           read ( unit,200,end=400 ) line
200        format ( a32 )
           print 300, i, line
300        format ( 1H , 'LINE ', i2.2, ': ', a32 )
       end do
400    continue
```

with the initial end-of-file line explicitly marked:

```
... file initially contains these lines
 LINE 01: First line.
 LINE 02: 2nd line.
 LINE 03: Initial EOF (line 3).
```

The file is closed and reopened, and additional data written directly to the end of the file:

```
       close ( unit=unit, status='KEEP' )
       open ( unit=unit, file='append.file', status='OLD',
      -        position='APPEND' )
       write ( unit,500 )
500    format ('Fourth line.'/'5th line.'/'Final EOF (line 6).')
```

Now the file has doubled in size with three new lines tacked on the end when reread:.

```
       rewind unit
       print *, " "
       print *, "... file APPENDed to now contains these lines"
       do i = 1, HUGE(i), 1
           read ( unit,200,end=600 ) line
           print 300, i, line
       end do
600    continue
       end program append
```

The file contains:

```
... file APPENDed to now contains these lines
 LINE 01: First line.
 LINE 02: 2nd line.
 LINE 03: Initial EOF (line 3).
 LINE 04: Fourth line.
 LINE 05: 5th line.
 LINE 06: Final EOF (line 6).
```

Opening a sequential file at the end without reading its existing contents is useful in concatenating output. It would allow a single comprehensive report file to be built-up during the course of running a sequence of analysis programs. At the other end, the first access to a sequential file tends to assume that it is open at the beginning, because nearly every Fortran implementation has respected that convention. Despite intuitive appeal and near-universal acceptance, this expected file position is not dictated by any Fortran standard. Fortran 90 allows this convention to be specified by explicitly setting REWIND as the value of OPEN's POSITION keyword. Lastly, POSITION='ASIS' is offered to reproduce Fortran 77 behavior, which left the decision up to the host system. ASIS remains the default.

Overwriting a File

Overwriting a file required some pretty clumsy Fortran 77 code sequences such as CLOSE-to-delete/OPEN/WRITE or REWIND/ENDFILE/WRITE. The REPLACE program demonstrates how this can be streamlined in Fortran 90 for existing files:

```
program replace
integer    ios
integer :: unit = 7
open  ( unit=unit, file='replace.file', status='NEW'     )
close ( unit=unit,                      status='KEEP'     )
open  ( unit=unit, file='replace.file', status='REPLACE',
-        iostat=ios                                        )
if ( ios .eq. 0 ) then
     print *, "... REPLACE.FILE has been replaced"
else
     print *, "... ERROR! replacing REPLACE.FILE!"
end if
```

displaying:

```
... REPLACE.FILE has been replaced
```

and for files that do not exist,

```
unit = 8
open  ( unit=unit, file='missing.file', status='NEW'     )
close ( unit=unit,                      status='DELETE'  )
open  ( unit=unit, file='missing.file', status='REPLACE',
-        iostat=ios                                        )
if ( ios .eq. 0 ) then
     print *, "... MISSING.FILE has been replaced"
else
     print *, "... ERROR! replacing MISSING.FILE!"
end if
end program replace
```

displaying:

```
... MISSING.FILE has been replaced
```

This simplifies opening files known to be empty or to contain useless data. If the file exists, STATUS='REPLACE" will delete it, create one with the same name, and connect this new file. If the file did not exist, STATUS='RE-PLACE' will create the file and connect it to the program.

Maximum Record Length in Formatted Files

Fortran 77 associates direct access files—but not sequential files—with the definition and enforcement of a fixed record length. Fortran 90 extends the approach to sequential formatted files by allowing the RECL specifier to be used when opening them, as with direct access files. For sequential files, RECL merely indicates a maximum length in characters, which the program enforces on each read and write.

The program RECLEN limits the record length of a sequential file and traps the error that ensues when an attempt is made to write past the end of the record. It creates a new file

```
       program reclen
       character*26 :: alphabet = 'abcdefghijklmnopqrstuvwxyz'
       integer         ios
       integer         recl
       character*32 :: string   = ' '
       integer      :: unit    = 7
     recl = len_trim ( alphabet )
       open     ( unit=unit, file='reclen.file', recl=recl )
       inquire ( unit=unit,                      recl=recl )
       print 100, recl
100    format ( 1H , 'RECLEN.FILE open and RECL = ', i5.5, ' bytes')
```

and reports the record length:

```
       RECLEN.FILE open and RECL = 00026 bytes
```

After writing a few records to the file, it then tries to write a record that is longer than the declared record length:

```
       write    ( unit,200 ) alphabet, alphabet
200    format ( a26 / a26 )
       print *, " "
       print *, "Wrote two records at declared record length"
       print *, " "
       string = 'xxx' // alphabet // 'xxx'
       write    ( unit,300,iostat=ios ) string, string
300    format ( a32 / a32 )
       if ( ios .eq. 0 ) then
             print *, "Wrote two records longer than declared ",
       -             "record length"
```

```
    else
        print *, "ERROR! Intended length exceeds ",
    -            "file's declared record length!"
    end if
    close ( unit=unit, status='DELETE' )
    end program reclen
```

which results in an error condition:

```
Wrote two records at declared record length

ERROR! Intended length exceeds file's declared record length!
```

Limiting the length of formatted records in sequential files is a preventative measure, but it is specific to one program's access to a file: it does not alter the operating system's view of the file or affect how another program will process the file. Just like PAD='NO' protects against trying to read more data from a record than the record contains, record lengths for sequential files prevent writing more data to a record than the file design permits. In both cases, file discipline is managed at the "record" rather than the "field" level. But given the absence of any control in Fortran 77, these two elements offer a significant gain in building "belt-and-suspenders" safe, robust Fortran 90 programs.

Information About a File

Once a file is connected to a program, all of its Fortran file attributes can be queried using the INQUIRE statement. Two dozen file attributes are defined for the INQUIRE statement and the F90OPEN program demonstrates how to retrieve information about each of them. Three uses of the INQUIRE statement in Fortran 90 are either new or changed enough to warrant extra attention: POSITION, IOLENGTH, and default values for selected attributes when no file is connected.

Location in a File

In sequential files, it is helpful to imagine a "file pointer" that moves through a file in step with each input/output operation. Depending on what kind of input/output operation just happened in a program, this pointer would be at the beginning or end of the file, or at the beginning, middle, or end of a record. Fortran 77 programs could not detect the location of that imaginary file pointer and had few tools—BACKSPACE, ENDFILE and REWIND—to force it to one location or another. The program POS demonstrates how Fortran 90's INQUIRE statement reports the POSITION of this file pointer. Initially, at the OPEN statement, the POSITION is "ASIS":

```
          program pos
          logical      error
          integer      iostat
          integer   :: unit = 7
          character*9  position
          open ( unit=unit, file='pos.file', status='NEW',
     —         iostat=iostat )
          if ( error ( 'OPEN', iostat ) ) go to 300
          inquire ( unit=unit, position=position, iostat=iostat )
          if ( error ( 'INQUIRE', iostat ) ) go to 300
          call location ( 'OPEN', position )
```

which changes to "APPEND" after a few lines have been written to the file:

```
          write ( unit,100 )
100       format ( ///// )
          inquire ( unit=unit, position=position, iostat=iostat )
          if ( error ( 'WRITE', iostat ) ) go to 300
          call location ( 'WRITE', position )
```

As expected, the POSITION is "REWIND" after the file is rewound:

```
          rewind unit
          inquire ( unit=unit, position=position, iostat=iostat )
          if ( error ( 'REWIND', iostat ) ) go to 300
          call location ( 'REWIND', position )
```

But after reading a few records, the POSITION becomes "UNKNOWN":

```
          read ( unit,200 )
200       format ( /// )
          inquire ( unit=unit, position=position, iostat=iostat )
          if ( error ( 'READ', iostat ) ) go to 300
          call location ( 'READ', position )
```

which is different from the POSITION of "UNDEFINED," which occurs after the file has been closed:

```
          close ( unit=unit, status='DELETE' )
          inquire ( unit=unit, position=position, iostat=iostat )
          if ( error ( 'CLOSE', iostat ) ) go to 300
          call location ( 'CLOSE', position )
          go to 400
300       continue
400       continue
```

Both subprograms—the ERROR function and the LOCATION subroutine—appear in Appendix D.

Once a sequential file is opened, by convention, the file pointer usually points to the beginning of the file. But neither Fortran 77 or Fortran 90 standards explicitly state this. Consequently, INQUIRE's POSITION keyword reports a pointer location of ASIS for freshly opened files. After each WRITE to a sequential file, it's positioned at the end-of-file which POSITION reports as APPEND. POSITION uses the string REWIND to signify file pointer placement at the beginning-of-file. After reading from a file, location of the pointer is not at the beginning-of-file and may not be at the end-of-file, so POSITION returns a processor-dependent value (for instance., UNKNOWN on the computer used with the POS program). Lastly, if no file is connected or a direct access file is connected to the file unit, the POSITION is shown to be UNDEFINED.

Computing Unformatted Direct Access File Record Length

Unformatted direct access files have fixed record lengths. This record length is specified in the OPEN statement with the RECL option and is measured in processor-dependent units. It has always been difficult to write portable source code when unformatted direct access files had to be implemented. For instance, one system might measure integers as 16-bit units and another in 32-bit units, while a third might use 8-bit units universally for all data types. A new INQUIRE keyword, IOLENGTH, takes a step towards more certainty in record lengths.

Program LENGTH measures the length of a record consisting of a character string and one of each type of number: double precision, integer, and real:

```
      program length
      character*26     :: c   = 'abcdefghijklmnopqrstuvwxyz'
      double precision :: d   = 1.2d0
      integer          :: i   = 3
      integer          :: iol = 0
      real             :: r   = 4.5
      inquire ( iolength = iol ) c, d, i, r
      print 100, iol
100   format ( / 1H , 'Record length for {c, d, i, r} is ',
     -                i2, ' units' )
      print 200, c, d, i, r
200   format ( 1H , a26, f8.1, i4, f4.1 / )
      end program length
```

Running this program results in the following display:

```
      Record length for {c, d, i, r} is 42 units
      abcdefghijklmnopqrstuvwxyz    1.2   3 4.5
```

Given the input/output list that constitutes a record, this new feature of the INQUIRE statement computes a record length suitable for OPEN's RECL keyword. IOLENGTH supports source code that can be moved more easily from computer to computer without hand-crafted changes.

New Fortran 90 Default Values for Some OPEN Keywords

Certain file attributes in Fortran 90 have slightly different values from Fortran 77 regarding connected files and file type. If a file or unit number was not connected, then Fortran 77 left the variables referenced by the ACCESS, BLANK, FORM, and NUMBER keywords undefined. Under the same conditions, however, Fortran 90 actually returns the string UNDEFINED for ACCESS, BLANK, and FORM and the value -1 for NUMBER. INQUIRE's OPENED keyword should be used to detect unconnected files or file unit numbers.

Record lengths are reported by the RECL keyword in the INQUIRE statement. Fortran 77 would measure records in direct access files, but leave undefined the record length of sequential access files. Now, Fortran 90 measures records in both direct and sequential files provided that the OPEN statement included a RECL specifier. Programs should use INQUIRE's ACCESS, DIRECT, or SEQUENTIAL to determine file type.

Position in a File

Fortran offers few tools to move about within a file. Direct access files are always able to read or write to a record anywhere in a file. Fortran 90 introduces a few options with OPEN's POSITION keyword to govern initial file position. But, the basic tools to cause wholesale movement within a file are the standard BACKSPACE, ENDFILE, and REWIND statements which are identical in form and function in both Fortran 77 and Fortran 90.

Read/Write Management

New flexibility in managing data transfers is always welcome. Fortran 90 adds two new facilities: nonadvancing formatted input and output, and NAMELIST input/output. That list is pretty tightly qualified so it doesn't sound like much, but nonadvancing input/output is very beneficial and (finally, after all these years and a thousand variations) NAMELIST makes it into the standard.

Nonadvancing Input

Nonadvancing input lets the programmer control when the next record will be processed. For input, a single file record can be READ as many times as necessary to trap and report errors. The new pieces of information provided by Fortran 90 can aid in processing input: the number of characters read, and the read statement has encountered the end of the record.

The program ADVANCE reads the following ten line file of scientific constants that has errors in lines four through seven:

Line	Value, Description
1	6.02 23N(o), Avogadro's number
2	1.38-23k, Boltzmann's constant
3	9.11-31m(e), mass of an electron
4	9.X1-31m(e),mass of an electron
5	9.11X31m(e), mass of an electron
6	9.11-31
7	
8	1.67-27m(p), mass of a proton
9	6.63-34h, Planck's constant
10	2.18-18Ry, Rydberg's constant

These constants were taken from page *xii* of *Physical Science for Biologists* by J. A. Edington and H. J. Sherman (1971, Hutchinson & Co. (Publishers) Ltd., 225 pages, London, England). Errors in this input file could be detected in Fortran 77, but there was no easy way to tell the user exactly where and in what field the failure occurred. Programmers had to rely on an involved procedure using BACKSPACE to reposition the file, reread the record as a character string, then use an internal file read to see if an individual field passed muster:

```
      character*3 :: buffer
      integer     :: record = 0
      integer     :: some_variable
      record = record + 1
      read ( buffer,100,err=200 ) some_variable
100   format ( i3 )
      go to 400
200   continue
      write ( 6,300 ) record
300   format ( 1H , 'ERROR! Field 1 in record ', i1,' is wrong!')
400   continue
```

This procedure had to be repeated with an internal file READ and FORMAT and error message tailored for each field. Reporting the position in the field where the offending byte occurred would require a character-by-character examination that further complicate the whole procedure by making it even more custommade for a particular field.

Fortran 90 makes this much easier. The ADVANCE program reports the mistakes per position, per field, and per record as:

```
6.02  23 N(o), Avogadro's number
1.38 -23 k, Boltzmann's constant
9.11 -31 m(e), mass of an electron
ERROR! Byte 3 in field 1 in record 4 is wrong!
ERROR! Byte 1 in field 2 in record 5 is wrong!
WARNING! Field 3 in record 6 is empty!
9.11 -31
WARNING! Record 7 is empty!
1.67 -27 m(p), mass of a proton
6.63 -34 h, Planck's constant
2.18 -18 Ry, Rydberg's constant
```

Reading One Field at a Time

The SIZE keyword, which is new in Fortran 90, records the actual number of characters taken in during a READ statement. This also represents the number of characters that the pointer has advanced within the record, so that the program can tell where the next read will come from. SIZE is permitted only with a formatted sequential file, and only in use with nonadvancing input. The mechanism is similar to IOSTAT, in that the program specifies a variable that is to hold the value returned by the READ statement.

If no field exists—that is, end-of-record has been reached—the SIZE variable will contain zero. Furthermore, if an IOSTAT variable is used, it will contain the end-of-record condition reported by the processor.

After a read controlled by a format specifier, if the SIZE variable contains fewer than the expected number of characters, the program can assume that an error occurred on the last character read. During list-directed I/O, where the program cannot predict the length of the input field, the SIZE variable reports this useful information.

Reading one field at a time, the ADVANCE program detects mistakes by relying on the standard ERR return and the byte count of characters successfully processed.

```
program advance
integer, dimension (3) :: bytes
real                   :: constant
integer                :: input = 7
integer, dimension (3) :: ios
integer                :: magnitude
character*26           :: name
integer                :: record = 0
open ( unit=input, file='advance.input', status='OLD' )
do
    bytes    = 99
    constant = 9.99
    ios      = 999
    magnitude = 999
    name     = 'XXXXXXXXXXXXXXXXXXXXXXXXXX'
```

The first field should be a real number occupying four characters. However, the READ statement stops if it encounters any character that does not fit the format for real input. MISTAKE is called with a hard-coded 1 to indicate that this is the first field, the number of characters, the error status, and the data itself (if any):

```
        read ( input,100,advance='NO',size=bytes(1),
     -          iostat=ios(1),err=200,eor=200,end=800 ) constant
100     format ( f4.2 )
200     continue
        record = record + 1
        call mistake ( 1, bytes(1), ios(1), record )
        if ( ios(1) .ne. 0 ) cycle
```

The record is now positioned at the beginning of the second field, a three character integer:

```
        read ( input,300,advance='NO',size=bytes(2),
     -          iostat=ios(2),err=400,eor=400            ) magnitude
300     format ( i3 )
400     continue
        call mistake ( 2, bytes(2), ios(2), record )
        if ( ios(2) .ne. 0 ) cycle
```

Finally, if no error occurred within the record so far, the rest of it is read, 26 characters of text:

```
        read ( input,500,advance='NO',size=bytes(3),
     -          iostat=ios(3),err=600,eor=600            ) name
500     format ( a26 )
```

```
600        continue
           call mistake ( 3, bytes(3), ios(3), record )
```

If no error had been detected, the record is displayed:

```
           print 700, constant, magnitude, name
700        format ( 1H , f4.2, 1x, i3, 1x, a26 )
       end do
800    continue
       end program advance
```

Error detection is handled in steps. First, empty records get a warning:

```
       subroutine mistake ( field, byte, io, record )
       integer byte
       integer field
       integer io
       integer record
       if ( io .lt. 0 .and. field .eq. 1 ) then
           print 100, record
100        format ( 1H , 'WARNING! Record ', i1, ' is empty!' )
           go to 400
       end if
```

Then, a bona fide mistake triggers the reporting of the specific location. It is safe to assume that the last character read is the source of the error:

```
       if (   io .gt. 0 .or.
     -      ( io .lt. 0 .and. field .ne. 3 ) ) then
           print 200, byte, field, record
200        format ( 1H , 'ERROR! Byte ', i1, ' in field ', i1,
     -                   ' in record ', i1, ' is wrong!' )
           go to 400
       end if
```

Finally, if the last field—a text field—is empty, the user is warned:

```
       if ( byte .le. 1 .and. field .eq. 3 ) then
           print 300, field, record
300        format ( 1H , 'WARNING! Field ', i1,
     -                   ' in record ', i1, ' is empty!' )
           go to 400
       end if
400    continue
       end subroutine mistake
```

Some Fortran 90 implementations can elect to return a string—NaN (not a number)—from the READ statement when the error happened processing a REAL number.

The ADVANCE program can be very specific about an error due to the new features of Fortran 90. When the fourth record is read, the first field is wrong: 9.X1 instead of 9.11. IOS(1), the IOSTAT variable, is set to a "processor-dependent" positive integer (140 in this implementation). BYTES(1) records the number of characters read, which is 3 because an error occurred on the 3rd character. Consequently, the exact position of the mistake can be trapped and reported. Note that the other two fields in this record—MAGNITUDE and NAME—are still set to their default values of 999 and Xs.

The error in the fifth record is handled like the one in the fourth. Everything is correct in the sixth record. But, from an application perspective, it doesn't make sense to input a CONSTANT without a NAME, so a warning is issued. The last field remains empty—BYTES(3) = 0—when the end-of-record is detected.

Reading the seventh record immediately flags an end-of-record condition because the record is empty. IOS(3) is set to a processor-dependent negative integer (-2 in this implementation) defined just for this situation. Again, from an application perspective, a warning should be given because empty records do not make sense.

Finally, when the program attempts to read an "eleventh" record, the end-of-file is detected, IOS(1) is set to a processor-dependent negative integer (-1 in this implementation), and control is passed out of the DO loop. Nonadvancing input gives a great boost to Fortran's ability to detect input errors and inform the user exactly where mistakes occur.

Nonadvancing Output

Nonadvancing output allows programmers to develop real prompt/response pairs and build-up a single line of output one field at a time. A standard Fortran 77 prompt/response pair would be:

```
      write ( 6,100 )
100   format ( 1H , 'Enter a whole number: ' )
      read ( 5,* ) i
```

which the user would see as:

```
      Enter a whole number:
      123
```

Since Fortran 77 had no way to stop a WRITE statement from advancing to the next line, the response from the user could never appear on the same line as the prompt. Granted, some implementations of Fortran 77 extended the definition of valid FORMAT edit strings to include some special character (typically $) that would arrest the carriage return and line feed pair at the end of a WRITE. But, by definition, extensions are not standard-conforming and cause portability headaches. Fortran 90 defines a new option for the WRITE statement, ADVANCE='NO', which makes the previous code fragment display:

```
Enter a whole number: 123
```

This looks a lot neater and much more conversational. Nonadvancing output also lets a single output line be written phrase-by-phrase.

The VIDEO program builds a "fill-in-the-blank" input screen for a file search program using a mixture of advancing and nonadvancing output from Fortran 90. This program also uses cursor control strings appropriate for an ANSI 3.64 compliant terminal—from page 39 of David Stephens' *A Programmer's Guide to Video Display Terminals* (1985, Atlantis Publishing Corp., 335 pages, Dallas, TX)—to clear the screen, move the cursor, and display characters in reverse video, plain text, or underlined. The program's purpose is to search a file containing some of the example code in the Fortran 90 standard document. If an example contains the user-entered keyword, the program displays the page number on which the code fragment appears in the standard, and the fragment itself:

```
program video
type attributes
      character ( len = 4 ) :: bold
      character ( len = 4 ) :: clear
      character ( len = 4 ) :: home
      character ( len = 4 ) :: normal
      character ( len = 4 ) :: up
      character ( len = 4 ) :: down
      character ( len = 4 ) :: left
      character ( len = 4 ) :: right
      character ( len = 4 ) :: underline
end type attributes
type ( attributes ) crt
character*03 :: answer
integer      :: crtin = 5
integer      :: crtout = 6
character*18 :: date_time
character*01 :: escape
integer      :: file = 7
integer      :: i
character*67 :: line
integer      :: line_count
character*32 :: keyword
integer      :: keyword_length
integer      :: search_count
integer      :: tab = 5
```

```
      real        :: version = 1.00
      escape      = achar(27)
      crt%bold      = escape // '[7m'
      crt%clear     = escape // '[J '
      crt%down      = escape // '[B '
      crt%home      = escape // '[H '
      crt%left      = escape // '[D '
      crt%normal    = escape // '[m '
      crt%right     = escape // '[C '
      crt%underline = escape // '[4m'
      crt%up        = escape // '[A '
      open ( unit=file, file='video.input', status='OLD' )
      search: do search_count = 1, HUGE(search_count), 1
      call display ( 1, crt%home )
      call display ( 1, crt%clear )
      call display ( 1,  crt%underline )
      write ( crtout,100,advance='NO' ) version
100   format ( 'VIDEO Version ', f4.2, 31 ( ' ' ) )
      call timestamp ( date_time )
      write ( crtout,200,advance='NO' ) date_time
200   format ( a18 )
      call display ( 1, crt%normal )
```

Initially, the program clears the screen and displays the program name and version number in underlined characters as:

VIDEO Version 1.00

It uses the DISPLAY routine to set terminal attributes:

```
      subroutine display ( count,  string )
      integer    :: count
      integer    :: j
      integer    :: length
      character*4 :: string
      character*5 :: a_format = "(aNN)"
      write ( a_format(3:4), fmt="(i2.2)" ) len_trim(string)
      do j = 1, count, 1
         write ( 6,advance='NO',fmt=a_format ) string
      end do
      end subroutine display
```

which relies on nonadvancing output to output the one to four characters that comprise a terminal escape sequence.

Then, TIMESTAMP is called to create a date and time string. Fortran 90's DATE_AND_TIME intrinsic function retrieves that information from the operating system and formats it into a string.

```
      subroutine timestamp ( date_time )
      character*18  date_time
```

```
      integer        elements(8)
      character*3    months(12)
      data months / 'Jan', 'Feb', 'Mar', 'Apr', 'May', 'Jun',
   -                 'Jul', 'Aug', 'Sep', 'Oct', 'Nov', 'Dec'    /
      call date_and_time ( VALUES=elements )
      invalid: if ( elements(1) .ne. -HUGE(0) ) then
          century: if ( elements(1) .lt. 2000 ) then
                      elements(1) = elements(1) - 1900
                  else
                      elements(1) = elements(1) - 2000
                  end if century
              write ( date_time,100 ) elements(3),
   -                      months ( elements(2) ),
   -                          elements(1),    elements(5),
   -                          elements(6),    elements(7)
100           format ( i2.2, 1x, a3, 1x, i2.2, 1x,
   -                   i2.2, ':', i2.2, ':', i2.2  )
      else invalid
          date_time = ' '
      end if invalid
      end subroutine timestamp
```

This date and time string is then written on the same line as the program name and version number with nonadvancing output so that it appears as follows:

```
VIDEO Version 1.00                            29 Apr 93 12:34:56
```

This small fragment clearly shows the convenience of nonadvancing output in its ability to create a single output line from multiple WRITE statements.

The following code allows the user to enter a string for searching in the file:

```
      print *, " "
      call display ( 2, crt%down )
      call display ( 5, crt%right )
      write ( crtout,300,advance='NO' )
300   format ( 'Enter keyword: ' )
      call display ( 1, crt%bold )
      do i = 1, 32, 1
         write ( crtout,400,advance='NO' )
400      format ( ' ' )
      end do
      call display ( 1, crt%normal )
      call display ( 32, crt%left )
      read ( crtin,500 ) keyword
500   format ( a32 )
```

The 32 spaces displayed in bold "paint" a reverse video bar to give a hint to the user about the length of the input field:

```
Enter keyword: ████████████████████████████████
```

The user's input is echoed:

```
        print *, " "
        call display ( tab, crt%right )
        write ( crtout, 600, advance='NO' )
600     format ( 'Searching for: ' )
        call display ( 1, crt%underline )
        write ( crtout, 700 ) keyword
700     format ( a32 )
        call display ( 1, crt%normal )
```

using an underlined field:

```
Searching for: integer_____
```

Finally, a line-by-line search through the input file uses the standard INDEX intrinsic

```
        print *, " "
        rewind file
        do i = 1, 2, 1
           read ( file, 800 ) line
800        format ( a67 )
           write ( crtout, 900 ) line
900        format ( a67 )
        end do
        keyword_length = len_trim ( keyword )
        do line_count = 1, HUGE(line_count), 1
           read ( file, 800, end=1000 ) line
           i = index ( line, keyword(1:keyword_length) )
           if ( i .ne. 0 ) write ( crtout, 900 ) line
        end do
1000    continue
```

and the first two input file records containing headings and all records containing the string are displayed:

```
Page  Example Code in FORTRAN 90 Standard [ ISO/IEC 1539 : 1991(E) ]
----  --------------------------------------------------------------
  54  implicit integer ( i - n ), real ( a - h, o - z )
  41  integer ( kind (0 )
  14  integer :: i
 266  integer q; parameter ( q = 8 ); real ( q ) b
  44  integer, dimension (3), parameter :: order = (/ 1, 2 3 /)
 168  integer, intent ( inout ) :: x, y
  41  integer, parameter :: short = selected_int_kind(4)
```

```
150 read *, integer_i, real_x, character_p, complex_z, logical_g
 35 type node; integer value; type (node), pointer; end type
```

The user is given a chance to search for another string:

```
     print *, " "
     call display ( tab, crt%right )
     write ( crtout,1100,advance='NO' )
1100 format ( 'Again (y=yes): ' )
     call display ( 1, crt%bold )
     do i = 1, 3, 1
        write ( crtout,1200,advance='NO' )
1200    format ( ' ' )
     end do
     call display ( 1, crt%normal )
     call display ( 3, crt%left )
     read ( crtin,1300 ) answer
1300 format ( a3 )
     if ( answer(1:1) .ne. 'Y' .and.
   -     answer(1:1) .ne. 'y'        ) exit
     end do search
```

using a reverse video field:

```
     Again (y=yes): n ▓▓▓▓
```

When the user finally elects to conclude the program:

```
     print *, " "
     call display ( tab, crt%right )
     call display ( 1, crt%bold )
     write ( crtout,1400,advance='NO' )
1400 format ( 'VIDEO is finished.' )
     call display ( 1, crt%normal )
     print *, " "
     print *, " "
     end program video
```

the program announces in reverse video that it is finished:

```
     VIDEO is finished.
```

NAMELIST Input/Output

NAMELIST became a very early part of Fortran, a form of interactive control that was unusually flexible and much appreciated in the pre-menu and pre-GUI era. Fortran 77 implementations were often extended to cover "namelist" input and output. Rules varied from system to system: value separators changed, NAMELIST input might be allowed but not output, and an end-of-record value was sometimes required, sometimes not. Portability of source code and input files suffered. Fortran 90 introduces NAMELIST input/output into the standard language.

As an example, program NLIST lists details about several probability distributions. Each probability distribution is characterized by a name and the number of parameters that define the distribution. This is followed by names and values for those parameters. A NAMELIST for a probability distribution, DIST, contains a TITLE and number, N, of parameters.

```
integer                    :: n
character*12               :: title
namelist / dist /             title, n
```

A NAMELIST for parameters, PARA, containing the NAMEs and values, Xs, for up to two parameters per probability distribution.

```
character*26, dimension(2) :: name
real,         dimension(2) :: x
namelist / para /             name,  x
```

The following input file is used:

```
&DIST title = 'None' n = 2 /
&PARA name = 2* x = 2*0.0 /
&DIST title = 'Bernoulli' n = 1 /
&PARA name(1) = 'p, success probability'  x(1) = 0.10 /
&DIST title = 'Binomial' n = 2 /
&PARA name(1) = 'n, trials' x=2.0,
 0.3, name(2) = 'p, success probability' /
&DIST title = 'Chi-Squared' n = 1 /
&PARA name = 'v, degrees of freedom', '' x = 4.0 /
&DIST title = 'Normal' n = 2 /
&PARA x = 5.60, 7.80 name = 'mu, mean' 'sigma, std. deviation' /
&DIST title = 'Poisson' n = 1 /
&PARA name(1) = 'lambda,
 mean'
 x(1) = 9.0 /
```

In general, each logical record in a NAMELIST file begins with an ampersand, &, followed by the name of a NAMELIST group, followed by individual variable names and values, and terminated with a slash, /.

A "throw away" distribution called NONE starts the input file and its parameter names are left to default values, 2*, but its parameter values are explicitly set to zero, 2*0.0.

```
&DIST title = 'None' n = 2 /
&PARA name = 2* x = 2*0.0 /
```

Only one parameter is defined for the Bernoulli distribution. So data about a second available parameter, NAME(2) and X(2), are not even specified in the input file. Consequently, these variables keep their default values.

```
&DIST title = 'Bernoulli' n = 1 /
&PARA name(1) = 'p, success probability'  x(1) = 0.10 /
```

Binomial variates are drawn from a distribution with two parameters. Details about both Binomial parameters are entered in the input file in an unusual order just to show the flexibility of NAMELIST input.

```
&DIST title = 'Binomial' n = 2 /
&PARA name(1) = 'n, trials' x=2.0,
 0.3, name(2) = 'p, success probability' /
```

The contents of DIST and PARA at this point are:

```
&DIST TITLE = Binomial    , N = 2/
&PARA NAME = n, trials                p, success probability    ,
 X =    2.0000000   0.3000000/
```

A space separates a new variable from the previous one, but commas separate values that are assigned to successive elements within a variable.

Although Chi-Squared random variables need only one parameter, the name for a second parameter is set to blank to prevent confusion in later displays, while its value is left at the default.

```
&DIST title = 'Chi-Squared' n = 1 /
&PARA name = 'v, degrees of freedom', '' x = 4.0 /
```

Names and values for both Normal distribution parameters appear with a comma separating X(1) from X(2) and the alternative value separator, a blank, used to keep NAME(1) and NAME(2) apart.

```
&DIST title = 'Normal' n = 2 /
&PARA x = 5.60, 7.80 name = 'mu, mean' 'sigma, std. deviation' /
```

Finally, three lines are used to document the single parameter for the Poisson distribution, demonstrating that data for a given variable (NAME(1) in this case) can span multiple physical records within one NAMELIST formatted logical record.

```
&DIST title = 'Poisson' n = 1 /
&PARA name(1) = 'lambda,
 mean'
 x(1) = 9.0 /
```

This particular file is read and displayed by this program:

```
        program nlist
        integer           :: n
```

```
      character*26, dimension(2) :: name
      character*12               :: title
      integer                    :: u = 7
      real,          dimension(2) :: x
      namelist / dist /             title, n
      namelist / para /             name,  x
      open ( unit=u, file='nlist.input', status='OLD' )
      distribution: do
         n     = 0
         title = ' '
         read   ( u,nml=DIST,end=100 )
         write ( *,nml=DIST         )
            parameters: if ( n .gt. 0 ) then
            name = ' '
            x    = -9.90
            read   ( u,nml=PARA )
            write ( *,nml=PARA )
            end if parameters
      end do distribution
100   continue
      end program nlist
```

Running this program results in the following display:

```
&DIST TITLE = None         , N = 2/
&PARA NAME =                                                ,
 X =    0.0000000E+00    0.0000000E+00/
&DIST TITLE = Bernoulli   , N = 1/
&PARA NAME = p, success probability                         ,
 X =    0.1000000  -9.9000000/
&DIST TITLE = Binomial     , N = 2/
&PARA NAME = n, trials                p, success probability ,
 X =    2.0000000   0.3000000/
&DIST TITLE = Chi-Squared , N = 1/
&PARA NAME = v, degrees of freedom                          ,
 X =    4.0000000  -9.9000000/
&DIST TITLE = Normal       , N = 2/
&PARA NAME = mu, mean                sigma, std. deviation   ,
 X =    5.6000000   7.8000000/
&DIST TITLE = Poisson     , N = 1/
&PARA NAME = lambda, mean                                   ,
 X =    9.0000000  -9.9000000/
```

NAMELIST output aims at the twin goals of readability and reusability. The processor can determine spacing and where to break the logical records into physical records, just as the user can do during input. The format allows the output to be read into another program through NAMELIST input, although some care may be needed in the case of strings, as described later in this section.

Different parts of any given sequential formatted file can be processed with normal, list-directed, or NAMELIST formatting depending on the needs of the program. Recall that the indicators of these different formatting conventions—FMT, *, and NML—are characteristics of individual READ and WRITE statements. They are not attributes set in the OPEN statement for a file. So, mixing records from each of these formatting conventions in a single file would be complicated, but permissible.

NAMELIST formatted strings are handled like list-directed strings. In this example, character data read into and displayed from the TITLE string and the NAME array are processed in the same way as list-directed character data. In general, these data are enclosed in apostrophes, quote marks, or nothing, according to the setting of DELIM in the OPEN statement. By default, strings need to be enclosed in apostrophes on input, but are written without delimiters on output. The DELIMIT program shown earlier in this chapter demonstrates the other possibilities for processing character data.

NAMELIST formatting does a good job of documenting relationships between variables names and the values they assume. Nowhere else in the Fortran language do the "internals" of source code reach out so explicitly to interact with something external to the program. For that reason, NAMELIST helps most when used to set those variables that are significant, key, or critical to the design and operation of a program.

Formats

Most advances in Fortran 90 file handling surround getting data to and from the user interface. Only a few change the outward appearance of data. Four areas of FORMATs are different in Fortran 90: new binary/hexadecimal/octal editing, engineering/scientific notation editing, generalized editing, and Hollerith editing.

ALL Fortran 77 Edits Work in Fortran 90

To provide instant relief, it should be noted that all Fortran 77 edit descriptors survive completely intact. Table 8-2 is a capsule review of all twenty-six edit descriptors. It shows the status of an edit descriptor if it is new in Fortran 90, if there is any restriction on use (i.e., just input or just

output), if it is repeatable (i.e., / is now repeatable in Fortran 90 so /////
can be appear as 5/), and a brief description.

Table 8-2: Fortran Edit Formats

Edit	New	Direction	Repeat	Description
' '		Output only	yes	Static character strings
/			yes	Skip line(s): *repeatable (new)*
:				Terminate input/output
a			yes	Character strings
b	yes		yes	Binary numbers
bn		Input only		Interpret blanks as null
bz		Input only		Interpret blanks as zero
d			yes	Double precision
e			yes	Explicit exponential notation
en	yes	Output only	yes	Engineering notation
es	yes	Output only	yes	Scientific notation
f			yes	Real
g			yes	*Generalized editing (new)*
h		Output only		Static character string *(obsolescent)*
i			yes	Integers
l			yes	Logical
o	yes		yes	Octal
p				Scale selection
s		Output only		Restore default + sign printing
sp		Output only		Print optional + sign
ss		Output only		Don't print optional + sign
t				Position in either direction
tl				Position to the left
tr				Position to the right

Table 8-2: Fortran Edit Formats (Continued)

Edit	New	Direction	Repeat	Description
x			yes	Spacing between fields
z	yes		yes	Hexadecimal

All of the edit rules established in Fortran 77 apply, without change, to their counterparts in Fortran 90. Character handling, positioning, and even the rather complicated patterns specified for floating point numbers under E and G editing are identical. There is every reason to believe that a standard-conforming Fortran 77 program will accept input or produce output in just the same way when it runs under Fortran 90.

Binary, Hexadecimal, and Octal Editing

A feature new in Fortran 90 is the ability to READ and WRITE positive whole numbers in bases other than 10. Many operating systems provide libraries of routines to provide system-level services: manipulating file directories, shared memory handling, semaphore management, etc. Usually some arguments to these routines are defined as bit fields, sums of individual octal numbers, or hexadecimal constants. Programmers have found it necessary to resort to hand calculators to convert the required binary, hexadecimal, or octal values to a decimal number that would be entered into the Fortran source code. Now those values can be handled directly in Fortran 90.

Program CONVERT prompts the user for a decimal, hexadecimal, or octal number and converts that value into the other bases.

```
      program convert
      integer, parameter       :: short = selected_int_kind ( 3 )
      character*8              :: bases = 'dDhHoOxX'
      integer                  :: crtin = 5
      integer                  :: crtout = 6
      integer                  :: decimal = 0
      character*1, dimension(6) :: edit=(/'I','I','Z','Z','O','O'/)
      character*1               frombase
      integer                   index
      integer(short)           :: left
      character*16              number
      integer(short)           :: right
      do
100   continue
```

The user must enter the letters in the BASES string, followed by a numeral
that is valid for that base. For instance, d99999 means 99999 in decimal.

```
      write ( crtout,200,advance='NO' )
200   format ( / 1H , 'Enter number [dho#]: ' )
      read ( crtin,300,advance='NO' ) frombase
300   format ( a1 )
      read ( crtin,400 ) number
400   format ( a16 )
```

The first character is now found in the BASES string. Its position is used as
an index into the EDIT array. For instance, since "d" is the first character in
BASES, it causes the first element of EDIT to be used. If the character is not
in the BASES string, the prompt is repeated. If the character is beyond the
sixth character in the BASES string—"x" or "X"—the program assumes the
user wants to exit.

```
      index = scan ( bases, frombase )
      if ( index .eq. 0 ) go to 100
      if ( index .gt. 6 ) go to 600
```

The element from EDIT plugs into the FMT string, producing a string such
as "(I16)" for decimal input.

```
      number = adjustr ( number )
      read ( number, FMT="("//edit(index)//"16)", err=100 ) decimal
      if ( decimal .lt. 0 ) go to 100
      left  = ishft      ( decimal, -bit_size(0_short) )
      right = transfer ( decimal,                0 )
      write ( crtout,500 ) left, right, decimal, decimal, decimal
500   format ( / 1H , 'binary        : ', b16, b16.16
     -           / 1H , 'decimal      : ', i32
     -           / 1H , 'hexadecimal : ', z32
     -           / 1H , 'octal         : ', o32                )
      end do
600   continue
      end program convert
```

Running this program results in the following display:

```
Enter number [dho#]: d99999

binary       :            11000011010011111
decimal      :                        99999
hexadecimal :                         1869F
octal        :                        303237

Enter number [dho#]: habcde
binary       :            10101011110011011110
decimal      :                          703710
```

```
hexadecimal  :                          ABCDE
octal        :                        2536336

Enter number [dho#]: o77777
binary       :            00111111111111111
decimal      :                          32767
hexadecimal  :                           7FFF
octal        :                          77777

Enter number [dho#]: x
```

Using these new formats is fairly straightforward with one exception. One of the new edit descriptors, B, is limited to positive integers in the range from zero to 32,767. Converting integers up to the high end (i.e., 2,147,483,647) of the integers allowed on most of today's computer systems takes a bit of trickery. The program accomplishes this feat by "splitting" the default 32-bit INTEGER variable, DECIMAL, into its two 16-bit components, LEFT and RIGHT. The two resulting numbers are shown in Figure 8-1.

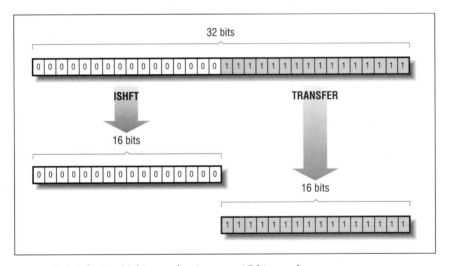

Figure 8-1: Splitting 32-bit number into two 16-bit numbers

A value for LEFT is extracted from DECIMAL using a technique shown in Chapter 11, *Intrinsic Functions*. The ISHFT function shifts bits in DECIMAL to the right (and zero fills vacated bits) by the number of bits defined in the special 16-bit INTEGER data type setup for LEFT. A value for RIGHT is extracted from DECIMAL using the TRANSFER function. It maps the storage allocated for DECIMAL over that for the special 16-bit INTEGER data type setup for RIGHT, thereby "chopping off" the left-most 16 bits of DECIMAL. This trickery results in two "short" INTEGERS that can be printed using the

B edit descriptor and, if recombined, would exactly mirror the value in the "regular" INTEGER variable, DECIMAL.

Engineering and Scientific Notation

Two other convenient edit descriptors are added in Fortran 90 to support engineering and scientific notation. The new engineering notation places special significance on the exponent of floating point numbers at every third power of ten. Laymen recognize these breakpoints in all sorts of measurements by commonly used prefixes:

Scale	Prefix	Example
$10 ** -9$	Nano	Nanosecond
$10 ** -6$	Micro	Microsecond
$10 ** -3$	Milli	Milliliter
$10 ** 3$	Kilo	Kilometer
$10 ** 6$	Mega	Megawatts
$10 ** 9$	Giga	Gigabyte

Using this idea of engineering notation, the EN edit prints the significand between 1 and 1000 and adjusts the exponent accordingly (i.e., 12345 becomes 12.345E+03). In Fortran 90, the ES edit supports scientific notation. It prints the significand between 1 and 10 and adjusts the exponent accordingly (i.e., 12345 prints as 1.2345E+04). Program NOTATION shows how these new edit descriptors compare with the old E descriptor:

```
program notation
integer exponent
integer i
real    variable
```

For completeness, NOTATION prints ten random numbers in the various formats such that every other exponent is negative and every third significand is also negative. Creating those random numbers is the job of the new Fortran 90 subroutine RANDOM_SEED. In this example, RANDOM_SEED is called without arguments, which asks the system to "seed" the random number stream. It could also be called with arguments to set the seed.

```
call random_seed
do i = 1, 10, 1
   call random_number ( variable )
   exponent = variable * 9.0
   if ( mod(i,2) .eq. 0 ) exponent = -exponent
   call random_number ( variable )
```

```
variable = variable * ( 10.0 ** exponent )
if ( mod(i,3) .eq. 0 ) variable = -variable
```

The variables are printed in traditional floating-point notation, engineering notation, and scientific notation.

```
        print 100, variable, variable, variable
100     format ( 1H , e20.5, 1x, en20.5, 1x, es20.5 )
    end do
    end program notation
```

Running this program results in the following display:

0.75093E+05	75.09268E+03	7.50927E+04
0.74454E-07	74.45371E-09	7.44537E-08
-0.99861E+03	-998.60712E+00	-9.98607E+02
0.35507E-05	3.55074E-06	3.55074E-06
0.99583E+06	995.83175E+03	9.95832E+05
-0.61159E-08	-6.11590E-09	-6.11590E-09
0.37497E+08	37.49674E+06	3.74967E+07
0.98524E+00	985.23778E-03	9.85238E-01
-0.94697E+08	-94.69734E+06	-9.46973E+07
0.58666E-07	58.66589E-09	5.86659E-08

Editing ANY Data Type with One Descriptor: G

In the Fortran 77 standard, the G descriptor handled REAL, DOUBLE PRECISION, and COMPLEX data types. In the Fortran 90 standard, G is extended to handle CHARACTER, INTEGER, and LOGICAL data types. Its name of "generalized" editing is now very appropriate, as demonstrated in the following program, GENERAL:

```
        program general
        character*10    :: a = 'string'
        double precision :: d = 1.2d-12
        real            :: e = 3.4e+34
        real            :: f = 5.6
        integer         :: i = 789
        logical         :: l = .TRUE.
        print 100, a, a, d, d, e, e, f, f, i, i, l, l
100     format ( 1H , 'A: <', a10,      '> <', g10.5, '>'
      -          / 1H , 'D: ', d10.5,    '  ', g10.5
      -          / 1H , 'E: ', e10.5E2, '  ', g10.5
      -          / 1H , 'F: ', f10.5,    '  ', g10.5
      -          / 1H , 'I: ', i10,      '  ', g10.5
      -          / 1H , 'L: ', l10,      '  ', g10.5       )
        end program general
```

Running this program results in the following display:

```
A: <string   > <string   >
D: .12000D-11   .12000E-11
E: .34000E+35   .34000E+35
F:    5.60000   5.6000
I:        789         789
L:          T           T
```

Different data types are displayed under G editing pretty much like their own type-specific edit descriptor. Comparing type-specific output to G edit output shows some slight changes: G uses an "E" rather than "D" to signal the exponent in DOUBLE PRECISION, and G puts in trailing blanks following the REAL display. Both these cases are treated the same in Fortran 77 and Fortran 90.

In the example, G10.5 is an instruction to print the fractional part of a number using five digits to the right of a decimal point in a field ten positions wide. When CHARACTER, INTEGER, and LOGICAL variables are printed using the G edit descriptor, the field width is meaningful but the fractional digits part is not. Thus, if the full "Gw.dEe" specification was used, CHARACTER, INTEGER, and LOGICAL variables would print in a field "w" positions wide; the "d" and "e"—fractional digits and exponent width—specifications would not apply.

G edits are useful when programs are being built. It is particularly important, during the nerve-racking business of software development, to trap and report mistakes concerning a variety of data items. To support users deprived of interactive symbolic debuggers and full-blown CASE environments, programmers have relied on homegrown error reporting routines. Fortran 90 eases the task of writing "generic" error reporting routines with G editing because G can display any data type, as shown in the program PANIC from Chapter 4, *Subroutines and Functions Revisited.*

Hollerith Edit Declared Obsolescent

Lastly, Fortran 90 declares the H edit descriptor obsolescent. Fortran 77 introduced the idea of enclosing strings in apostrophes (i.e., "this is a string") which is easy to do compared to the old Fortran 66 standard. Fortran 66 required programmers to count characters and set-off each string with a count followed by the H edit descriptor (e.g., 16Hthis is a string). H is still supported in Fortran 90, but declared obsolescent because using apostrophes is such a superior technique. Although H editing is not an error, only obsolescent, Fortran 90 compilers must elect to warn the user each time it is used.

Note that making the H edit obsolescent has nothing to do with and has no effect on its use as a carriage control indicator. Single space, double space, top-of-form, and no advance are equally valid expressed as ' ', 0, 1, and + as they are when written as 1H, 1H0, 1H1, and 1H+.

9

Numeric Models

A critical requirement in scientific programming, the ability to specify the range and precision of data, has finally been standardized and made portable in Fortran 90.

In earlier versions of Fortran, the traditional trade-offs of adequate range and precision versus memory requirements and efficiency had to be made on the basis of a particular machine architecture, and could not be easily ported. For instance, depending on the machine architecture, a compiler might offer either two or three kinds of floating-point data type. REAL and DOUBLE PRECISION were the standard ways of specifying two such kinds. But the standard did not guarantee what actual range and precision were offered, and provided no way for the program to query the limits.

Thus, it is a relief to find, in Fortran 90, that the programmer can specify the range and precision of data in decimal form, and let the compiler allocate the proper amount of space to meet the requirements. Programmers can also query the processor for the characteristics of its data representation. Most interestingly perhaps, they can compensate for the inherent fuzziness of floating-point calculations by comparing numbers for comparable range rather than equality. The cost of these achievements is some extra over-head for the programmer to learn and apply the new attribute of data introduced by Fortran 90, called KIND.

Table 9-1 briefly summarizes the new Fortran 90 intrinsics that deal with the computer representation of numbers.

Table 9-1: Numeric Model Fortran 90 Intrinsics

Intrinsic	Description
INTEGERS	
SELECTED_INT_KIND	Select integer KIND
INTEGERS and REALS	
DIGITS	Significant digits
HUGE	Largest value
KIND	Code for numeric representation
RADIX	Radix of numerical model
RANGE	Decimal exponent range
REALS	
EPSILON	Number negligible compared to one
EXPONENT	Exponent part of real number
FRACTION	Fraction part of real number
MAXEXPONENT	Largest exponent
MINEXPONENT	Smallest exponent
NEAREST	Representable number nearest to target
PRECISION	Digits of precision
RRSPACING	Relative real number spacing
SCALE	Scale real number by constant
SELECTED_REAL_KIND	Select real KIND
SET_EXPONENT	Set exponent part
SPACING	Absolute spacing or real model
TINY	Smallest value

The discussion in this section is not meant to be a guide to choosing the precision appropriate to a given application; that is a mathematical thread within the discipline of computer science outside the scope of this book. Many programmers can get by with the techniques documented in the next two sections. For those who need to apply more sophisticated techniques, subsequent sections show how to query the processor for the characteristics of data. All of the numeric intrinsics are demonstrated with extracts from the program NUMERIC, which appears in its entirety in Appendix D, *Selected Source Code Listings.*

The Concept of Kind

A kind can be considered a subset of a data's type. Thus, if a machine architecture offers integers in sizes of one byte, two bytes, and four bytes, the compiler can make available three kinds of integers. The concept of multiple kinds of integers and reals parallels the familiar extension of Fortran 77 to declare INTEGER*1, *2, *4, and REAL*4 and *8.

Fortran 90 requires the compiler to arbitrarily assign three numbers that designate the sizes. It is reasonable to assume that compiler writers might chose 1, 2, and 3 as the KINDs of INTEGERs. But, since the choice of numbers is entirely arbitrary, they should not normally appear in a Fortran program. The following code forces the processor to show what is associated to the basic kinds of character, complex, double precision, integer, logical, and real data, simple to reveal the mechanics behind kind selection:

```
        character            a
        complex              c
        double precision :: d
        integer          :: i
        logical              l
        real             :: x
        print 100, "Character (KIND)",        kind(a)
100 format ( a40, ': ', g24.10 )
        print 100, "Complex (KIND)",          kind(c)
        print 100, "Double precision (KIND)", kind(d)
        print 100, "Integer (KIND)",          kind(i)
        print 100, "Logical (KIND)",          kind(l)
        print 100, "Real (KIND)",             kind(x)
```

This displays:

```
        Character (KIND):                 1
        Complex (KIND):                   1
        Double precision (KIND):          2
        Integer (KIND):                   3
        Logical (KIND):                   2
        Real (KIND):                      1
```

Note that there is some overlap in KIND numbers. For example, COMPLEX variables and REAL variables can be declared with the same precision as the DOUBLE PRECISION data type using the following syntax:

```
        complex (kind=2) c
        real    (kind=2) d
```

Selecting a Kind

Specifying a kind directly is contrary to the intent of the standard. That is why there are two SELECTED_X_KIND intrinsic functions. The programmer specifies the greatest value that must be represented by an integer or a real and the compiler reports the kind number it has assigned to such a representation.

This section shows the basic steps to selecting kinds, as well as a program that can display the available ranges and precisions on any system.

Integer Selection

The choice for integer formats depends simply on the integer's range. This is measured as the largest number of decimal digits that are needed to specify a given number. Thus, the first step in declaring integers is to submit the number of required digits for a particular set of data to the SELECTED_INT_KIND function.

```
integer, parameter  :: small  = selected_int_kind(2)
integer, parameter  :: large  = selected_int_kind(8)
```

The second and final step is to place the integers SMALL and LARGE in type statements declaring the data manipulated by the program.

```
integer (small)     :: specimen_type
integer (large)     :: input_store, store1, store2
```

In this hypothetical example, SPECIMEN_TYPE records different classes available within the program, and is assured always to remain very small. Thus, any data type that can range up to 99 can be used to hold the variable. The number of digits (in this case two) becomes the input to SELECTED_INT_KIND. The resulting kind will almost certainly be the smallest data type on the system, which is 8 bits for some architectures and 16 in others.

By contrast, INPUT_STORE, STORE1, and STORE2 take enormous data values. They are sometimes expected to exceed 999999 (seven digits) but never to exceed 99999999 (eight digits) and therefore are specified with a different integer KIND. The integers holding them will probably be 32 bits.

If the value submitted to SELECTED_INT_KIND is too large for any integer on the system, the compiler returns -1. All valid return values are positive. While it is not feasible to test for -1 in a type declaration statement, the test shown later in this chapter can be run to find the limits on the system.

Floating-point Selection

Floating-point offers two parameters that vary: range and precision.

The range is the largest magnitude required, and thus can be derived from the number of digits to the left of the decimal point in the largest number that must be represented. For instance, if numbers from 0.0 to 7500.0 are required, the range is 4.

Precision refers to the decimal exponent for the largest number that must be represented accurately when the number is stored.

The SELECTED_REAL_KIND function accepts the precision as the first argument, and the range as the second:

```
integer, parameter   :: real4   = selected_real_kind(6,37)
integer, parameter   :: real8   = selected_real_kind(15,307)
```

On most systems, REAL4 will correspond to Fortran 77's REAL and REAL8 will correspond to DOUBLE PRECISION. As with integers, the remaining step is to declare the data used by the program using the REAL4 and REAL8 kinds.

```
real    (real4)   :: thirty_two_bit_calc
real    (real8)   :: sixty_four_bit_calc
```

The SELECTED_REAL_KIND function, like its integer counterpart, returns negative values to signal errors: -1 indicates that the precision is unavailable, -2 indicates the same problem for the range, and -3 indicates that both are out of bounds. The return values are exercised by the test program later in this chapter.

Forcing Constants to the Proper Range and Precision

Constants can be forced to a larger size if necessary, for instance:

```
sixty_four_bit_calc = sixty_four_bit_calc + 0.5_real8
```

Since 0.5 cannot be represented exactly in any number of bits, the programmer here wishes to create the most accurate representation possible. In Fortran 77, the construct 0.5D1 would be used for this. But the interpretation of the D is just as vague as that of the DOUBLE PRECISION data type for which it stands. Since the code shown earlier in this chapter selected the REAL8 precision directly, that can be used instead.

The general format for specifying a real or numeric constant is *constant_kind*, where the *kind* is a number or an integer chosen through

SELECTED_INT_KIND or SELECTED_REAL_KIND. Thus, an integer can be forced to a larger size:

```
99_large
```

But, this should rarely be necessary, because the compiler selects the necessary size and performs conversions automatically as needed during calculations.

DOUBLE PRECISION is now an outmoded concept, although still supported in Fortran 90 like all Fortran 77 constructs. In its place, the program can specify the necessary precision of floating-point numbers in decimal digits, and the necessary range in decimal exponents. If it is important to represent at least 12 digits accurately and then hold values up to 1,000,000,000 (i.e., 10^9), then

```
i_real_size = selected_real_kind ( 12, 9 )
```

would return the necessary KIND, probably an eight-byte REAL on any system.

Precision is guaranteed only when the compiler stores a specified constant or input value. Naturally, it is a basic tenet of engineering computation that precision decreases during the course of calculations.

Retrieving KINDs

The KIND intrinsic function returns the kind of its input. For instance, KIND(0.0) returns the default kind associated with REAL on the system, while KIND(0.0D0) returns the default kind associated with DOUBLE PRECISION. Thus, the following declaration:

```
real    ( kind(0.0d0) ) :: xyz
```

has the same effect as

```
double precision xyz
```

but neither offers the certainty that can be achieved through the use of SELECTED_REAL_KIND. The KIND intrinsic is useful mostly in combination with other numerical intrinsics, shown later in this chapter, that query the processor about its numerical model.

KIND returns an integer, since the compiler uses integers internally to represent kinds. The function accepts any data type that is intrinsic (that is, not a derived type, which is defined by the user).

Testing the System

The format promulgated by the IEEE 754 standard is becoming more and more dominant on floating-point processors. But enough people still use IBM mainframes, VAX systems, and other non-IEEE processors to warrant a test program that shows what a system provides in the way of floating-point kinds. For the sake of completeness, integer kinds are also tested.

```
integer                    :: current_kind
integer                    :: digits_precision
integer                    :: exponent_range
integer                    :: old_kind
type kind_structure
      integer precision
      integer range
end  type kind_structure
type ( kind_structure )    :: types(10)
```

For integers, the first step is to select the kind large enough to hold a single digit—the smallest range that is valid as input to SELECT_INT_KIND.

```
old_kind = selected_int_kind(1)
```

A loop now increments the number of digits and compares the newly selected kind with the old one. Moving from one digit to two will not change the selected kind. But moving from two to three can well change it, because that is the point where eight bits are no longer sufficient and 16 are required. The loop prints a message wherever a change between OLD_KIND and CURRENT_KIND is detected.

```
     do exponent_range = 2, 128, 1
        current_kind = selected_int_kind(exponent_range)
        if ( current_kind .ne. old_kind ) then
            print 300, "Valid kind (SELECTED_INT_KIND)",
     -                  old_kind, exponent_range-1
300         format ( a40, ':      ', i5, ' => +/- 10**', i3.3 )
```

On each pass, the new number of digits is stored in OLD_KIND so that the process can be repeated:

```
            old_kind = current_kind
        end if
```

A value that exceeds the largest available integer on the system causes the loop to terminate.

```
        if ( current_kind .eq. -1 ) exit
     end do
```

The output of this loop on the author's system is:

```
Valid kind (SELECTED_INT_KIND):        1 => +/- 10**002
Valid kind (SELECTED_INT_KIND):        2 => +/- 10**004
Valid kind (SELECTED_INT_KIND):        3 => +/- 10**009
```

This is consistent with two's-complement integers in eight-bit, 16-bit, and 32-bit sizes.

The same process can now be repeated for floating-point numbers. The existence of two parameters—range and precision—brings more complexity to the strategy. A double loop is required.

```
print *, " "
types(:)%precision = 0
types(:)%range     = 0
R: do exponent_range = 1, 512, 1
   P: do digits_precision = 1, 128, 1
        current_kind = selected_real_kind(digits_precision,
    -                                       exponent_range   )
```

A positive return value indicates that the precision and range are available. The TYPES array reserves 10 places—a generously large number—for the different kinds. Each precision and range was initialized to zero at the start of the program. Whenever the loop uncovers a new precision or range that can be handled by the kind, the proper component of TYPES is updated with the new value.

```
if ( current_kind .gt. 0 ) then
   if ( digits_precision .gt.
 -        types(current_kind)%precision )
 -        types(current_kind)%precision=digits_precision
   if ( exponent_range .gt.
 -        types(current_kind)%range )
 -        types(current_kind)%range = exponent_range
end if
```

The value -1 is checked within the P loop because it indicates an excessive request for precision, while -2 is checked in the R loop because it denotes the same condition for range.

```
        if ( current_kind .eq. -1 ) exit
   end do P
   if ( current_kind .eq. -2 ) exit
end do R
```

Now that all kinds have been found, the non-zero kinds are displayed.

```
do i = 1, 10, 1
   if (types(i)%precision .eq. 0 .or.
        types(i)%range     .eq. 0    ) cycle
```

```
                print 500, "Valid kind (SELECTED_REAL_KIND)",
     -                 i, types(i)%precision,
     -                    types(i)%range
  500          format ( a40, ':      ', i5, ' => p=',i3.3,
     -                                  ' r=',i3.3  )
       end do
```

Since the book was developed with an IEEE processor, these kinds are valid on that system:

```
     Valid kind (SELECTED_REAL_KIND):        1 => p=006 r=037
     Valid kind (SELECTED_REAL_KIND):        2 => p=015 r=307
```

Character Sets

It is beyond the scope of this book to discuss varieties of character sets, since the current Fortran 90 compiler offerings are based entirely on the ASCII set. But it can be noted that the language contains hooks for implementing multiple sets and, therefore, some support for internationalization.

Multiple kinds for character data are allowed in Fortran 90, just as for numeric types. Thus, different alphabets can be assigned to different kinds. When a character from such an alphabet is passed to the KIND function, it returns the kind corresponding to the proper set.

What Is Available?

There is a subtle difference between specifying and selecting numeric precision. Fortran 90 programmers can only choose from a limited set of implemented precisions. Compiler writers craft a compiler to take advantage of the target computer platform. They specify what precision to implement. They control what precision will be available.

Thus, SELECTED_INT_KIND(2) requests an integer large enough to hold numbers in the range (-99,99), but it does not limit integers to that range. The compiler will probably return an eight-bit size capable of holding integers from -128 to 127. If byte addressing is not supported, it may return an even larger size. In this sense, Fortran 90 selects but does not specify range.

Finding the Nearest Representable Value

Fortran compilers complain when code compares two floating-point numbers for equality. And for good reason: such comparisons are not exact, because the underlying representation of floating-point numbers is not exact. Now, Fortran 90 allows the programmer to replace code like the following:

```
real :: x = 123.56
real :: y = 123.56
if ( y .eq. x ) print *, y, "equals", x
```

by recoding the comparison as

```
if ( y .ge. nearest ( x, -1.0 ) .and.
-     y .le. nearest ( x,  1.0 )        )
-     print *, y, "is close enough to", x
```

NEAREST in reports the closest machine representable number that is distinct from its first argument. In the second argument, only the sign is significant. It indicates which direction to move away from the first argument. Graphically, NEAREST's results for this example are shown in Figure 9-1.

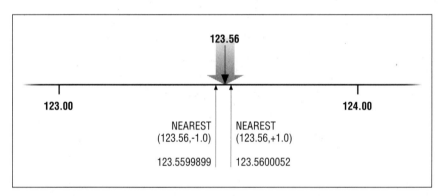

Figure 9-1: NEAREST floating-point numbers

Alternatives to using NEAREST to measure convergence are

```
if ( abs ( x - y ) .le. spacing ( x ) )
-     print *, y, "is close enough to", x
```

or

```
if ( x - y .le. epsilon ( x ) )
-     print *, y, "is close enough to", x
```

In the first version, the SPACING intrinsic returns the difference between successive floating-point numbers that have X's exponent. In the second version, EPSILON returns the mean spacing between successive floating-point numbers (the spacing around 1.0). These intrinsic functions, and the floating-point model that supports them, are explained below.

Once again, these comparison techniques account only for variations in storage. They cannot compensate for inevitable divergences when numbers undergo repeated additions or multiplications.

The Numeric Models

For average programming needs, the functions shown in the previous section give the necessary control. However, analysts might want to use the functions described below to determine the exact characteristics and behavior of numbers on their systems. It is unlikely that the information returned by these queries could be used to make decisions at run time; they are useful just for forcing a particular compiler on a particular system to display its numerical aptitude.

The INTEGER Numeric Model

INTEGER variables of three different lengths can be declared using the following syntax.

```
integer (kind=1) narrow
integer (kind=2) medium
integer (kind=3) long
```

These three kinds differ in the parameters, r and q, specified in the mathematical model of an integer, as shown in Table 9-2.

Table 9-2: Parameters of the Integer Number Model

Parameter	Range	Meaning
$i = s \sum_{k=1}^{q} w_k r^{k-1}$	$1 < r$ $1 \leq q$ $s = -1$ or $+1$ $0 \leq w_k < r$	Radix (number base) Number of bits less one Sign bit sequence

The RADIX intrinsic reports the base of the model. While this is almost certain to be two for any scientific processor, the Fortran 90 standard leaves open the possibility for other bases, such as ten.

BIT_SIZE returns the number of bits in the integer, which is 32 for the default integer on the author's system. In addition, DIGITS reports q, the number of bits used to represent the magnitude of the integer. Since one bit is always reserved for the sign, DIGITS in this case is 31.

HUGE returns the largest number that can be represented by this model, which is r^q-1. In a 32-bit word that works out to 2^{31}-1, or 2,147,483,647. Finally, RANGE returns the number of digits that can be fully represented in the integer. This is defined as the largest integer exponent that does not exceed $\log_{10}$(HUGE(I)). Since $\log_{10}$(2147483647) is 9.3319, the exponent range for this integer kind is 9.

```
      integer          :: i = 789
      print *,   "INTEGER components"
      print *,   " "
      print 200, "Base of model (RADIX)", radix(i)
  200 format ( a40, ': ', g24.10 )
      print 200, "Bits defined in model (BIT_SIZE)", bit_size(i)
      print 200, "Significant digits (DIGITS)", digits(i)
      print *,   " "
      print *,   "INTEGER extrema"
      print *,   " "
      print 200, "Largest value (HUGE)", huge(i)
      print 200, "Decimal exponent range (RANGE)", range(i)
```

This displays:

```
INTEGER components

            Base of model (RADIX):              2
   Bits defined in model (BIT_SIZE):           32
      Significant digits (DIGITS):             31

INTEGER extrema

         Largest value (HUGE):        2147483647
  Decimal exponent range (RANGE):             9
```

The REAL Numeric Model

Turning to the REAL numbers, Table 9-3 implements the mathematical model used in Fortran 90:

Table 9-3: Parameters of the Real Number Model

Parameters	Range	Meaning
$1 < b$	Radix (number base)	
p	$e_{min} \le e \le e_{max}$	Exponent
$r = sb^e \sum f_k b^{-k}$	$0 \le f_k < b$	Bit sequence
$k{=}1$	$1 < p$	Number of bits
	s = -1 or +1	Sign

The equation models a left-justified fraction in f (f_1 must be set) multiplied by the exponent in e and the sign bit. The value zero is specially represented by a bit string containing all zeroes. Fundamental parameters for this model are b, p, e_{min}, and e_{max}, which Fortran 90 reports with the RADIX, DIGITS, MINEXPONENT, and MAXEPONENT functions. In the default four-byte REAL provided by the author's system (IEEE standard), these values are 2, 24, -125, and 128 respectively.

Fully 11 intrinsic functions exist to query the processor about its representation of real numbers. To understand what each intrinsic says, a trivial example using decimal numbers can help. A typical decimal floating-point number might be printed in this format:

```
1.23E+31
```

where the mantissa is arbitrarily restricted to a maximum of three digits and the exponent to two. Were this format to be described in terms of the new Fortran 90 intrinsic functions, they would report the following characteristics:

- The base is 10, the number of digits (reported by the RADIX intrinsic).

- The minimum exponent is -99 and the maximum exponent is +99 (MINEXPONENT and MAXEXPONENT in the model).

- The range is -9.99*99 through 9.99*99, and these are also the greatest representable numbers in each direction (RANGE and HUGE).

- The smallest representative value is -1.00E-99 or 1.00E-99 (TINY).

- The number of significant digits is three, which is also the precision (DIGITS, PRECISION).

- In the number 1.23E+31, the exponent is 31 and the fraction—mantissa—is 123 (EXPONENT, FRACTION).

- The binary floating-point formats used for internal storage have exactly the same elements. But since PRECISION, RANGE, HUGE, and TINY are reported in decimal, their relation to the lower-level statistics is less intuitively obvious than in the hypothetical decimal model just shown.

Here is a query of a standard REAL number:

```
real            :: x = 123.56
print *,    "REAL components"
print *,    " "
print 400, "Base of model (RADIX)", radix(x)
400 format ( a40, ': ', g24.10 )
print 400, "Significant digits (DIGITS)", digits(x)
print 400, "Minimum exponent (MINEXPONENT)", minexponent(x)
```

```
print 400, "Maximum exponent (MAXEXPONENT)", maxexponent(x)
print *,    " "
print *,    "REAL extrema"
print *,    " "
print 400, "Smallest value (TINY)", tiny(x)
print 400, "Largest value (HUGE)", huge(x)
print 400, "Decimal exponent range (RANGE)", range(x)
print *,    " "
print *,    "REAL precision"
print *,    " "
print 400, "Decimal precision (PRECISION)", precision(x)
print 400, "Negligible value (EPSILON)", epsilon(x)
print *,    " "
print *,    "REAL fit"
print *,    " "
print 400, "Value of x", x
print 400, "Exponent part (EXPONENT)", exponent(x)
print 400, "Scale (SCALE)", scale(x,radix(x))
print 400, "Nearest + infinity (NEAREST)", nearest(x, 1.0)
print 400, "Nearest - infinity (NEAREST)", nearest(x,-1.0)
print 400, "Fractional part (FRACTION)", fraction(x)
print 400, "Absolute spacing (SPACING)", spacing(x)
print 400, "Relative spacing (RRSPACING)", rrspacing(x)
print 400, "Exponent form (SET_EXPONENT)",
     -        set_exponent(fraction(x),exponent(x))
```

On an IEEE-compliant system, this generates the display:

```
REAL components

                Base of model (RADIX):                   2
          Significant digits (DIGITS):                  24
     Minimum exponent (MINEXPONENT):                 -125
     Maximum exponent (MAXEXPONENT):                  128

REAL extrema

              Smallest value (TINY):   0.1175494351E-37
               Largest value (HUGE):   0.3402823466E+39
      Decimal exponent range (RANGE):                 37

REAL precision

          Decimal precision (PRECISION):                6
            Negligible value (EPSILON):  0.1192092896E-06
```

REAL fit

Value of x:	123.5599976
Exponent part (EXPONENT):	7
Scale (SCALE):	494.2399902
Nearest + infinity (NEAREST):	123.5600052
Nearest – infinity (NEAREST):	123.5599899
Fractional part (FRACTION):	0.9653124809
Absolute spacing (SPACING):	0.7629394531E-05
Relative spacing (RRSPACING):	16195256.00
Exponent form (SET_EXPONENT):	123.5599976

A further level of sophistication comes in measuring the distance between representable values. To return to the trivial decimal model, consider the following two numbers at the top of the range:

9.89E+99, 9.99E+99

The difference between them is 0.01E+99, exactly the same as between the following numbers, which are the smallest that have an exponent of 99:

1.00E+99, 1.01E+99

In short, the absolute difference between two neighboring numbers is always constant, given the same exponent. The intrinsic SPACING returns this difference for the given input value. When the exponent is less, the absolute difference is also less, so at the bottom of the exponent range:

1.00E-99, 1.01E-99, ..., 9.98E-99, 9.99E-99

the difference is only 0.01E-99. Halfway between these extremes is the value called EPSILON, which is the change between 1.0 and the next higher or lower number. In this decimal model, EPSILON is the difference between 1.00E+00 and 1.01E+00, or 0.01.

While the absolute spacing is the same for any given exponent, there is still an enormous difference between the spacing around 1.00E+99 and that around 9.99E+99, in a relative sense. 0.01E+99 is 1% of the former value, but only slightly above 0.001% of the latter. The RRSPACING function reports such relative spacing.

Step-by-step calculation of the major instrinsics for the real numeric model is shown in Table 9-4.

Table 9-4: Calculation of Values Reported in Program NUMERIC for Real Numeric Model Intrinsics

Intrinsic	Formula	Step-by-Step Calculations
TINY	$b^e min^{-1}$	$2^{-125 - 1}$ 2^{-126} 1.1755x10-38
HUGE	$(1-b^{-p})b^e max$	$(1 - 2^{-24}) \times 2^{128}$ $(1 - 1/16777216) \times 2^{128}$ $(1 - 5.9605 \times 10^{-8}) \times 3.4028 \times 10^{38}$ $9.9999 \times 10^{-1} \times 3.4028 \times 10^{38}$ 3.4028×10^{38}
RANGE	min(logHUGE, -logTINY)	min (log 3.4028×10^{38}, -log 1.1755×10^{-38}) min (38.5318, 37.9298) 37.9298 37
PRECISION[1]	$(p-1)(\log b)+k$	$(24 - 1) \times (\log 2) + 0$ 23 x 0.3010 6.9237 6
EPSILON	b^{1-p}	2^{1-24} 2^{-23} 1/8388608 1.1921×10^{-7}
SCALE[2]	Xb^i	$123.56 \times b^2$ 123.56×2^2 123.56 x 4 494.24
EXPONENT[3]	$X = fx\ b^e$	$123.56 = f \times b^7$ $123.56 = f \times 2^7$ 123.56 = f x 128 $9.6531 \times 10^{-1} = f$

Table 9-4: Calculation of Values Reported in Program NUMERIC for Real Numeric Model Intrinsics (Continued)

Intrinsic	Formula	Step-by-Step Calculations
FRACTION[3]	$X = f \times b^e$	$123.56 = f \times b^7$
		$123.56 = f \times 2^7$
		$123.56 = f \times 128$
		$9.6531 \times 10^{-1} = f$
SPACING	b^{e-p}	2^{7-24}
		2^{-17}
		$1/131072$
		7.6929×10^{-6}
RRSPACING	$\lvert X \times b^{-e} \rvert \, b^p$	$\lvert\ 123.56 \times 2^{-7}\ \rvert \times 2^{24} \rvert\ 123.56 \times 1/128\ \rvert \times 16777216$
		$123.56 \times 7.8125 \times 10^{-3} \times 16777216$
		$0.9653125 \times 16777216$
		16195256

[1] PRECISION returns the decimal precision of the model and is the largest integer that does not exceed $(p\text{-}1)(\log_{10}(b)+k$ where k is 1 if b is an integral power of 10 and zero otherwise.

[2] SCALE returns the value of X by b^i where i is any integer that keeps the result between TINY(X) and HUGE(X). Since the number base, b, is 2, then SCALE multiplies X by 2 to the i-th power.

[3] In an IEEE complaint system, a thirty-two bit REAL number is comprised of a sign bit, seven bits for the exponent, and twenty-four bits for the significand. EXPONENT reports the value of the seven exponent bits as 7 and FRACTION reports the value of the twenty-four significand bits as 9.6351×10^{-1}. So the value for X is $2^7 \times 0.9653124809$ or 123.56.

SET_EXPONENT allows the program to play with a number's exponent without changing the fraction. In any floating-point number with a binary radix, the value doubles as the exponent increments. This activity is demonstrated in SET_EXPONENT. In SET_EXPONENT(X, I), where the first argument is the input number, and the second is an exponent. The return value is the value of the number that produced from the fractional part of X combined with the exponent I.

For example, a first argument of 123.56 produces the following outputs for a variety of values in the second argument. When normalized, the binary

exponent for 123.56 is 7. Therefore, a second argument of 7 in SET_EXPO-
NENT produces 123.56 without a change, as shown in Table 9-5.

Table 9-5: Effects of SET_EXPONENT Intrinsic

X	I	SET_EXPONENT(X,I)
123.56	0	0.9653
123.56	1	1.9306
123.56	2	3.8612
123.56	3	7.7225
123.56	4	15.4450
123.56	5	30.8900
123.56	6	61.7800
123.56	7	123.5600

Of course, the result of SET_EXPONENT(X,I) must lie between TINY(X)
and HUGE(X). Otherwise, the return value is undefined.

The intrinsics appropriate for REAL numbers also apply to the DOUBLE
PRECISION data type:

```
      double precision :: d = 123.56d0
      print *,   "DOUBLE PRECISION components"
      print *,   " "
      print 600, "Base of model (RADIX)", radix(d)
  600 format ( a40, ': ', g24.10 )
      print 600, "Significant digits (DIGITS)", digits(d)
      print 600, "Minimum exponent (MINEXPONENT)", minexponent(d)
      print 600, "Maximum exponent (MAXEXPONENT)", maxexponent(d)
      print *,   " "
      print *,   "DOUBLE PRECISION extrema"
      print *,   " "
      print 600, "Smallest value (TINY)", tiny(d)
      print 600, "Largest value (HUGE)", huge(d)
      print 600, "Decimal exponent range (RANGE)", range(d)
      print *,   " "
      print *,   "DOUBLE PRECISION precision"
      print *,   " "
      print 600, "Decimal precision (PRECISION)", precision(d)
      print 600, "Negligible value (EPSILON)", epsilon(d)
      print *,   " "
      print *,   "DOUBLE PRECISION fit"
      print *,   " "
      print 600, "Value of d", d
      print 600, "Exponent part (EXPONENT)", exponent(d)
      print 600, "Scale (SCALE)", scale(d,radix(d))
      print 600, "Nearest + infinity (NEAREST)", nearest(d, 1.0)
```

```
print 600, "Nearest - infinity (NEAREST)", nearest(d,-1.0)
print 600, "Fractional part (FRACTION)", fraction(d)
print 600, "Absolute spacing (SPACING)", spacing(d)
print 600, "Relative spacing (RRSPACING)", rrspacing(d)
print 600, "Exponent form (SET_EXPONENT)",
    -           set_exponent(fraction(d),exponent(d))
```

On an IEEE-compliant system, this generates this display:

```
DOUBLE PRECISION components

              Base of model (RADIX):                        2
          Significant digits (DIGITS):                     53
     Minimum exponent (MINEXPONENT):                    -1021
     Maximum exponent (MAXEXPONENT):                     1024

DOUBLE PRECISION extrema

              Smallest value (TINY):      0.2225073859-307
               Largest value (HUGE):      0.1797693135+309
       Decimal exponent range (RANGE):                   307

DOUBLE PRECISION precision

         Decimal precision (PRECISION):                   15
           Negligible value (EPSILON):    0.2220446049E-15

DOUBLE PRECISION fit

                     Value of d:         123.5600000
         Exponent part (EXPONENT):                       7
                 Scale (SCALE):           494.2400000
     Nearest + infinity (NEAREST):        123.5600000
     Nearest - infinity (NEAREST):        123.5600000
        Fractional part (FRACTION):       0.9653125000
        Absolute spacing (SPACING):       0.1421085472E-13
     Relative spacing (RRSPACING):        0.8694762031E+16
       Exponent form (SET_EXPONENT):      123.5600000
```

10

Bit Functions

As a high-level programming language, Fortran shields programmers from the need to manage data at the bit level. Indeed, Fortran 77 shielded programmers too well, offering no bit manipulation functions. Fortran 90 introduces eleven functions and one subroutine to manage variables at the bit level. They are essentially the ones in the U. S. Department of Defense's MIL-STD-1753 standard, which has been part of many Fortran implementations since 1978, but extended to accept array arguments as well as scalars.

Table 10-1: Fortran 90 Bit Intrinsics

Intrinsic	Description	Page
BIT_SIZE	Number of bits in integer	235
BTEST	Test whether bit is on or off	235
IAND	Logical and	239
IBCLR	Clear bit	237
IBITS	Extract bit	241
IBSET	Set bit	236
IEOR	Exclusive or	239
IOR	Inclusive or	239
ISHFT	Logical bit shift	237
ISHFTC	Circular bit shift	239
MVBITS	Combination of bits from target to source	242
NOT	Logical complement	240

All of the bit routines described in Table 10-1 are new in Fortran 90. They will be warmly received by those programmers who must invoke operating system routines, interpret system level data structures, and, where supported, interface with other programming languages. Also, they will benefit programs designed to manage very large quantities of small-valued data such as presence/absence information, values ranging from zero to three fitting into two bits, values ranging from zero to 15 fitting in four bits, etc. The memory storage ramifications of packing eight, sixteen, or thirty-two observations into one array element could be staggering.

Bit level code in Fortran rarely appears outside the applications listed above. Regrettably, none of these applications are remotely portable between computer platforms. So, although this chapter exercises all of the new Fortran 90 bit routines, it is somewhat artificial.

What programmers can count on is the small set of categories that their bit manipulations will fall into. These are the categories into which this chapter is divided:

- Sorting, clearing, and testing individual bits
- Shifts (circular and end-off)
- Boolean operations
- Extracting bit fields

The Bit Model

The program BITS shows the special meaning assigned by Fortran 90 to an integer when it is used in bit functions. Later parts of this program illustrate each function.

```
program bits
integer            :: from
integer            :: frompos
integer            :: i          = 456
integer (kind=1) :: kind_one
integer (kind=2) :: kind_two
integer (kind=3) :: kind_three
integer            :: j          = 789
integer            :: k
integer (kind=2) :: left
integer            :: length
integer            :: pos
integer (kind=2) :: right
integer            :: shift
integer            :: to
```

```
integer          :: topos
integer          :: zero      = 0
```

In this program, data is manipulated both as bits and as integers, in order to help the reader develop a model for bit representation. The relation between bit fields and integers is guaranteed to be portable so long as the integer is positive (the most significant bit is clear).

The program reports the size of each KIND of INTEGER variable in bits.

```
print *, " "
print *, "BIT_SIZE for KIND 1, 2, and 3 integers:",
-          bit_size(kind_one),   bit_size(kind_two),
-          bit_size(kind_three)
```

This corresponds to some Fortran implementations that support INTEGER*1, INTEGER*2, and INTEGER*4 data types. Their bit length is what this program displays: 8, 16, and 32 bits for integer KINDs 1, 2, and 3.

```
BIT_SIZE for KIND 1, 2, and 3 integers: 8 16 32
```

All Fortran 90 bit routines assume a bit addressing scheme where the high bit number is at the low memory address and the zeroth bit is at the high memory address. It is hard to talk about microscopic memory locations without confusion. Concepts of "left" and "right" do not refer to what one would see by inspecting a memory chip; they are just convenient ways to orient the bit stream. The bottom line here is that the Fortran 90 bit routines assume that bits become more significant as one moves left, and less significant as one moves right. That means that Fortran 90 views the 32 bit binary representation of the decimal positive integer 456 as follows:

Bit value	0 0 0 0 0 ... 1 1 1 0 0 1 0 0 0
Bit place	31 30 29 28 27 ... 08 07 06 05 04 03 02 01 00

That is why the BTEST function:

```
      print *, " "
      do pos = 0, bit_size(i)-1, 1
         if ( btest(i,pos) ) then
            write ( 6,100,advance='NO' ) pos, i
100         format ( 1h , 'Bit ', i2.2, ' of ', i3, ' ' )
            call binary ( i )
            print *, "is set"
         else
            cycle
         end if
      end do
```

reports that bits 3, 6, 7, and 8 are set for the integer 456.

```
Bit 03 of 456 ( 00000000 00000000 00000001 11001000 ) is set
Bit 06 of 456 ( 00000000 00000000 00000001 11001000 ) is set
Bit 07 of 456 ( 00000000 00000000 00000001 11001000 ) is set
Bit 08 of 456 ( 00000000 00000000 00000001 11001000 ) is set
```

This program uses a subroutine, BINARY, to display all thirty-two bits in groups of eight. Note that the calling program examines bits in numerical order (i.e., right to left) where this subroutine prints a 1 or 0 for on or off bits in address order (i.e., left to right).

```
      subroutine binary ( i )
      integer    i
      character onoff
      integer    pos
      write ( 6,100,advance='NO' )
100   format ( '( ' )
      do pos = bit_size(i)-1, 0, -1
         if ( btest(i,pos) ) then
            onoff = '1'
         else
            onoff = '0'
         end if
         if ( mod ( pos,8 ) .eq. 0 ) then
            write ( 6,200,advance='NO' ) onoff
200         format ( a1, ' ' )
         else
            write ( 6,300,advance='NO' ) onoff
300         format ( a1 )
         end if
      end do
      write ( 6,400,advance='NO' )
400   format ( ')' )
      end subroutine binary
```

Individual Bits

Bits can be set or cleared by IBSET and IBCLR. An application would give a concrete reason to manage individual bits, but here they are used in an artificial setting to add 32K to the integer 456 and then subtract it by clearing the fifteenth bits.

```
      pos = 15
      k   = ibset(i,pos)
      print *, " "
      print *, "Adding 32K to", i, "yields", k
      pos = 15
      print *, " "
```

```
print *, "Subtract 32K from", k, "by clearing bit fifteen",
    -         " yielding", ibclr(k,pos)
```

These results are displayed.

```
Adding 32K to 456 yields 33224

Subtract 32K from 33224 by clearing bit fifteen yielding 456
```

Shifting

ISHFT is a classic bit shifting routine. A shift of 3 moves all bits to the left (increasing the integer's value). A shift of -3 moves them to the right (decreasing the value). In each case, 3 bits are lost, shifted off the end into the empty ether.

A thirty-two bit integer can be "split" into its two 16-bit components with the ISHFT and TRANSFER intrinsics. For example, the number 889,938,024 has two components, left-side and right-side, as shown below:

Base	"Left" side	"Right" side
Decimal	13579	24680
Binary	0011010100001011	0110000001101000
Octal	32413	60150
Hexadecimal	350B	6068

By design these components have an integer comprised of the odd decimal digits on the left and an integer containing the even decimal digits on the right. Using ISHFT to isolate the 16-bit integer on the left and TRANSFER to get the one on the right:

```
k     = 889938024
left  = ishft ( k, -bit_size(left) )
right = transfer ( k, zero )
print *, " "
print *, "Splitting the 32-bit integer", k, "into"
print *, "its two 16-bit halves gives", left, "and", right
```

gives the following display:

```
Splitting the 32-bit integer 889938024 into
its two 16-bit halves gives 13579 and 24680
```

The bits in K representing 889,938,024 are shifted right by sixteen bits, leaving original bits 31 through 16 right-justified in the result of 13,579.

TRANSFER is necessary because K and RIGHT are different sizes; the function provides a portable alternative to EQUIVALENCE. Here, the need is to store the least significant bits of a 32-bit integer (K) into a 16-bit integer (RIGHT). ZERO is simply a reference variable used in the second argument of TRANSFER. Figure 10-1 shows the result. So, the "leading part" of K is copied into RIGHT, giving 24,680.

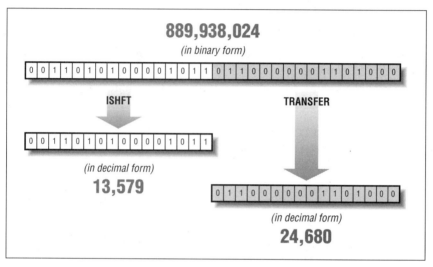

Figure 10-1: TRANSFER intrinsic

Fortran 90's restrictions on no-mixed mode EQUIVALENCEs clearly demands a solution such as the one just discussed. It is very familiar for programmers using a Fortran providing INTEGER*2 and INTEGER*4 data type extensions to align arrays of both type as

```
      INTEGER*2 SMALL(16)
      INTEGER*4 LARGE( 8)
C     ---------------------------------------- FORTRAN 77 CORRECT
      EQUIVALENCE ( SMALL(1), LARGE(1) )
C     ---------------------------------------- FORTRAN 77 CORRECT
```

because the Fortran 77 standard did not prohibit mixing data types in the EQUIVALENCE list. In contrast, the Fortran 90 standard explicitly constrains members in the EQUIVALENCE list to be all the same type. However, both ISHFT and TRANSFER accept and return array values, so the old Fortran 77 practice can be implemented.

```
      integer (kind=2), dimension(16) :: small
      integer (kind=3), dimension( 8) :: large
```

.
.
.

```
small(1:size(small):2) = ishft ( large, -bit_size(left) )
small(2:size(small):2) = transfer ( large,(/size(large)*0/) )
```

With EQUIVALENCE, a change in one value changes causes the other to change as well because they share storage. With TRANSFER, the variables remain separate in memory, so changing one has no effect on the other.

Another shift function, ISHFTC, moves bits around the boundaries of an integer. It is defined as ISHFTC(I,SHIFT,SIZE) which moves the SIZE's right-most bits in I to the right or the left depending on whether SHIFT is negative or positive, respectively. If SIZE is not specified,

```
k = 1
print *, " "
do shift = 0, 7, 1
    print *, "Powers of 2:", shift, ishftc(k,shift)
end do
```

then SIZE is assumed to equal to the value of BIT_SIZE(I), and displays

```
Powers of 2: 0 1
Powers of 2: 1 2
Powers of 2: 2 4
Powers of 2: 3 8
Powers of 2: 4 16
Powers of 2: 5 32
Powers of 2: 6 64
Powers of 2: 7 128
```

If SIZE is less than BIT_SIZE(I), then shifting takes place only within a "window" of the SIZE's right-most digits. This is one way to isolate a bit field within an integer—for instance, a field having a particular significance within a network packet header. Figure 10-2 illustrates the results of shifting the whole integer, and just the three right-most bits. Of course, SHIFT must be less than or equal to SIZE for this windowing to make any sense.

Boolean Operations

Other fundamental bit functions perform logical conjunctions and bit toggling. IAND, IEOR, and IOR apply AND, exclusive OR, and inclusive OR operations on pairs of variables or arrays:

```
print *, " "
print *, "Logical AND and exclusive/inclusive OR ..."
```

```
        print 200, "AND", i, i, j, j, iand(i,j), iand(i,j)
        print 200, "EOR", i, i, j, j, ieor(i,j), ieor(i,j)
        print 200, "IOR", i, i, j, j,  ior(i,j),  ior(i,j)
200     format ( 1H , a3, 3 ( 1x, i3, 1x, b16.16 ) )
```

and the following display results.

```
Logical AND and exclusive/inclusive OR ...
AND 456 0000000111001000 789 0000001100010101 256 0000000100000000
EOR 456 0000000111001000 789 0000001100010101 733 0000001011011101
IOR 456 0000000111001000 789 0000001100010101 989 0000001111011101
```

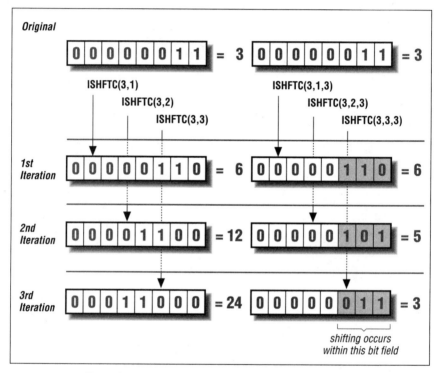

Figure 10-2: Effects of ISHFTC intrinsic

NOT "toggles" each bit in an INTEGER variable or array by performing a logical complement,

```
        print *, " "
        write ( 6,300,advance='NO' ) i
300     format ( 1H , "Flipping bits ", i5, ' ' )
        call binary ( i )
        print *, " "
        write ( 6,300,advance='NO' ) not(i)
        call binary ( not(i) )
        print *, " "
```

which yields the following output:

```
Flipping bits   456 ( 00000000 00000000 00000001 11001000 )
Flipping bits  -457 ( 11111111 11111111 11111110 00110111 )
```

Extracting Bit Fields

Many situations that require bit manipulation subdivide an integer into several fields. For instance, an address might occupy the right-most nine bits of a 32-bit integer; a 3-bit code might be located in bits 9, 10, and 11 (see Figure 10-3). Isolating fields, and moving them to another integer, are important operations that the specialized IBITS and MVBITS functions make easier.

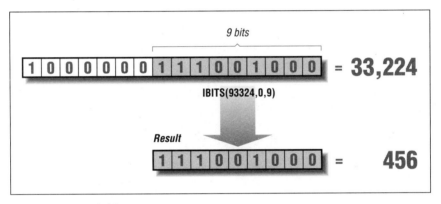

Figure 10-3: Bit fields

IBITS extracts certain bits from an integer value and returns the result as an integer. In the following code fragment, 32K is extracted from an integer

```
k      = 33224
pos    = 0
length = 9
print *, "isolate the rightmost nine bits from", k,
-          "yielding", ibits(k,pos,length)
```

yielding this result;

```
isolate the rightmost nine bits from 33224 yielding 456
```

Arguments for the IBITS intrinsic are tricky. IBITS(33224,0,9) extracts the value of the nine right-most bits of 33224—bits zero through eight—and returns them right-justified yielding a result of 456. IBITS(14,1,3) returns the value seven, which is the value in the three bits starting at bit one. In general, IBITS(K,POS,LENGTH) returns the value of LENGTH right-justified bits: the bit in position POS and the next LENGTH-1 bits to its left.

The subroutine MVBITS copies a sequence of bits from one INTEGER variable or array to another.

```
          from    = i
          frompos = 4
          length  = 3
          to      = j
          topos   = 4
          call mvbits ( from, frompos, length, to, topos )
          print *, " "
          write ( 6,400) length, frompos,
     —                   from,   from,    topos,
     —                   j, j,
     —                   to, to
400   format ( 1H , 'Moving ', i2.2, ' bits',
     —                ' from position ', i2.2
     —        / 1H , 'of ', i3, ' (', b16.16, ')',
     —                ' to position ', i2.2
     —        / 1H , 'in ', i3, ' (', b16.16, ')'
     —        / 1H , 'is ', i3, ' (', b16.16, ')' )
          print *, " "
          end program bits
```

It takes LENGTH bits out of FROM starting at position FROMPOS, and inserts them in TO starting at position TOPOS. In the example just shown, the three bits "100" in positions six, five, and four, respectively, are extracted from the number 456 and inserted into the number 789, thereby changing the target value from 789 to 837 (see Figure 10-4).

```
Moving 03 bits from position 04
of 456 (0000000111001000) to position 04
in 789 (0000001100010101)
is 837 (0000001101000101)
```

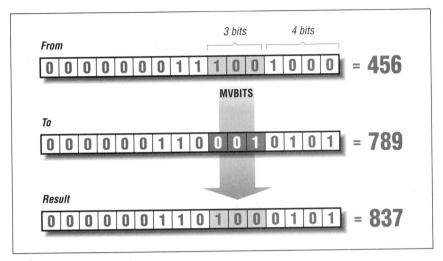

Figure 10-4: MVBITS subroutine

11

Intrinsic Functions

As examples in preceding chapters have shown, intrinsic functions provide a large part of the access to new Fortran 90 features. To some extent, the benefits arise simply from providing array functions that are likely to be faster and easier to maintain than user written alternatives (i.e., TRANSPOSE, SUM, COUNT, etc.).

But some heavily-used functions in this book evince an entirely new role for intrinsics, where they query for attributes of the processor or user data. Thus, where earlier programs would employ ad hoc methods to maintain and communicate information about arrays, Fortran 90 programs can use the new intrinsics in a standardized and portable way to retrieve such information.

Fortran 90 provides more intrinsic functions than Fortran 77. Many intrinsics defined in Fortran 90 are familiar and have changed little from their Fortran 77 incarnation. But nearly half are new. A census of all 160 Fortran 90 intrinsics shows:

30   Are familiar Fortran 77 generic functions

47   Are familiar specific names for Fortran 77 generic functions

8   Are familiar Fortran 77 functions with one new option

75   Are genuinely new Fortran 90 intrinsics

This chapter provides details about each new intrinsic that may not have been appropriate for earlier chapters. A comprehensive treatment of each new Fortran 90 function can be found here, with guidelines for using the rarer optional arguments and subtler effects. But the first order of business is to explain exactly what has remained the same in the language, and where things have changed since Fortran 77.

Familiar Fortran 77 Intrinsic Functions

First, a number of intrinsic functions are identical in Fortran 77 and Fortran 90. Table 11-1 lists these functions.

Table 11-1: Intrinsics Identical in Fortran 77 and Fortran 90 (Count=30)

Name	Description
ABS	Absolute value: real
ACOS	Arccosine: real
AIMAG	Imaginary part of complex
ASIN	Arcsine: real
ATAN	Arctangent: real
ATAN2	Arctangent: quotient of reals
CONJG	Conjugate of complex number
COS	Cosine: real
COSH	Hyperbolic cosine: real
DBLE	Type conversion: miscellaneous/double
DIM	Positive difference: real
DPROD	Double precision product
EXP	Exponential: real
ICHAR	Type conversion: character/integer
LEN	Length of character entity
LGE	Lexically greater than or equal
LGT	Lexically greater than
LLE	Lexically less than or equal
LLT	Lexically less than
LOG	Natural logarithm: real
LOG10	Common logarithm: real
MAX	Choosing largest value
MIN	Choosing smallest value
MOD	Remaining: integer
SIGN	Transfer of sign: real
SIN	Sine: real
SINH	Hyperbolic sine: real

Table 11-1: Intrinsics Identical in Fortran 77 and Fortran 90 (Count=30) (Continued)

Name	Description
SQRT	Square root: real
TAN	Tangent: real
TANH	Hyperbolic tangent: real

What is new is that nearly all of these functions accept array valued arguments. So, if A and B were arrays, then A = SIN (B) accepts an array argument and returns an array valued result. The lone exception is the LEN intrinsic: it takes a character scalar or character array argument but always returns an integer scalar.

Second, Fortran 77 and Fortran 90 define type specific names for certain generic functions. For example, CABS, DABS, and IABS are data type specific names—COMPLEX, DOUBLE PRECISION, and INTEGER—for the generic absolute value routine, ABS. Generic functions have long been a convenience in Fortran. They permit a single function call to accept various type arguments (i.e., ABS works with all numeric data types). But twenty-five generic intrinsic functions have counterparts with specific types. As a group, these functions are the same in Fortran 90 as they were in Fortran 77. Table 11-2 lists the intrinsics in the specific/generic name category.

Table 11-2: Specific Names for Generic Intrinsic Functions (Count=47)

Generic	Integer	Real	Double Precision	Complex
ABS	IABS		DABS	CABS
ACOS			DACOS	
AINT			DINT	
ANINT			DNINT	
ASIN			DASIN	
ATAN			DATAN	
ATAN2			DATAN2	
COS			DCOS	CCOS
COSH			DCOSH	
DIM	IDIM		DDIM	
EXP			DEXP	CEXP
INT		IFIX	IDINT	
LOG		ALOG	DDLOG	CLOG
LOG10		ALOG10	DLOG10	
MAX [1]	(A)MAX0	(A)MAX1	DMAX1	

Table 11-2: Specific Names for Generic Intrinsic Functions (Count=47) (Continued)

Generic	Integer	Real	Double Precision	Complex
MIN [1]	(A)MIN0	(A)MIN1	DMIN1	
MOD		AMOD	DMOD	
NINT			IDNINT	
REAL	FLOAT		SNGL	
SIGN	ISIGN		DSIGN	
SIN			DSIN	CSIN
SINH			DSINH	
SQRT			DSQRT	CSQRT
TAN			DTAN	
TANH			DTANH	

[1] Entries for integer and real specific counterparts to MAX and MIN refer to two intrinsics. (A)MAX0 is a compact way to record both the AMAX0 and the MAX0 specific intrinsic (i.e., a real function and an integer function returning the maximum value of a list of integers, respectively).

All of these functions accept array valued arguments and, when invoked in such a manner, return an array.

Third, a few intrinsics have been outfitted with one new argument in Fortran 90. Table 11-3 lists the intrinsics in this category.

Table 11-3: Intrinsics With New Argument in Fortran 90 (Count=8)

Name	New Argument	Description
AINT	KIND	Truncation: real
ANINT	KIND	Nearest whole number: real
CHAR	KIND	Type conversion: integer/character
CMPLX	KIND	Type conversion: miscellaneous/complex
INDEX	BACK	Index character substring (BACK)
INT	KIND	Type conversion: integer/integer
NINT	KIND	Nearest integer: real
REAL	KIND	Type conversion: real/real

All of these functions accept array valued arguments and, when invoked in such a manner, return an array. The KIND argument identifies the result as a variant of a basic data type. For example, many implementations of Fortran 77 allow variants of the INTEGER type such as INTEGER*1 and INTEGER*2, to specify 8- and 16-bit integers. respectively. These "kinds" are used in this Fortran 90 code fragment

```
integer, parameter :: bit_08 = selected_int_kind ( 2 )
integer, parameter :: bit_16 = selected_int_kind ( 4 )
```

```
integer ( bit_08 ) :: i = 0
integer ( bit_16 ) :: j = 0
x = 126.0
y = 32766.0
i = int ( x, KIND=1 )
j = int ( y, KIND=2 )
print *, i, j
x = x + 10.0
y = y + 10.0
i = int ( x, KIND=1 )
j = int ( y, KIND=2 )
print *, i, j
```

in which different bit lengths for integers are distinguished. The first PRINT statement would show that I and J are 126 and 32766, respectively. After overflow, the second PRINT statement shows its values as -120 and -32760. Chapter 9, *Numeric Models* discusses character and numeric KINDs.

Character strings and substrings are the province of the last intrinsic in this group, INDEX. In Fortran 77, it takes two arguments—the string and the substring—and returns the starting position of the substring within the string. So, INDEX ('MISSISSIPPI', 'X') is zero to signify that the letter X does not appear in the state name, but INDEX ('MISSISSIPPI', 'ISS') is 2 to mark the first occurrence of that substring. Fortran 90 adds a third optional argument, BACK, which can reverse the starting point and direction of the search. So, INDEX ('MISSISSIPPI', 'ISS', BACK=.FALSE.) is still two because the search is from left-to-right, but INDEX ('MISSISSIPPI', 'ISS', BACK=.TRUE.) is five because the search is from right-to-left and the I in the second "ISS" sequence begins in the fifth position.

The program FILENAME is a practical example of this new functionality for the INDEX intrinsic. Given a fully qualified pathname,

```
      program filename
      character* 1 :: delimit = '>'
      character*64 :: file
      integer      :: finish
      character*64 :: path
      integer      :: start
      print *, "Enter pathname: " )
      read ( 5,100 ) path
100   format ( a )
      print *, "PATH ", path
      start = index    ( path, delimit, BACK = .TRUE. )
      finish = len_trim ( path )
```

```
file(1:finish-start) = path(start+1:finish)
print *, "FILE ", file
end program filename
```

the program extracts the terminal component: the filename.

```
Enter pathname:
```
system>directory>subdirectory>MyFile
```
PATH system>directory>subdirectory>MyFile
FILE MyFile
```

All eight of the intrinsic functions in this category have changed slightly from their Fortran 77 implementations for a reason: to align with other, related features and functions within Fortran 90. For example, Fortran 90 introduces a standard-conforming way of identifying variants of a data type (i.e., the SELECTED_INT_KIND of a previous example), so it only makes sense to make the basic type conversion intrinsics sensitive to this feature. Fortran 90 introduces two new character search functions—SCAN a string for a character in a set and VERIFY the set of characters in a string—which are effective only if they search both from left-to-right and from right-to-left (i.e., BACK=.TRUE.). So it is reasonable to extend the third string search function, INDEX, to permit bidirectional searches.

New Fortran 90 Intrinsic Functions

Seventy-five intrinsic functions are new in Fortran 90. They range from the trivial ADJUSTL and ADJUSTR string alignment functions, through the macro-level SUM summation function, to system subroutines that retrieve a time stamp (i.e., DATE_AND_TIME and SYSTEM_CLOCK). Most of these new intrinsic functions take array arguments or return same.

Nearly all new intrinsics are functions, with a few scattered subroutines. Some incorporate the new optional argument syntax. Table 11-4 lists all of the new intrinsics, their calling sequence with underlined optional argments, the function type, a page reference where they are used in some example program, and a concise summary of their functionality.

Table 11-4: Concise Summary of New Fortran 90 Intrinsics (Count=75)

NAME (positional, OPTIONAL arguments)	Type	Page	Description
ACHAR (I)	Character	277	Returns character in I-th position in ASCII collating sequence. It is the ASCII counterpart of CHAR, which works with the host processor's collating sequence.
ADJUSTL (STRING)	Character	277	Returns STRING left-adjusted. Leading blanks are removed and trailing blanks are inserted.
ADJUSTR (STRING)	Character	277	Returns STRING right-adjusted. Trailing blanks are removed and leading blanks are inserted.
ALL (MASK, DIM)	Logical	268	Returns true if all values pass MASK along dimension DIM.
ALLOCATED (ARRAY)	Logical	139, 292	Returns true if ARRAY is allocated. ARRAY may be of any data type but must be an allocatable array.
ANY (MASK, DIM)	Logical	268	Returns true if one or more values pass MASK along dimension DIM.
ASSOCIATED (POINTER, TARGET)	Logical	143, 292	Returns true if POINTER is associated with any target. Optionally, returns true if POINTER is associated with a specific, named TARGET. POINTER may be of any data type.
BIT_SIZE (I)	Integer	235	Returns number of bits defined for integer I.
BTEST (I, POS)	Logical	235	Returns true if bit is one at position POS in integer I.
CEILING (R)	Integer	284	Returns smallest integer greater than or equal to real R.
COUNT (MASK, DIM)	Integer	268	Returns the number of values passing MASK along dimension DIM.
CSHIFT (ARRAY, SHIFT, DIM)	Any	32, 272	Performs a circular shift of ARRAY along dimension DIM, where the direction is left if SHIFT is positive or right if SHIFT is negative. Elements shifted off one end are filled in on the other. Result is the same type as ARRAY which may be of any data type.

Table 11-4: Concise Summary of New Fortran 90 Intrinsics (Count=75)
(Continued)

NAME (positional, OPTIONAL arguments)	Type	Page	Description
DATE_AND_ TIME (**DATE, TIME, ZONE, VALUES**)		286	Subroutine returns information from system clock. **DATE** is an eight character date in the form CCYYMMDD (CC is the century like 19, 20, 21, etc.). **TIME** is a ten character time in the form HHMMSS.SSS. **ZONE** is a five character time in the form +HHMM or -HHMM to designate difference between local time and UTC (i.e., Greenwich Mean Time). **VALUES** is an eight element integer array containing year, month, day, difference between local time and UTC in minutes, hour in 24-hour clock notation (i.e., "military time"), minute, second, and milliseconds.
DIGITS (X)	Integer, Real	224, 225	Returns number of significant digits in numeric model for X, where X is either an integer or a real.
DOT_PRODUCT (VECTOR_A, VECTOR_B)	Numeric	273	Performs a dot product of one-dimensional arrays VECTOR_A and VECTOR_B. Result is the same type as both of its numeric arguments.
EOSHIFT (ARRAY, SHIFT, **BOUNDARY, DIM**)	Any	35, 272	Performs end-off shift of ARRAY along dimension **DIM**, where the direction is left if SHIFT is positive or right if SHIFT is negative. Elements shifted off one end are filled in by **BOUNDARY** values. If not present, **BOUNDARY** is assumed to be zero for numeric ARRAYs, .FALSE. for logical ARRAYs, and blanks for character ARRAYs. Result is the same type and kind as ARRAY which may be of any data type.
EPSILON (R)	Real	228	Difference between 1 and the next nearest representable number among reals of the same type and kind as R.
EXPONENT (R)	Integer	228	Returns exponent part of real R.
FLOOR (R)	Integer	284	Returns largest integer less than or equal to real R.

Table 11-4: Concise Summary of New Fortran 90 Intrinsics (Count=75) (Continued)

NAME (positional, OPTIONAL arguments)	Type	Page	Description
FRACTION (R)	Real	228	Returns fractional part of real R.
HUGE (X)	Integer, Real	224, 228	Returns largest number that can be represented by a number of the same type and kind as X, which can be an integer or a real. Result is the same type and kind as X.
IACHAR (C)	Integer	277	Returns position of character C in ASCII collating sequence character. It is the ASCII counterpart of ICHAR which works with the host processor's collating sequence.
IAND (I, J)	Integer bit	239	Returns the logical AND of integers I and J.
IBCLR (I, POS)	Integer bit	237	Returns the value of I with the bit in position POS set to zero. Inverse of IBSET.
IBITS (I, POS, LEN)	Integer bit	241	Returns LEN bits from I ending at position POS. That is, it returns LEN-1 bits to the left of position POS and the bit in position POS itself.
IBSET (I, POS)	Integer bit	236	Returns the value of I with the bit in position POS set to one. Inverse of IBCLR.
IEOR (I, J)	Integer bit	239	Returns the exclusive OR of I and J.
IOR (I, J)	Integer bit	239	Returns the inclusive OR of I and J.
ISHFT (I, SHIFT)	Integer bit	237	Returns I shifted by SHIFT bits, where the direction is right for a positive SHIFT and left for negative SHIFT. Any bits shifted off the end are replaced by zeros.
ISHFTC (I, SHIFT, SIZE)	Integer bit	239	Returns the right-most SIZE bits from I shifted by SHIFT bits, where the direction is right for a positive SHIFT and left for a negative SHIFT. Any bits shifted off the end wrap around to the other side.
KIND (V)	Integer	215	Returns the kind type parameter corresponding to variables of the same type and kind as V. V may be of any data type.

*Table 11-4: Concise Summary of New Fortran 90 Intrinsics (Count=75)
(Continued)*

NAME (positional, OPTIONAL arguments)	Type	Page	Description
LBOUND (ARRAY, **DIM**)	Integer	263	Integer function returns the lower bound(s) declared for ARRAY along dimension **DIM**. ARRAY may be of any data type.
LEN_TRIM (STRING)	Integer	277	Returns the number of characters in STRING excluding any trailing blanks.
LOGICAL (L, **KIND**)	Logical	281	Converts logical L to a logical of logical type KIND.
MATMUL (MATRIX_A, MATRIX_B)	Numeric, Logical	57, 273	Returns a matrix representing the matrix multiplication of MATRIX_A by MATRIX_B. Arguments must have one or two dimensions. Arguments can be of any numeric or logical data type but must be conformable: last dimension of MATRIX_A must be the same as the first dimension of MATRIX_B. Result is the same type and kind as its two arguments.
MAXEXPONENT (R)	Integer	225	Returns the largest exponent for real numbers of the same type and kind as R.
MAXLOC (ARRAY, **MASK**)	Integer	49, 274	Returns a vector holding the location (i.e., subscripts) of the largest integer or real ARRAY element that passes the **MASK**. Location is always reported with reference to a lower bound of one(s) for ARRAY regardless of the actual lower bounds with which ARRAY was declared.
MAXVAL (ARRAY, **DIM**, **MASK**)	Integer, Real	49, 274	Returns the value of the largest element of integer or real ARRAY along dimension **DIM** that passes the MASK. Result is the same type and kind as ARRAY.
MERGE (TSOURCE, FSOURCE, MASK)	Any	268	Returns values from the TSOURCE array where MASK is true and values from the FSOURCE array where MASK is false. TSOURCE and FSOURCE must be the same data type and kind. Result is the same type and kind as TSOURCE.

Table 11-4: Concise Summary of New Fortran 90 Intrinsics (Count=75) (Continued)

NAME (positional, OPTIONAL arguments)	Type	Page	Description
MINEXPONENT (R)	Integer	225	Returns the smallest exponent for real numbers of the same type and kind as R.
MINLOC (ARRAY, **MASK**)	Integer	49, 274	Returns a vector holding the location (i.e., subscripts) of the smallest integer or real ARRAY element that passes the **MASK**. Location is always reported with reference to a lower bound of one(s) for ARRAY regardless of the actual lower bounds with which ARRAY was declared.
MINVAL (ARRAY, **DIM**, **MASK**)	Integer, Real	49, 274	Returns the value of the smallest element of integer or real ARRAY along dimension **DIM** that passes the MASK. Result is the same type and kind as ARRAY.
MODULO (X, Y)	Integer, Real	285	Returns the value, rounded towards negative infinity, of X modulo Y when Y is not zero. X and Y must be the same type and kind and may be integers or reals. Result is the same type and kind as X.
MVBITS (FROM, FROMPOS, LEN, TO, TOPOS)		242	Subroutine moves LEN bits out of FROM ending at position FROMPOS and into TO ending at position TOPOS. All arguments are integers.
NEAREST (R, S)	Real	222	Returns the nearest representable number to R in the direction of the infinity with the same sign as S. Both R and S must be real.
NOT (I)	Integer	240	Returns the logical complement of integer I.
PACK (ARRAY, MASK, **VECTOR**)	Any	270	Returns a one-dimensional representation of all elements of ARRAY that pass the MASK. The result has as many elements in it as elements of ARRAY that pass the MASK. If **VECTOR** is present, it must have at least as many elements as elements of ARRAY that pass the MASK.

Table 11-4: Concise Summary of New Fortran 90 Intrinsics (Count=75) (Continued)

NAME (positional, OPTIONAL arguments)	Type	Page	Description
PACK (ARRAY, MASK, **VECTOR**) (Continued)			If **VECTOR** is present and has more elements than the number of elements of ARRAY that pass the MASK, then the result of this function is augmented by values from **VECTOR**. Result is the same type and kind as ARRAY which may be of any type.
PRECISION (Z)	Integer	228	Returns the decimal precision for real or complex numbers of the same type and kind as Z.
PRESENT (A)	Logical	101	Returns true if optional argument A is present in the subprogram calling sequence and otherwise returns false.
PRODUCT (ARRAY, **DIM**, **MASK**)	Numeric	273	Returns the product of all elements of ARRAY along dimension **DIM** that passes the **MASK**. Result is the same type and kind as ARRAY which can be integer, real, or complex.
RADIX (X)	Integer	224, 225	Returns the radix of the numeric model for integer or real numbers of the same type and kind as X.
RANDOM_ NUMBER (HARVEST)		290	Subroutine sets argument to pseudorandom number from the uniform distribution over the range $0 \leq x < 1$.
RANDOM_SEED (**SIZE**, **PUT**, **GET**)		289	Subroutine accepts just one of the three optional arguments at a time. **SIZE** sets the number of parameters in the seed; **PUT** sets the seed to an input vector; **GET** places the current seed in the output vector.
RANGE (X)	Integer	224, 225	Returns the decimal exponent range for integer or real numbers of the same type and kind as X.
REPEAT (STRING, I)	Character	281	Returns I concatenated copies of STRING.

Table 11-4: Concise Summary of New Fortran 90 Intrinsics (Count=75) (Continued)

NAME (positional, OPTIONAL arguments)	Type	Page	Description
RESHAPE (SOURCE, SHAPE, **PAD**, **ORDER**)	Any	30, 263	Returns an array constructed out of the elements of array SOURCE in an array shape specified by positive integers in the vector SHAPE. Optionally, the resulting array may be padded by values from the array **PAD**. The order in which the dimensions are traversed can be changed with the vector **ORDER**. Result is the same type and kind as ARRAY which may be of any data type.
RRSPACING (R)	Real	228	Real function returns the reciprocal of the relative spacing for real numbers with the same exponent as R, a real number.
SCALE (R, I)	Real	228	Returns the value of R multiplied by the base of the real numeric model raised to the I-th power.
SCAN (STRING, SET, **BACK**)	Integer	279	Returns the left-most position in STRING of any character in SET if **BACK** is absent or present and false. If **BACK** is present and true, it returns the right-most position in STRING of any character in SET. It returns zero if no character in SET can be found in STRING.
SELECTED_INT_ KIND (I)	Integer	216	Returns the kind type parameter for integers in the range $-10^i < n < 10^i$.
SELECTED_ REAL_KIND (I, J)	Integer	217	Returns the kind type parameter for any real in the range with at least I digits of precision and a decimal exponent range of at least J. PRECISION and RANGE report values for I and J for any given real.
SET_EXPONENT (R, I)	Real	229	Returns the number with the same fractional part as the real R, but with an exponent of the integer I.
SHAPE (SOURCE)	Integer	41, 263	Returns a vector in which each element indicates the number of elements in the corresponding dimension of SOURCE. ARRAY may be of any data type.

Table 11-4: Concise Summary of New Fortran 90 Intrinsics (Count=75) (Continued)

NAME (positional, OPTIONAL arguments)	Type	Page	Description
SIZE (ARRAY, DIM)	Integer	41, 263	Returns the number of elements in ARRAY along dimension **DIM**. ARRAY may be of any data type.
SPACING (R)	Real	228	Returns the absolute spacing between real numbers having the same exponent as R, a real number.
SPREAD (SOURCE, DIM, I)	Any	264	Returns an array of the same type as SOURCE, but with one more rank than the rank of SOURCE. The new dimension is filled with I copies of whatever is in dimension DIM of SOURCE. SOURCE may be of any data type.
SUM (ARRAY, **DIM, MASK**)	Numeric	273	Returns the sum of all elements of ARRAY along dimension **DIM** that pass the **MASK**. ARRAY must be numeric. The result is the same type and kind as ARRAY.
SYSTEM_CLOCK (**COUNT, COUNT_RATE, COUNT_MAX**)		287	Subroutine returns information about the clock on the host system. Information includes the current **COUNT**, the **COUNT_RATE** in counts per second, and the **COUNT_MAX** which is the highest number of counts that can be obtained before the count rolls over to zero and continues. All arguments are integers.
TINY (R)	Real	228	Returns smallest number that can be represented by a real of the same type and kind as R.
TRANSFER (SOURCE, MOLD, **SIZE**)	Any	206, 281	Returns a result with the same physical representation of SOURCE interpreted according to the data type represented by MOLD. If **SIZE** is present, then TRANSFER returns a vector of the length specified by **SIZE**. SOURCE and MOLD may be of any data type. Result is the same type and kind as MOLD.
TRANSPOSE (MATRIX)	Any	52, 275	Returns the transpose of a two-dimensional array MATRIX. MATRIX may be of any data type. Result is the same type and kind as MATRIX.

Table 11-4: Concise Summary of New Fortran 90 Intrinsics (Count=75) (Continued)

NAME (positional, OPTIONAL arguments)	Type	Page	Description
TRIM (STRING)	Character	277	Returns STRING with all trailing blanks removed.
UBOUND (ARRAY, DIM)	Integer	263	Returns the upper bound(s) declared for ARRAY along dimension DIM. ARRAY may be of any data type.
UNPACK (VECTOR, MASK, FIELD)	Any	269	Function constructs an array from the vector VECTOR. It takes as many elements from VECTOR as pass the MASK and fills in any remaining elements from FIELD. VECTOR and MASK may be of any data type, but must be the same data type. Result is the same type and kind as VECTOR and the same shape as MASK.
VERIFY (STRING, SET, BACK)	Integer	278	Returns the left-most position in STRING of any character not in SET, if **BACK** is absent or false. If **BACK** is true, it returns the right-most position in STRING of any character not in SET. It returns zero if each character in STRING is in SET.

Groups of Related Functions

The new Fortran 90 intrinsics can be classified into six groups. Each group addresses one broad application (i.e., arrays, bit manipulation, character handling, etc.). Within some groups, there may be distinct topics (i.e., dimensionality as a topic in the array group). This chapter will present most of these groups (numeric model and bit functions were discussed in the two preceding chapters). Table 11-5 lists the groups.

Table 11-5: Groups of New Fortran 90 Intrinsics

Group/Topic	Intrinsic	Description
Array Functions		
Array dimensions	LBOUND	Vector of lower bounds of array
	UBOUND	Vector of upper bounds of array

Table 11-5: Groups of New Fortran 90 Intrinsics (Continued)

Group/Topic	Intrinsic	Description
	SIZE	Number of elements in an array
	SHAPE	Vector of elements per dimension in array
Extending arrays	RESHAPE	Array cast into different dimensions
	SPREAD	Replicate parts of array
Combining arrays	MERGE	Combination of two arrays using a mask
Finding values	ALL	Determine if all elements pass mask
	ANY	Determine if any elements pass mask
	COUNT	Number of elements passing mask
Packaging arrays	PACK	Pack array into vector
	UNPACK	Unpack vector into array
Shifty functions	CSHIFT	Circular shift of elements
	EOSHIFT	End-off shift of elements
Array mathematics	DOT_PRODUCT	Dot product of two vectors
	MATMUL	Matrix multiplication
	PRODUCT	Product of all elements
	SUM	Sum of elements passing mask
Array extrema	MAXLOC	Location in array of maximum value
	MAXVAL	Value of largest element in array
	MINLOC	Location in array of minimum value
	MINVAL	Value of smallest element in array
Array transposition	TRANSPOSE	Transpose of a matrix

Bit Routines (see Chapter 10, *Bit Functions*)

	BIT_SIZE	Number of bits in integer
	BTEST	Test whether bit is on or off
	IAND	Logical and
	IBCLR	Clear bit

Table 11-5: Groups of New Fortran 90 Intrinsics (Continued)

Group/Topic	Intrinsic	Description
	IBITS	Extract bit
	IBSET	Set bit
	IEOR	Exclusive or
	IOR	Inclusive or
	ISHFT	Logical bit shift
	ISHFTC	Circular bit shift
	MVBITS	Combination of bits from target to source
	NOT	Logical complement
Character Functions		
Character	ACHAR	Character in position in ASCII code
	ADJUSTL	Left-adjust string
	ADJUSTR	Right-adjust string
	IACHAR	Position of character in ASCII code
	LEN_TRIM	Count characters less trailing blanks
	REPEAT	Repeat multiple copies of string
	SCAN	Scan string for characters
	TRIM	Trim trailing blanks
	VERIFY	Verify string contains characters
Conversions		
Conversions	LOGICAL	Convert between different logical types
	TRANSFER	Convert data physical representations
Numeric Model Functions (See Chapter 9)		
Integer model	SELECTED_INT_KIND	Select integer KIND
Both models	DIGITS	Significant digits
	HUGE	Largest value
	KIND	Code for numeric representation
	RADIX	Radix of numerical model
	RANGE	Decimal exponent range

Table 11-5: Groups of New Fortran 90 Intrinsics (Continued)

Group/Topic	Intrinsic	Description
Real model	EPSILON	Number negligible compared to one
	EXPONENT	Exponent part of real number
	FRACTION	Fraction part of real number
	MAXEXPONENT	Largest exponent
	MINEXPONENT	Smallest exponent
	NEAREST	Representable number nearest to target
	PRECISION	Digits of precision
	RRSPACING	Relative real number spacing
	SCALE	Scale real number by constant
	SELECTED_REAL_KIND	Select real KIND
	SET_EXPONENT	Set exponent part
	SPACING	Absolute spacing or real model
	TINY	Smallest value
Nearest integers	CEILING	Least integer greater or equal to number
	FLOOR	Largest integer less than or equal to number
	MODULO	Modulo of integer or real

System Routines

Calendars and clocks	DATE_AND_TIME	System date and time
	SYSTEM_CLOCK	System time measures
Random numbers	RANDOM_NUMBER	Pseudo random number
	RANDOM_SEED	Initialize random number stream
Existence	ALLOCATED	Determine if array is allocated
	ASSOCIATED	Determine if pointer is associated
	PRESENT	Determine if argument is present

Array Functions

Array Dimensionality

Never before has the layout of an array been available to the programmer. Fortran 90 intrinsics report the upper and lower bounds, size, and shape of an array.

```
real,    dimension ( -1:2,-3:4 ) :: array
integer, dimension ( 2 )         :: bound_lower
integer, dimension ( 2 )         :: bound_upper
integer, dimension              :: elements
integer, dimension ( 2 )         :: form
bound_lower = lbound ( array )x
bound_upper = ubound ( array )
elements    = size   ( array )
form        = shape  ( array )
```

In the example above, BOUND_LOWER is the vector {-1, -3}, BOUND_UPPER is the vector {2, 4}, ELEMENTS is the scalar 32, and FORM is the vector {4, 8}. The SIZE intrinsic can also compute the number of elements individually in each dimension so that SIZE (ARRAY, DIM=1) is 4 and SIZE (ARRAY, DIM = 2) is 8. Note that the SHAPE intrinsic always returns an array. So, a variable established to hold the return value of SHAPE (FORM) must be a single element vector of one dimension (i.e., DIMENSION (1).

Extending Arrays

An array can be extended with the RESHAPE and SPREAD intrinsics. In its simplest form, a vector can be turned into an array, or a list can be joined to another list to add a dimension resulting in an array:

```
integer, dimension ( 3 ) :: lista = (/ (i,i=1,6,2) /)
integer, dimension ( 3 ) :: listb = (/ (i,i=2,6,2) /)
integer, dimension ( 2,3 ) :: new_array
integer, dimension ( 2,3 ) :: two_array
integer, dimension ( 6 ) :: vector = (/ (i,i=1,6,1) /)
new_array = reshape (    vector,
-                     (/ shape(new_array) /) )
two_array = reshape ( (/ lista, listb    /),
-                     (/ shape(two_array) /) )
```

Both arrays, NEW_ARRAY and TWO_ARRAY, are the same:

```
1  3  5
2  4  6
```

It is certainly convenient to initialize VECTOR with the implied DO loop, but that still adheres to the standard, column-major array element storage order for filling NEW_ARRAY. If it is useful to employ a row-major order, RESHAPE can ignore underlying storage order and traverse the array in any specified order. NEW_ARRAY can be created in row-major order through:

```
integer, dimension (  2  ) :: disposition = (/ 2,1 /)
integer, dimension ( 2,3 ) :: new_array
integer, dimension (  6  ) :: vector      = (/ (i,i=1,6,1) /)
new_array = reshape (     vector,
  -                   (/ shape(new_array) /),
  -                   ORDER=disposition    )
```

to produce:

```
1  2  3
4  5  6
```

If NEW_ARRAY had been declared as a 2-by-4 array, then the output is larger than the source. PAD is used to set the last two elements of NEW_ARRAY with signature values to indicate that they are not original:

```
integer, dimension (  2  ) :: missing = 99
integer, dimension ( 2,4 ) :: new_array
integer, dimension (  6  ) :: vector = (/ (i,i=1,6,1) /)
new_array = reshape (     vector,
  -                   (/ shape(new_array) /),
  -                   PAD=missing          )
```

which would result in these values for NEW_ARRAY:

```
1  3  5 99
2  4  6 99
```

A new array can be formed of multiple copies of an original array. The SPREAD intrinsic does this and is particularly useful in broadcasting a single set of initial values throughout an array created (i.e., ALLOCATED) at run time. In the example below, the three element vector ORIGINAL is duplicated ten times.

```
      integer, allocatable, dimension(:,:) :: copy
      integer,              dimension(3)    :: original=(/12,34,56/)
      allocate ( copy(10,3) )
      copy = spread ( original, DIM=1, NCOPIES = 10 )
      write ( 6,100 ) original
100   format ( 1H , 'ORIGINAL     ", 3i4 )
      print *, " "
      do i = 1, 10, 1
         write ( 6,200 ) i, ( copy(i,j), j = 1, 3  )
200      format ( 1H , 'COPY row ', i2.2, ': ', 3i4 )
```

```
      end do
      deallocate ( copy )
```

The array COPY results.

```
ORIGINAL        12  34  56

COPY row 01:    12  34  56
COPY row 02:    12  34  56
COPY row 03:    12  34  56
COPY row 04:    12  34  56
COPY row 05:    12  34  56
COPY row 06:    12  34  56
COPY row 07:    12  34  56
COPY row 08:    12  34  56
COPY row 09:    12  34  56
COPY row 10:    12  34  56
```

Entire arrays can be distributed. For example, in the DSPREAD program, the SPREAD intrinsic distributes a table along different dimensions of a three-dimensional array.

```
      program dspread
      integer                    :: i, j, k
      integer, dimension ( 2,3   ) :: source_2d
      integer, dimension ( 4,2,3 ) :: result_dim1_3d
      integer, dimension ( 2,4,3 ) :: result_dim2_3d
      integer, dimension ( 2,3,4 ) :: result_dim3_3d
      source_2d = reshape ( (/ 101, 102, 201, 202, 301, 302 /),
     -                      (/ 2, 3 /)                          )
      print *, " "
      print *, "SOURCE (2x3) array ..."
      do i = 1, 2, 1
          write ( *,100 ) ( source_2d(i,j), j = 1, 3 )
100       format ( 1H , 4x, 3i4 )
      end do
```

The original table is the 2-by-3 matrix called SOURCE:

```
SOURCE (2x3) array ...
    101 201 301
    102 202 302
```

The SPREAD intrinsic is used to make four copies of the original table down the first dimension of a 4-by-2-by-3 array.

```
      result_dim1_3d = spread ( source_2d, dim=1, ncopies=4 )
      print *, " "
      print *, "RESULT (4,2,3) spreading SOURCE on dimension 1"
      do k = 1, 3, 1
          write ( *,200 ) k
200       format ( / 1H , 5x, 'Plane ', i1 )
```

```
        do i = 1, 4, 1
            write ( *,300 ) ( result_dim1_3d(i,j,k), j = 1, 2, 1 )
300         format ( 1H , 4x, 2i4 )
        end do
      end do
```

SPREAD takes the first column of SOURCE and copies it into the first plane of the 3-D array as rows, moves the second column into the second plane, etc. The result is as follows:

```
RESULT (4,2,3) spreading SOURCE on dimension 1

    Plane 1
    101 102
    101 102
    101 102
    101 102

    Plane 2
    201 202
    201 202
    201 202
    201 202

    Plane 3
    301 302
    301 302
    301 302
    301 302
```

Then, SPREAD distributes the table along the second dimension of the array.

```
        result_dim2_3d = spread ( source_2d, dim=2, ncopies=4 )
        print *, " "
        print *, "RESULT (2,4,3) spreading SOURCE on dimension 2"
        do k = 1, 3, 1
            write ( *,200 ) k
            do i = 1, 2, 1
                write ( *,400 ) ( result_dim2_3d(i,j,k), j = 1, 4, 1 )
400             format ( 1H , 4x, 4i4 )
            end do
        end do
```

It takes the first column of SOURCE and copies it into the first plane of the 3-D array as columns, moves the second column into the second plane, etc. The result is as follows:

```
RESULT (2,4,3) spreading SOURCE on dimension 2

      Plane 1
      101 101 101 101
      102 102 102 102

      Plane 2
      201 201 201 201
      202 202 202 202

      Plane 3
      301 301 301 301
      302 302 302 302
```

Then, SPREAD distributes the table along the third dimension of the array.

```
      result_dim3_3d = spread ( source_2d, dim=3, ncopies=4 )
      print *, " "
      print *, "RESULT (2,3,4) spreading SOURCE on dimension 3"
      do k = 1, 4, 1
         write ( *,200 ) k
         do i = 1, 2, 1
            write ( *,500 ) ( result_dim3_3d(i,j,k), j = 1, 3, 1 )
500         format ( 1H , 4x, 3i4 )
         end do
      end do
      end program dspread
```

It takes the entire SOURCE table and copies it intact into each plane of the 3-D array. The result is as follows:

```
RESULT (2,3,4) spreading SOURCE on dimension 3

      Plane 1
      101 201 301
      102 202 302

      Plane 2
      101 201 301
      102 202 302

      Plane 3
      101 201 301
      102 202 302

      Plane 4
      101 201 301
      102 202 302
```

Combining Arrays

Arrays can be combined with the MERGE intrinsic. Given two arrays with the same shape and data type, MERGE (TSOURCE, FSOURCE, MASK) fills the array with elements of TSOURCE where MASK is true and elements of FSOURCE where MASK is false. The MASK can be a logical statement:

```
integer, dimension ( 3,3 ) :: numbers, positive
integer                    :: zero = 0
positive = merge ( numbers, zero, numbers.gt.zero )
```

or a logical array

```
real,    dimension ( 3,3 ) :: a, b, combined
logical, dimension ( 3,3 ) :: selection
combined = merge ( a, b, selection)
```

where SELECTION(I,J) is .TRUE. when it is desired to have COMBINED(I,J) equal A(I,J) and .FALSE. to have it equal B(I,J).

Finding Certain Values

Entire arrays can be examined for the existence of certain values. ALL will report whether every array value meets a certain criterion throughout the array or along a specified dimension. ANY will show if any array value meets the criterion. COUNT will enumerate the number of array values meeting the criterion. In a medical setting, if the morning body temperature for three patients for each day in a week is held in an array arranged with patients for columns and days for rows,

```
integer, parameter              :: days     = 7
integer, parameter              :: patients = 3
logical                         :: all_sick
logical                         :: any_sick
logical, dimension ( days )     :: by_day
logical, dimension ( patients ) :: by_patient
integer                         :: count_sick
real, dimension ( days, patients ) :: temperature
:
all_sick   = all   ( temperature.gt.98.6 )
any_sick   = any   ( temperature.gt.98.6 )
count_sick = count ( temperature.gt.98.6 )
:
by_day     = any   ( temperature.gt.98.6, dim=2 )
by_patient = all   ( temperature.gt.98.6, dim=1 )
```

then ALL_SICK would be .TRUE. if every patient had an elevated temperature every day. ANY_SICK would be .TRUE. if any of the patients had a fever on any day. COUNT_SICK would range from 0 to 21—zero through DAYS x PATIENTS—and counts the number of patients running fevers throughout the week.

BY_DAY is a logical vector containing DAYS elements where each element is .TRUE. if any patient ran a fever on that day and .FALSE. otherwise. BY_PATIENT is a logical vector containing PATIENT elements where each element is .TRUE. if a patient ran a fever all week, and .FALSE. otherwise. The COUNT intrinsic also can enumerate along dimensions, with a syntax identical to the ANY and ALL intrinsics.

Packaging Arrays

Many applications perform a single operation uniformly over the whole array; these are much easier to code if they can be performed linearly instead of dealing with the columns and rows of a multidimensional array. Fortran 90 provides the PACK and UNPACK intrinsics for converting between vectors and multidimensional arrays. Additionally, an array can be built from a combination of two separate arrays through the MERGE intrinsic.

PACK places some or all elements of an array into a vector, always maintaining the column-major storage order. UNPACK reverses this operation. Given the following arrays and vectors:

```
integer, dimension ( 3,4 ) :: array
logical, dimension ( 3,4 ) :: filter = .TRUE.
integer, dimension (  12 ) :: fillin
integer                    :: missing = 99
integer, dimension (  12 ) :: vector = (/ (i,i=1,12) /)
fillin = vector * 10
```

the UNPACK intrinsic:

```
array = 0
array = unpack ( vector, filter, missing )
```

populates ARRAY with the following values:

```
1  4  7 10
2  5  8 11
3  6  9 12
```

In this trivial case, where every element of the mask is true, PACK and UNPACK are equivalent to RESHAPE. Here, MISSING is optional because FILTER is .TRUE., and that ensures that every output value is filled with a value from VECTOR. If any element of FILTER had been .FALSE., then the corresponding element of ARRAY would be set to the value of MISSING.

The whole process can be reversed with the PACK intrinsic.

```
vector(1:count(filter)) = pack ( array, filter )
```

The result contains only as many values as the number of true elements in FILTER. If FILTER were replaced in the invocation of PACK with the scalar .TRUE., then the result would contain all the elements from ARRAY. In this example, there is protection against the risk that some elements of FILTER are false, which would lead to fewer than 12 values of output. The COUNT(FILTER) intrinsic returns the number of true elements in FILTER, thus ensuring that the number of elements on the left side of the assignment statement matches the number on the right side. Any higher-numbered elements of VECTOR keep their original values.

PACK and UNPACK seem simple, but with a combination of MASK and MISSING arguments they are among the most powerful intrinsics in Fortran 90. Missing values are managed with this syntax:

```
vector = 0
vector = pack ( array, filter, VECTOR=fillin )
```

when every element of FILTER is .TRUE., then the results are the same. Missing values are indicated by setting the corresponding values of FILTER to .FALSE. For example, the second column and second row of ARRAY can be bypassed.

```
vector(1:count(filter)) = pack ( array, filter )
filter(:,2) = .false.
filter(2,:) = .false.
```

Now the output is larger than the input, which is reduced to six elements of ARRAY. Those elements of ARRAY that are transferred to VECTOR are shown in Figure 11-1. These elements fill the first six elements of VECTOR, and the scalar MISSING expands to fill the rest.

```
1   3   7   9 10 12 99 99 99 99 99 99
```

The vector could have been created with a similar mask and merged with the FILLIN list using the following code:

```
vector=pack(array,filter,VECTOR=fillin)
```

which would yield the following result:

```
1 2 3 4 5 6 70 80 90 100 110 120
```

Going in the other direction:

```
filter(:,2) = .false.
filter(2,:) = .false.
vector = (/ ( i, i = 1, 12 ) /)
array = unpack ( vector, filter, missing )
```

produces ARRAY values as follows:

```
1 99  3  5
99 99 99 99
2 99  4  6
```

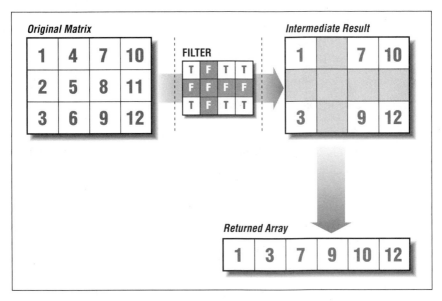

Figure 11-1: MASK in PACK intrinsic

This is kind of surprising. However, the UNPACK intrinsic extracts from VECTOR only the number of elements that it needs; if N elements of FILTER are .TRUE., then the first N elements of VECTOR are used regardless of their final location in ARRAY. UNPACK works nicely in undoing a previous PACK: whatever elements were previously extracted by PACK can be restored, after intervening calculations, into their original places in the array by UNPACK.

Productive use of PACK and UNPACK is promoted by this rule: use PACK with a mask followed by UNPACK with the same mask, or vice versa.

What was surprising about the previous UNPACK operation was that the original row and column position of values in ARRAY was changed. Rows and columns can be masked with less intuitive code that yields a more common sense result. After reinitializing FILTER and ARRAY, set ARRAY's second row and column to MISSING

```
filter = .TRUE.
array = unpack ( (/ (i,i=1,12) /), filter, missing )
array(:,2) = missing
array(2,:) = missing
```

to produce a new set of values for ARRAY.

```
1 99 7 10
99 99 99 99
3 99  9 12
```

Then, the nonmissing values from ARRAY can be packed into VECTOR

```
vector = 0
vector(1:count(array.ne.missing)) =
-     pack(array,array.ne.missing)
```

which produces the following values:

```
1 3 7 9 10 12 0 0 0 0 0 0
```

As before, non-missing values from ARRAY can be merged with the FILLIN list using the FILTER and PACK's third argument

```
filter(:,2) = .false.
filter(2,:) = .false.
vector=pack(array,filter,VECTOR=fillin)
```

to populate VECTOR as follows:

```
1 3 7 9 10 12 70 80 90 100 110 120
```

Shifty Functions

While shifts are usually known in connection with bit manipulation, Fortran 90 offers two intrinsics for shifting around the elements within an array: CSHIFT for circular shifts and EOSHIFT for end-off shifts.

The CSHIFT function moves all elements on a particular array dimension along a conveyer belt. In the simplest case, CSHIFT (VECTOR, -1) slides each element of VECTOR one position to the right and moves the last element, VECTOR(N), around to the beginning to take the place vacated by VECTOR(1).

EOSHIFT differs only in that it discards any element that has shifted beyond the limits of an array. That is, EOSHIFT (VECTOR, -1) slides each element of VECTOR one position to the right so that VECTOR(1) is now zero (or .FALSE. if LOGICAL, and blank if CHARACTER), VECTOR(2) holds the value that was originally in the first element, VECTOR(3) holds the value that was originally in the second element, and the last element of VECTOR holds the old penultimate value. EOSHIFT discards elements shifted out-of-bounds. If desired, EOSHIFT can replace discarded positions with a signal value so that if GREEK were {'alpha', 'beta', 'gamma'}, then EOSHIFT (GREEK, -1, BOUNDARY = 'missing') yields {'missing', 'alpha', 'beta'}.

Fortran 77 was not well suited to manage array index sequences that over-lapped array boundaries. When this happened, Fortran 77 programmers had to isolate the condition as a special case or craft complicated array index computations involving the MOD intrinsic. Fortran 90's CSHIFT and EOSHIFT intrinsics simplify the task.

Array Mathematics

Fortran 90 introduces four intrinsics that apply mathematical operators to an entire array: DOT_PRODUCT, MATMUL, PRODUCT, and SUM. Using vectors A = {1,4,7} and B = {2,5,3}, DOT_PRODUCT (A, B) is 43, the sum of the three products 1x2, 4x5, and 7x3.

Multiplying the two vectors requires that they be cast as two-dimensional arrays. In matrix terms, C is a column vector and D is a row vector.

```
integer, dimension ( 3,1 ) :: c
integer, dimension ( 1,3 ) :: d
integer, dimension ( 3,3 ) :: e = 0
integer, dimension ( 1,1 ) :: f = 0
data c / 1, 4, 7 /
data d / 2, 5, 3 /
e = matmul ( c, d )
f = matmul ( d, c )
```

This allows the MATMUL intrinsic to multiply C by D yielding E, a full 3-by-3 matrix, and D by C yielding F, a "1-by-1" array. MATMUL is fully aware of the conformability requirements for matrix multiplication.

C	D	E=CD	F=DC
1		2 5 3	
4	2 5 3	8 20 12	43
7		14 35 21	

PRODUCT multiplies and SUM adds together all of the elements of a vector or an array. So, PRODUCT (A) equals 28 while PRODUCT (E) equals

592,704,000. SUM (A) equals 12, while SUM (E) equals 120. Both PRODUCT and SUM can operate on specific dimensions and under masks.

```
integer                      :: big_product
integer                      :: big_sum
integer, dimension (   3 ) :: columns
integer, dimension ( 3,3 ) :: e
integer, dimension ( 3   ) :: rows
columns     = product ( e, dim=1 )
rows        = sum     ( e, dim=2 )
big_product = product ( e, MASK = e .gt. 8 )
big_sum     = sum     ( e, MASK = e .gt. 8 )
```

The four results are shown below:

Variable	Intermediate Results	Final Results
COLUMNS	{2x8x14, 5x20x35, 3x12x21}	{224, 3500, 756}
ROWS	{2+5+3, 8+20+12, 14+35+21}	{10, 40, 70}
BIG_PRODUCT	14x20x35x12x21	2,469,600
BIG_SUM	14+20+35+12+21	102

Array Extrema by Value and Location

The largest and smallest array values and their locations can be discovered with the MAXVAL, MINVAL, MAXLOC, and MINLOC functions. Using the 3-by-3 array from the section above, MAXVAL (E) is 35, MINVAL (E) is 2, MAXLOC (E) is {3, 2}, and MINLOC is {1,1}. All four intrinsics accept a mask. MAXVAL and MINVAL also accept a DIM argument, which restricts the search to a particular dimension. (For instance, MINVAL(E,DIM=1) is the vector {2, 5, 3}).

A tricky bit of the two "location" intrinsics is that they always return coordinates relative to a lower dimension bound of one. So, MAXLOC (E) will return {3, 2} if E had been declared DIMENSION (-3:-1, 128:130) or any other set of dimensional bounds that would yield a 3-by-3 matrix. This distraction can be overcome by combining the MAXLOC and LBOUND intrinsics.

```
integer, dimension(-3:-1,128:130) :: e
e = reshape ( (/ 2,8,14,5,20,35,3,12,21 /), (/ 3,3 /) )
print *,   maxloc ( e )
print *, ( maxloc ( e ) + lbound ( e ) ) - 1
```

The combination converts MAXLOC's row-and-column reference based on a unitary lower bound

3 2

to a row-and-column reference based on the range of subscripts by which the array was originally declared.

−1 129

Array Transposition

Two-dimensional arrays can have their rows and columns reversed with the TRANSPOSE intrinsic. From the example above, C is the 3-by-1 column vector {1, 4, 7} so TRANSPOSE (C) carries the same values but is cast into a 1-by-3 row vector. Again, using E from above, TRANPOSE (E) is shown below.

E   TRANSPOSE (E)
```
|  2  5  3 |        |  2  8  14 |
|  8 20 12 |        |  5 20  35 |
| 14 35 21 |        |  3 12  21 |
```

Character Functions

Many implementations of Fortran 77 have provided extensions to adjust, measure, trim, scan, and verify character strings. But as with any extension, the precise syntax and definition of return value was not standardized across computing platforms. The nine character intrinsics described in this section can replace hand crafted code or system-dependent routines, and will facilitate porting Fortran programs among different computer systems.

The SOUNDEX program uses these new character intrinsics to implement the Soundex method of coding surnames so as to collect similar sounding names into the same group. This method was originally developed in 1918 in conjunction with work by the U.S. Bureau of the Census and it is described on pages 391 through 393 of Donald E. Knuth's *The Art of Computer Programming*: Volume 3—Sorting and Searching (1973, Addison-Wesley Publishing Company, 722 pages, Reading, MA). This implementation is patterned after a C language program placed in the public domain in January, 1989, by Dean Pentcheff (now with the Department of Biology at the University of South Carolina, Columbia, SC) and used here with his permission. It begins by declaring several variables and arrays:

```
program soundex
character (len=52)                        :: alphabet
integer                                   :: ascii_la
integer                                   :: ascii_lz
integer                                   :: ascii_ua
integer                                   :: ascii_uz
integer,           dimension(0:127) :: code
character (len= 4), dimension(12)   :: key
integer,           dimension(3)     :: key_code
integer                                   :: key_count
character (len= 1)                        :: key_letter
integer                                   :: last
character (len=12), dimension(12)   :: name
integer                                   :: position
integer                                   :: trial
integer                                   :: upper_case_quantum
```

and filling an array as long as the ASCII character set with the Soundex code for that character.

```
    data code /
    -65*0,0,1,2,3,0,1,2,0,0,2,2,4,5,5,0,1,2,6,2,3,0,1,0,2,0,2,
   -  6*0,0,1,2,3,0,1,2,0,0,2,2,4,5,5,0,1,2,6,2,3,0,1,0,2,0,2,5*0/
c          a b c d e f g h i j k l m n o p q r s t u v w x y z
```

Nonalphabetic characters and vowels are coded as zero. Consonants that have similar vocalization patterns are given the same value (i.e., b, f, p, and v are coded as 1, m and n as 5, etc.). Upper- and lowercase letters have the same code.

A full Soundex value for a surname is the first letter followed by three digits corresponding to the first three unique consonants. Twelve sample names and their assigned Soundex codes follows and were taken from the Knuth text.

```
    data name / 'Euler',  'Gauss',  'Hilbert', 'Knuth',
   -            'Lloyd',  'Lukasiewicz',
   -            'Ellery', 'Ghosh',  'Heilbronn', 'Kant',
   -            'Ladd',   'Lissajous'                        /
    data key  / 'E460',   'G200',   'H416',     'K530',
   -            'L300',   'L222',
   -            'E460',   'G200',   'H416',     'K530',
   -            'L300',   'L222'                             /
```

The KEY array is included in this program to verify the results.

The encoding algorithm is not sensitive to case, so Fortran 90's ACHAR and IACHAR intrinsics are used to build a 52-element string containing every letter. ACHAR and IACHAR are identical to Fortran 77's CHAR and ICHAR, respectively. However, the former pair is bonded to the ASCII collating sequence where the latter pair works with the host processor's collating sequence. ASCII places the letters A through Z in positions 65 through 90 and letters a through z in positions 97 through 122. Consequently, a lower-case letter is always 32 positions above its upper case counterpart.

```
ascii_ua = iachar ( 'A' )
ascii_uz = iachar ( 'Z' )
j = 1
do i = ascii_ua, ascii_uz, 1
   alphabet(j:j) = achar(i)
   j = j + 1
end do
ascii_la = iachar ( 'a' )
ascii_lz = iachar ( 'z' )
do i = ascii_la, ascii_lz, 1
   alphabet(j:j) = achar(i)
   j = j + 1
end do
upper_case_quantum = ascii_lz - ascii_uz
```

For each name in the test data set, count its actual length, ignore if blank, and confirm that it begins with a letter.

```
print *, " "
data_entry: do i = 1, 12, 1
   name(i) = adjustl ( name(i) )
   length = len_trim ( name(i) )
   if ( length .eq. 0 ) then
       print *, "... name is NULL"
       cycle data_entry
   end if
```

Fortran 90 introduces two string adjustment functions, two trimming functions, and a string verification function. ADJUSTL and ADJUSTR align a character string flush left or flush right. Leading blanks are moved to trailing blanks for ADJUSTL, and just the opposite occurs in ADJUSTR.

LEN_TRIM reports the number of characters in a string, ignoring trailing blanks. Another function, TRIM, not shown in SOUNDEX, truncates a string after the last nonblank character. It is especially useful to "compress" a series of character tokens into one long string without resorting to complex runtime FORMATs. For example, Fortran's character editing FORMAT, A, will left-justify a token in an output field as long as the character variable. In output from the following program:

```
      program compress
      character*10, dimension (5) : sentence
      data sentence / 'This', 'is', 'a', 'compressed', 'sentence' /
      do i = 1, 5, 1
          write ( 6,100,advance='NO' ) sentence(i)
100       format ( 1H , a )
      end do
      print *, " "
```

SENTENCE appears disjointed:

```
This      is        a            compressed sentence
```

Using the TRIM intrinsic to excise trailing blanks

```
      do i = 1, 5, 1
          write ( 6,100,advance='NO' ) trim ( sentence(i) )
      end do
      print *, " "
      end program compress
```

lets each token follow the previous one without a break.

```
This is a compressed sentence
```

TRIM helps implement complex prompts for interactive programs and facilitates preparing output files containing variable length character strings.

Continuing with the SOUNDEX program:

```
          position = verify ( name(i)(1:1), alphabet )
          if ( position .ne. 0 ) then
              print *, "...first character not alphabetic"
              cycle data_entry
          end if
```

VERIFY confirms that all characters in the search string are in the set of reference characters. The first argument is a string to be verified, while the second is a string of valid characters. A zero return value means that the string consists purely of the valid characters. That is what the SOUNDEX program is looking for to be certain that the first character of NAME(I) really is a letter. A nonzero return value pinpoints the location of a nonconforming character, in the same manner as the Fortran 77 INDEX function. While SOUNDEX is simply interested in the presence or absence of a nonconforming character, other programs could use a nonzero return value to truncate or split the string where the nonconforming character lies.

VERIFY can also be invoked with an optional argument to specify the search direction. VERIFY (NAME(I), ALPHABET, BACK=.TRUE.) returns the position of the right-most non-alphabetic character, if there happen to be any. VERIFY (NAME(I), ALPHABET, BACK=.FALSE.) returns the position of the left-most non-alphabetic character, if any.

A Soundex code begins with the first letter of the surname in upper case. Fortran 90's SCAN function finds the first alphabetic character in a surname. In this particular program, NAME is already assured of beginning with a letter, but SCAN is used for purposes of illustration. If that character is lower case, as determined by comparing it to "a" and "z" in the ASCII collating sequence, then it is converted to upper case. The following code uses IACHAR to represent a lowercase character as a numeric value, subtracts the necessary amount, then uses ACHAR to change the value back to a character, as shown in Figure 11-2.

```
position = scan ( name(i), alphabet )
key_letter = name(i)(position:position)
if ( iachar(key_letter) .ge. ascii_la .and.
-       iachar(key_letter) .le. ascii_lz       ) then
        key_letter = achar ( iachar(key_letter) -
-                            upper_case_quantum    )
    end if
```

Initialize the numeric part of the Soundex code to all zeros and keep searching the surname until it is exhausted or all three Soundex numbers have been generated.

```
last       = code ( iachar ( key_letter ) )
key_code   = (/ 0, 0, 0 /)
key_count  = 0
encode: do while ( key_count .le. 2 )
    position = position + 1
    if ( position .gt. length ) exit encode
```

Finally, complete the Soundex code by skipping nonalphabetic characters, adjacent letters with the same code, and zero-coded characters (i.e., vowels).

```
trial = scan ( name(i)(position:position), alphabet )
if ( trial .eq. 0 ) cycle encode
trial = code ( iachar(name(i)(position:position) ) )
if ( last .eq. trial ) then
        cycle encode
else
        last = trial
    end if
```

```
           if ( last .ne. 0 ) then
               key_count           = key_count + 1
               key_code(key_count) = last
           end if
       end do encode
```

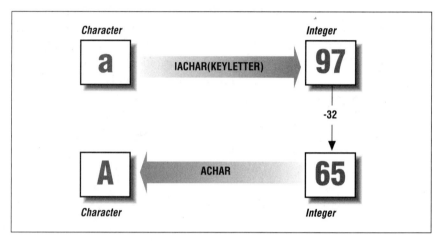

Figure 11-2: Arithmetic operation on character

Given the twelve sample surnames, display the results.

```
       write (6,200) key_letter, key_code, key(i), name(i)
200    format (   1H , 'Soundex code is ', a1, 3i1,
       -                    ' (should be ', a4, ')',
       -                    ' for ', a12                  )
       end do data_entry
       print *, " "
       end program soundex
```

Each result contains the Soundex code generated by this program, the correct Soundex code, and the surname.

```
Soundex code is E460 (should be E460) for Euler
Soundex code is G200 (should be G200) for Gauss
Soundex code is H416 (should be H416) for Hilbert
Soundex code is K530 (should be K530) for Knuth
Soundex code is L300 (should be L300) for Lloyd
Soundex code is L222 (should be L222) for Lukasiewicz
Soundex code is E460 (should be E460) for Ellery
Soundex code is G200 (should be G200) for Ghosh
Soundex code is H416 (should be H416) for Heilbronn
Soundex code is K530 (should be K530) for Kant
Soundex code is L300 (should be L300) for Ladd
Soundex code is L222 (should be L222) for Lissajous
```

A final character intrinsic makes multiple copies of a string. While the concatenation operator stitches together several tokens into one string,

```
character (len = 10) :: concatenated = ' '
character ( len =  5 ) :: token       = 'abcde'
concatenated = token // token
```

REPEAT copies a token several times into one string.

```
character (len = 10) :: repeated = ' '
character ( len =  5 ) :: token       = 'abcde'
repeated     = repeat ( token, 2 )
```

In the above example, both CONCATENATED and REPEATED are identical. For a few copies, either the concatenation operator or the REPEAT intrinsic are adequate. For many copies, the REPEAT intrinsic is certainly more compact.

Conversions

Fortran 90 introduces two new conversion intrinsics, LOGICAL and TRANSFER. LOGICAL is just like the other type conversion intrinsics listed earlier in Table 11-2 (i.e., AINT, ANINT, ..., REAL) except it is completely restricted to the LOGICAL data type. Its full syntax is:

```
logical either_or, true_false:
either_or = logical ( true_false, KIND=1 )
```

and its sole purpose is to convert between different KINDs of variables of LOGICAL data type. Since programs need only one kind of LOGICAL data type, this intrinsic might not be of much use.

On the other hand, the TRANSFER intrinsic will be used regularly. It fills the gap between the capabilities of Fortran 77's and Fortran 90's EQUIVA-LENCE statement. Recall that Fortran 77 allows variables of different data type in an EQUIVALENCE statement but Fortran 90 forbids it. The TRANSFER intrinsic covers this difference.

Its basic syntax:

```
result = transfer (source, mold)
```

sets RESULT to the value of SOURCE interpreted as the same KIND as MOLD. Just like Fortran 77 EQUIVALENCE statement, TRANSFER does not affect a mathematical conversion: it re-interprets the bit pattern of SOURCE according to the design of MOLD. If the physical representation of SOURCE is larger than RESULT, then the right-most—high address—bits are used. If the physical representation of SOURCE is smaller than RESULT, then

SOURCE's bit pattern is copied into the right-most—high address—bits of RESULT and the left-most, low address bits of RESULT are undefined. For example, in the code shown below,

```
        integer (kind=2) :: i, i0 = 0
        integer (kind=3) :: j, j0 = 0
c
c       CODE                    CASE    RESULT
        i = HUGE ( i0 )
        j = j0
        j = transfer ( i, i0 ) !   A      32767
        j = j0
        j = transfer ( i, j0 ) !   B      2147483647
        r = HUGE ( r0 )
        j = HUGE ( j0 )
        i = i0
        i = transfer ( j, i0 ) !   C.     32767
        i = i0
        i = transfer ( j, j0 ) !   D      -1
```

cases A and B demonstrate the TRANSFER of a small SOURCE into a larger RESULT and cases D and F demonstrate the TRANSFER of a large SOURCE into a smaller RESULT. Conversions between data types are viable. For example, TRANSFER (1082130432, 0.0) is 4.0 because the large integer produces the exact bit pattern that a MOLD of type REAL would interpret as 4.0. Earlier, the BIT program in Chapter 10 used the TRANSFER intrinsic to "split" a 32-bit integer into its two 16-bit components.

There is a third, optional, argument to the TRANSFER intrinsic. When the MOLD is a scalar, the SIZE optional argument determines the length of the resulting vector. Its basic syntax is

```
        result = transfer (source, mold, SIZE=length)
```

where the data in SOURCE is transferred, as a vector LENGTH elements long, to the one dimensional array RESULT.

For example, in the following TSIZE program, all four numbers stored in a small COMPLEX array are transferred into a longer REAL vector. Data types are as follows:

```
        program tsize
        complex, dimension ( 2 ) :: c       = (/ (1.1,2.2),
        _                                       (3.3,4.4)  /)
        real,    dimension ( 4 ) :: r        = 0
        integer                  :: r_length = 0
        real                     :: r_zero   = 0
        print *, " "
        print *, "Before TRANSFER ..."
```

```
print *, " C ", c
print *, " R ", r
```

and the initial values display as follows.

```
Before TRANSFER ...
C  (  1.1000000,  2.2000000) (  3.3000000,  4.4000001)
R    0.0000000E+00   0.0000000E+00   0.0000000E+00   0.0000000E+00
```

The TRANSFER intrinsic populates the R_LENGTH elements of the R vector:

```
r_length = size ( r )
r = transfer ( c, r_zero, SIZE=r_length )
print *, " "
print *, "After TRANSFER ..."
print *, " C ", c
print *, " R ", r
print *, " "
end program tsize
```

with the following results:

```
After TRANSFER ...
C  (  1.1000000,  2.2000000) (  3.3000000,  4.4000001)
R    1.1000000   2.2000000   3.3000000   4.4000001
```

Without a SIZE argument, the length of the MOLD argument determines the rank of the result. If MOLD is a scalar, then TRANSFER returns a scalar. Otherwise, MOLD must be a vector or array that has a sufficient number of elements to effect the transfer. That is, MOLD must be long enough to measure the result of the TRANSFER.

For example, in the following TARRAY program, three full-sized integers are split into six "short" integers. After declaring two KINDs of INTEGERs:

```
      program tarray
      integer, parameter          :: small =selected_int_kind(2)
      integer, parameter          :: large =selected_int_kind(4)
      integer (small), dimension (6) :: choose=0
      integer (small), dimension (6) :: narrow=0
      integer (large), dimension (3) :: wide
      wide = (/ 3106, 14414, 23052 /)
      print *, " "
      print *, "Before TRANSFER ..."
      write ( *,100 ) "NARROW", narrow
100   format ( 1H , 1x, a, 6i6 )
      write ( *,200 ) "WIDE  ", wide
200   format ( 1H , 1x, a, 3i12 )
```

the three full-sized integers are initialized and their base values displayed:

```
Before TRANSFER ...
  NARROW     0     0     0     0     0     0
  WIDE          3106      14414      23052
```

TRANSFER breaks apart the three full-size integers into six "short" integers. Using the first number as an illustration, TRANSFER splits WIDE(1) into values for NARROW(1) and NARROW(2).

WIDE(1)

Decimal	3106
Binary	000011000100010

NARROW(1) AND NARROW(2)

"Split" Binary	00001100	00100010
Decimal	12	34

All three elements of WIDE are split:

```
        narrow = transfer ( wide, choose )
        print *, " "
        print *, "After TRANSFER ..."
        write ( *,100 ) "NARROW", narrow
        write ( *,200 ) "WIDE  ", wide
        print *, " "
        end program tarray
```

and displayed as follows:

```
After TRANSFER ...
  NARROW    12    34    56    78    90    12
  WIDE          3106      14414      23052
```

Nearest Integers and Divisors

Fortran 90 provides two functions to detect the nearest whole number to a real number and a full-blown MODULO function. CEILING and FLOOR return the nearest INTEGER to a REAL number. CEILING gives the next larger INTEGER compared to the number (i.e., greater than or equal to the argument). FLOOR provides the next smallest INTEGER compared to the number (i.e., less than or equal to the argument). Some examples are:

REAL	CEILING	FLOOR
-2.5	-2	-3
-2.0	-2	-2

REAL	CEILING	FLOOR
-1.5	-1	-2
-1.0	-1	-1
-0.5	0	-1
0.5	1	0
1.0	1	1
1.5	2	1
2.0	2	2
2.5	3	2

The new MODULO intrinsic will be confused with the old MOD remainder intrinsic. Both take two REAL or two INTEGER arguments and, in many cases, will return the same value:

(A, P)	MODULO	MOD
(8, 5)	3	3
(-8, 5)	2	-3
(8, -5)	-2	3
(-8, -5)	-3 -3	

MOD is defined as [A-INT(A/P)*P] when P is not zero. MODULO is defined as [A-FLOOR(A/P)*P] when P is not zero. So, the difference is in the use of INT versus FLOOR. Consequently, when A and P are the same sign, then MOD and MODULO are interchangeable. Otherwise, when A and P are different signs, then MOD and MODULO results will differ by both magnitude and sign.

System Routines

Calendars and Clocks

A vexing problem in porting Fortran code from one platform to another is the tremendous variety of techniques to examine the clock on the target system. It is very frustrating to have all of the mathematics and most of the file handling convert right away and end up stuck on trying to find out the time of day. Fortran 90 resolves the issue with the DATE_AND_TIME and SYSTEM_CLOCK subroutines. The program WATCH begins by starting an execution timer with the SYSTEM_CLOCK subroutine and then calls a user-written routine to format the current date time which gets the current date and time from the system.

```
program watch
integer, dimension ( 3 ) :: clock
character*26            :: date_time
integer                 :: finish
character* 5            :: greenwich
real                    :: hours
character* 8            :: plain_date
character*10            :: plain_time
real                    :: seconds
integer                 :: start
call system_clock ( COUNT=start )
call timestamp2 ( date_time )
```

TIMESTAMP2 is just slightly different from its original incarnation as TIMESTAMP in Chapter 8, *File Handling*, as part of the VIDEO example program. Here it has been modified to return the day and fractions of seconds in addition to date and time.

```
subroutine timestamp2 (date_time)
character*26  date_time
character*3   days(0:6)
integer       elements(8)
character*3   months(12)
integer       m, y, w
data days   / 'Sun', 'Mon', 'Tue', 'Wed', 'Thu', 'Fri',
     -             'Sat'                                      /
data months / 'Jan', 'Feb', 'Mar', 'Apr', 'May', 'Jun',
     -             'Jul', 'Aug', 'Sep', 'Oct', 'Nov', 'Dec'   /
call date_and_time ( VALUES=elements )
invalid: if ( elements(1) .ne. -HUGE(0) ) then
    y = elements(1)
    m = elements(2)
    if ( m .lt. 3 ) then
        m = m + 12
        y = y - 1
    end if
    w = mod ( ( elements(3) +
     -                (13*m-27)/5 +
     -                y + y/4 - y/100 + y/400 ),
     -                7                              )
    century: if ( elements(1) .lt. 2000 ) then
                 elements(1) = elements(1) - 1900
             else
                 elements(1) = elements(1) - 2000
    end if century
    write ( date_time,100 ) days(w),
     -                         elements(3),
```

```
        -                        months ( elements(2) ),
        -                               elements(1),     elements(5),
        -                               elements(6),     elements(7),
        -                               elements(8)
100          format ( a3, 1x, i2.2, 1x, a3, 1x, i2.2, 1x,
        -               i2.2, ':', i2.2, ':', i2.2, '.', i3.3 )
     else invalid
          date_time = ' '
     end if invalid
     end subroutine timestamp2
```

It returns a twenty-six character string as:

```
The current date and time is Fri 20 Aug 93 09:33:35.500
```

DATE_AND_TIME can also return a compact representation of the date, time, and difference between the local time zone and "Greenwich" or UTC time

```
call date_and_time (DATE=plain_date)
call date_and_time ( TIME=plain_time )
call date_and_time ( ZONE=greenwich  )
print *, " "
print *, "The current date and time is ", date_time
print *, " "
print *, "Other formats are ", plain_date,
  -                         " and ", plain_time
print *, " "
print *, "Difference from UTC is ", greenwich
```

which display as:

```
Other formats are 19930820 and 093335.540

Difference from UTC is -0400
```

The difference of negative four results from running the program on the east coast of the United States during daylight savings time. Finally, the system clock can be queried to detect its "heart beat" and determine when it will roll over:

```
print *, " "
call system_clock ( COUNT_RATE = clock(2),
  -                  COUNT_MAX  = clock(3)  )
print *, "System clock runs at", clock(2),
  -          "ticks per second and"
hours = (( float(clock(3))+1.0 ) / float(clock(2))) / 3600.0
print *, "runs up to", hours, "hours before resetting"
```

which, on one particular system, displays:

```
System clock runs at 50 ticks per second and
runs up to  24.0000000 hours before resetting
```

Last, SYSTEM_CLOCK can be used to clock the execution timer

```
print *, " "
call system_clock ( COUNT=finish )
if ( finish .ge. start ) then
    seconds = float ( finish - start ) / float ( clock(2) )
else
    seconds = 0.0
end if
print *, "This job has taken", seconds, "seconds to execute"
print *, " "
end program watch
```

and report the wall clock time necessary to complete program WATCH.

```
This job has taken 5.9999999E-02 seconds to execute
```

Both DATE_AND_TIME and SYSTEM_CLOCK go a long way towards making a Fortran program aware of the calendar and the clock. But more precise time measures are beyond the immediate capabilities of Fortran 90. Measures not based on wall clock time such as system time, user time, input/output time, etc., remain the province of the host system.

Random Numbers

An impediment to porting simulation code is the wide range of random number generators available on systems that support Fortran. Fortran 90 introduces two subroutines, RANDOM_SEED and RANDOM_NUMBER, that standardize the selection and acquisition of random number streams.

The Fortran 90 standard does not say how random numbers should be generated, but the calling sequences of the new intrinsics reflect the common pseudo random number algorithms offered by most contemporary operating systems. These algorithms generate a fixed sequence of numbers that repeat after a large number of iterations. Invocations that start with the same seed will always produce the same sequence of iterations. Since the algorithm can be different on every system, a single seed can produce different results on different systems.

The new random number intrinsics are exercised in the program RANDOM. Random number generators begin with one or more seed values depending on the underlying generating algorithm. The RANDOM_SEED intrinsic is used to detect the number of seeds and retrieve their default values.

```
program random
integer, parameter                      :: draws = 6
real, dimension ( draws )               :: bernoulli
real, dimension ( draws )               :: erlang
real, dimension ( draws )               :: geometric
integer, dimension ( : ), allocatable   :: seed
integer                                 :: seed_size
real, dimension ( draws )               :: standard_normal
real, dimension ( draws )               :: uniform
call random_seed ( SIZE=seed_size )
print *, " "
print *, "Default seed integer array length is", seed_size
allocate ( seed(seed_size) )
seed = 0
call random_seed ( GET=seed(1:seed_size) )
print *, "and the array is {", seed, "}"
```

On one particular system, only one seed is required, so the length of the seed array is one and its default value is 714,478,811,

```
Default seed integer array length is 1
and the array is { 714478811 }
```

which, as is typical, changes with the time of day. When simulations are tested, it is essential to have an ability to draw the same series of random numbers at each and every invocation of the program. Invoking RANDOM_SEED with the PUT argument sets the seed, and the GET argument retrieves the seed.

```
seed   (1) = 16307
call random_seed ( PUT=seed(1:seed_size) )
seed = 0
call random_seed ( GET=seed(1:seed_size) )
print *, " "
print *, "Now using a seed value of", seed
```

This sequence results in the following display:

```
Now using a seed value of 16307
```

A stream of random numbers greater than or equal to zero and less than one is now available. Random numbers for various probability density distributions (PDF) can be generated from these samples from the unit rectangular uniform PDF. Algorithms that do so are concisely covered in the thin volume *Statistical Distributions* by N. A. J. Hastings and J. B. Peacock (1975, John Wiley & Sons, Inc., 130 pages, New York, NY).

Bernoulli (1,0.5) variates are 1 if the Uniform (0,1) variate is less than or equal to 0.5, and is 0 otherwise. Fortran 90's WHERE statement is a convenient way to apply the test against the Bernoulli success probability.

```
      print *, " "
      call random_number ( uniform )
      where ( uniform .le. 0.5 )
            bernoulli = 1.0
      elsewhere
            bernoulli = 0.0
      end where
      print 100, "BERNOULLI (1,0.5)", bernoulli
100   format ( a20, ': ', 6f7.3 )
```

RANDOM_NUMBER can generate several numbers in sequence during one call, a potentially large savings in execution time. It will accept a scalar or an array as its only argument. Furthermore, the argument can be tagged so that

```
      call random_number (HARVEST = uniform)
```

is an alternative to the CALL RANDOM_NUMBER (UNIFORM) line in the example program.

Erlang (0.5,6) variates are equal to -0.5 times the log of the product of six Uniform (0,1) variates. Fortran 90's PRODUCT intrinsic makes it easy to multiply together the six numbers drawn by RANDOM_NUMBER.

```
      do i = 1, draws, 1
         call random_number ( uniform )
         x = product ( uniform )
         erlang(i) = -0.5 * log ( x )
      end do
      print 100, "ERLANG (0.5,6)", erlang
```

Geometric (0.5) variates are equal to the integer next larger than the ratio of log of a Uniform (0,1) variate to log of 0.5. Since Fortran 90's CEILING and LOG function can both accept and return arrays, all six Geometric variates can be created in a single statement.

```
      call random_number ( uniform )
      geometric = ceiling ( log ( uniform ) / log ( 0.5 ) )
      print 100, "GEOMETRIC (0.5)", geometric
```

Normal (0,1)—standard normal—variates are six less than the sum of twelve Uniform (0,1) variates. Fortran 90's SUM intrinsic makes quick work of summing values of the Uniform (0,1) variates.

```
      do i = 1, draws, 1
         call random_number ( uniform )
```

```
    x = sum ( uniform )
    call random_number ( uniform )
    standard_normal(i) = ( x + sum ( uniform ) ) - 6
end do
print 100, "NORMAL (0,1)", standard_normal
```

Uniform (0,1) variates are returned directly by the RANDOM_NUMBER function.

```
call random_number ( uniform )
print 100, "UNIFORM (0,1)", uniform
```

Lastly the program DEALLOCATEs the vector containing the random number seed, and exits.

```
deallocate ( seed )
print *, " "
end program random
```

Six independent samples from each of the five PDFs are displayed in the course of executing this program.

```
BERNOULLI (1,0.5):   1.000  0.000  0.000  1.000  0.000  0.000
ERLANG    (0.5,6):   5.080  1.372  1.982  1.986  4.996  1.679
GEOMETRIC (0.5)  :   2.000  1.000  2.000  2.000  4.000  1.000
NORMAL    (0,1)  :  -0.896 -2.819  0.266  0.053  2.143 -0.802
UNIFORM   (0,1)  :   0.779  0.709  0.914  0.880  0.272  0.028
```

Note that the Fortran 90 standard does not specify the method by which random numbers are generated, is silent on the run length of random numbers before the cycle repeats, and provides no minimum standard of "randomness" for the number stream that RANDOM_NUMBER generates. All three of these issues are important to the success and veracity of simulation programs. So, although the interface to a random number generator has been standardized, the implementation of such generators remains system specific and worthy of the programmer's close scrutiny.

Existence

The very existence of program elements can be detected by ALLOCATED, ASSOCIATED, and PRESENT. ALLOCATED determines if an allocatable array is indeed allocated. ASSOCIATED reports if a pointer is associated, optionally checking for a specific target. PRESENT confirms that an optional subprogram argument has been specified. All three intrinsics are demonstrated in the program EXISTS.

```
program exists
interface
```

```
        subroutine accountedfor ( always, sometimes )
            integer            :: always
            integer, optional :: sometimes
        end subroutine accountedfor
    end interface
    integer, dimension ( : ), allocatable :: runtime
    integer, dimension ( : ), pointer     :: a_pointer
    integer, dimension ( 3 ), target      :: a_target
    print *, " "
    allocate ( runtime(3) )
    print *, "RUNTIME is allocated? ", allocated ( runtime )
    deallocate ( runtime )
    print *, "RUNTIME is allocated? ", allocated ( runtime )
    print *, " "
    call accountedfor ( 1, SOMETIMES=2 )
    call accountedfor ( 1 )
    print *, " "
    print *, "A_POINTER associated? ", associated ( a_pointer )
    a_pointer => a_target
    print *, "A_POINTER associated? ", associated ( a_pointer )
    print *, "A_POINTER & A_TARGET? ", associated ( a_pointer,
  -                                     TARGET = a_target  )
    nullify ( a_target )
    print *, "A_POINTER associated? ", associated ( a_pointer )
    print *, " "
    end program exists
    subroutine accountedfor ( always, sometimes )
    integer            :: always
    integer, optional :: sometimes
    print *, "SOMETIMES is present? ", present ( sometimes )
    end subroutine accountedfor
```

The results are:

```
RUNTIME is allocated? T
RUNTIME is allocated? F

SOMETIMES is present? T
SOMETIMES is present? F

A_POINTER associated? F
A_POINTER associated? T
A_POINTER & A_TARGET? T
A_POINTER associated? F
```

ALLOCATED is useful as a "first time" flag in a subprogram to sense when memory needs to be allocated. ASSOCIATED is useful to check if pointer is still associated with some target before being nullified. PRESENT is useful to let a subprogram take a different path of execution if the argument exists, or assign a default value when the argument does not exist.

Fortran 90 Compilers

This appendix lists all full Fortran 90 compilers known as of this writing. Inclusion in this list does not represent an endorsement. The following list is provided as a convenience to the reader.

Note that the performance of several of these compilers in a computationally intensive series of benchmarks has been published by John K. Prentice (1993, "A Performance Benchmark Study of Fortran 90 Compilers", Fortran Journal, Volume 5, Number 3, May/June issue, pages 2 - 7, Fullerton, CA).

Absoft Corporation
2781 Bond Street
Rochester Hills, MI 48309
(313) 853 - 0050

- Fortran 90 (available in the second half of 1994)

- Fortran 90 compiler for Intel platforms (DOS, Unixware, SCO Unix, Windows NT) and Macintosh (Motorola and PowerPC)

Applied Parallel Research
5500 Lambeth Road
Bethesda, MD 20814
(301) 718 - 3733

- xHPF (available now)

- High Performance Fortran (see preface) compiler for Intel PARAGON, IBM SPI, NCube, DEC, IBM, SGI, and HP.

Cray Research, Inc.
655F Lone Oak Drive
Eagan, MN 55121
(612) 683 - 7100

- CF90 (available in late 1993)

- Fortran 90 compiler for Cray computers (Y-MP, C90, EL, and Super servers) and Sun SPARC under Solaris

Edinburgh Portable Compilers Ltd.
20 Victor Square17 Alva Street
Scotts Valley, CA 95066
Edinburgh EH2 4PH Scotland
(408) 438 - 1851031 - 225 - 6262

- EPC Fortran 90 (available now)

- Fortran 90 compiler for Sun SPARC (Solaris 1.X and 2.X), IBM RS/6000, SVR4 (Sun SPARC, Intel), and Intel Solaris 2.X

Fujitsu Systems Business of America, Inc.
5200 Patrick Henry Drive
Santa Clara, CA 95054
(408) 988 - 8012

- Fortran 90 compiler (available mid-1994)

- Fortran 90 compiler for Sun SPARC platform under SOLARIX 2.x

Gesellschaft für Mathematik und Datenverarbeitung mbh
Rudower Chaussee 5
O-1199 Berlin
Germany
49-30-63921800

- Fortran 90 (available December, 1993)

- Fortran 90 to C translator for Intel i860 parallel computer (MANNA)

International Business Machines
Old Orchard Road
Armonk, NY 10504
(914) 765-1900

- AIX Fortran Version 3.1 (available late 1993)

- Fortran 90 compiler for the RS/6000

Intel Scientific
14924 N. W. Greenbrier Parkway
Beaverton, OR 97006
(503) 629 - 7843

- HPF compiler (available now)
- High Performance Compiler (see preface) for Intel PARAGON

Lahey Computer Systems, Inc.
P. O. Box 6091
Incline Village, NV 89450
(702) 831 - 2500

- Fortran 90 (available now)
- Fortran 90 compiler for Intel platforms

MicroWay, Inc.
Research Park
P. O. Box 79
Kingston, MA 02364
(508) 746 - 7341

- Fortran 90 (available now)
- Fortran 90 compiler for Intel 386, 486, and 860 under Protected Mode DOS, OS/2, or Unix

Numerical Algorithms Group, Inc.
1400 Opus Place, Suite 200
Downers Grove, IL 60515
(708) 971 - 2337

- NAGWare Fortran 90 (available now)
- Fortran 90 through C compiler for HP Domain and HP-UX, DEC VMS and Ultrix, IBM RS/6000, NEXT, PC DOS, Silicon Graphics, and Sun SunOS 4.1

Pacific-Sierra Research Corp.
Computer Products Group
2901 28th Street
Santa Monica, CA 90405
(310) 314 - 2300

- VAST-90 (available now)

- Fortran 90 to Fortran 77 translator for Cray (2, 3, XMP, YMP), Convex, DEC VMS and Ultrix, HP 9000/700, Silicon Graphics, and Sun

ParaSoft Corporation
2500 E. Foothill Boulevard, Suite 205
Pasadena, CA 91107
(818) 792 - 9941

- Fortran 90 (available now)
- Fortran 90 to Fortran 77 translator for Convex, DEC Ultrix, HP 9000, IBM (3090/AIX, ES9000/ESA, RS/6000), PCs, Silicon Graphics, and Sun SPARC

The Portland Group, Inc.
9150 S. W. Pioneer Court, Suite H
Wilsonville, OR 97070
(503) 682 - 2806

- HPF (available in late 1993)
- High Performance Fortran (see preface) compiler for Intel PARAGON, Meiko CS-2, and Sun SPARC workstation clusters

Salford Software Marketing Ltd.
Venables Building
5 Cockcroft Road
Salford M5 4NT
England
44-061-745-5678

- PC 90 (available now)
- PC platforms running DOS or UNIX

Sun Microsystems, Inc.
2550 Garcia Avenue
Mountain View, CA 94043
(415) 960 - 1300

- Fortran 90 (available now)
- Fortran 90 compiler for Sun SOLARIS-based platforms

B

Fortran 77 Compilers with Fortran 90 Features

This appendix lists all partial Fortran 90 compilers known as of this writing. Inclusion in this list does not represent an endorsement. The following list is provided as a convenience to the reader.

Absoft Corporation
2781 Bond Street
Rochester Hills, MI 48309
(313) 853–0050

Absoft FORTRAN 77 and MacFortran II incorporates the following Fortran 90 features as extensions:

- Binary, octal, hex, engineering, and generic G format edits
- RECURSIVE subprograms
- IMPLICIT NONE
- DO WHILE, CYCLE and EXIT
- CASE
- INCLUDE
- NAMELIST
- POINTERs
- Symbolic representations of for relational operators
- Free form source
- Quote marks (" ") to delimit character constants
- 31-character names including underscore

Control Data Corporation
4201 North Lexington Avenue
Arden Hills, MN 55126
(612) 482–2100

Currently released compiler supports long names and selected array extensions.

Convex Computer Corp.
3000 Waterview Parkway
Richardson, TX 75083
(214) 497–4000

Currently released compiler supports the following major Fortran 90 features:

- Limited array notation (i.e., array names and sections in assignment statements)
- 18 of the Fortran 90 array intrinsic functions
- ALLOCATABLE and automatic arrays

The next major release, currently under development, will add:

- Vector valued subscripts
- Array valued expressions permitted as actual arguments to subprograms
- Array valued functions
- Array constructors
- Array sections/expressions in input/output statements
- Array sections in DATA statements
- Some additional array intrinsic functions
- Limited support for INTERFACE blocks
- Assumed shape arrays
- Optional arguments
- Keyword arguments
- The new type declaration statement syntax ("entity" form)

Future releases will add incrementally:

- Support for MODULEs
- Free form source
- Derived types
- Remainder of Fortran 90 features
- Support for HPF

Cray Research, Inc.
655F Lone Oak Drive
Eagan, MN 55121
(612) 683–7100

CF77 compiler Release 6.0 includes support for common Fortran 90 features:

- INCLUDE line
- DO WHILE, END DO, non-labeled DO
- WHERE constructs
- Array intrinsics
- Automatic arrays
- A subset of the array syntax including whole and partial array
- Assignment and subscript triplet notation
- 31-character names plus underscores and upper/lower case
- Exclamation mark for inline comments
- IMPLICIT NONE
- NAMELIST
- RECURSIVE functions and subroutines
- Vectorizable math functions (i.e., sin, sqrt, max, and abs)
- MIL-STD 1753 bit intrinsics
- Quotes (" ") as string delimiters
- Hexademical (Z) and octal (O) constants
- Character and non-character data may be mixed in the same
- COMMON block
- Character string edit descriptor can be delimited with quotes
- Repeat count count for slash editor (ie., 3///)

Fujitsu Systems Business of America, Inc.
5200 Patrick Henry Drive
Santa Clara, CA 95054
(408) 988–8012

Fortran 90 compiler for Sun SPARC platform under SOLARIS 2.X including these Fortran 90 extensions:

- Free form source
- Inline comments
- Lowercase letters
- Symbolic names that are up to 31 characters
- IMPLICIT NONE
- Derived types
- New type declaration statement syntax
- INTENT statements
- ALLOCATE/DEALLOCATE statements
- Array sections with triplet subscripts
- Intrinsic operations and assignments of arrays
- New symbolic relational operators
- DO and CASE constructs
- Construct names
- EXIT and CYCLE statements
- NAMELIST input/output
- New specifiers in input/output statements (i.e., POSITION, DELIM, PAD, etc.)
- Elemental intrinsic functions
- Bit intrinsic functions

Hewlett-Packard Company
3000 Hanover Street
Palo Alto, CA 94304
(415) 857–1501

FORTRAN/9000 compiler includes the following Fortran 90 features:

- The CYCLE and EXIT statement
- The DO WHILE and DO "forever" loops
- The CASE statement

- Automatic arrays and character strings
- Allocatable arrays
- Array expressions and array assignment
- Array sections
- WHERE statement
- Attributes in type declarations

International Business Machines
Old Orchard Road
Armonk, NY 10504
(914) 765–1900

AIX XL Fortran Compiler/6000 Version 2.3 implements the following Fortran 90 extensions:

- Array language features
- Derived data types
- INTERFACE blocks
- DO construct enhancements
- Internal procedures
- CASE construct
- EXIT and CYCLE statements for DO contructs

Language Systems Group
441 Carlisle Drive
Herndon, VA 22070
(703) 478–0181

Language Sytems Fortran supports the following Fortran 90 extensions:

- Control statements ... CYCLE, DO WHILE, DO forever, EXIT, and CASE
- Declaration statements ... IMPLICIT NONE
- Format specifications ... EN
- Relational operators ... symbolic representations
- Intrinsic functions ... ADJUSTL, ADJUSTR, BTEST, EPSILON, HUGE, IACHAR, IAND, IBCLR, IBITS, IBSET, IEOR, IOR, ISHFT, ISHFTC, MVBITS, NOT, and TRIM

MasPar Computer Corporation
749 North Mary Avenue
Sunnyvale, CA 94086
(408) 736–3300

MasPar FortranVersion 2.0 includes the following extensions derived from Fortran 90:

- Array constructs including whole array manipulation, array
- Sections, and array constructors
- Assumed shape arrays
- Vector-values array subscripts
- WHERE statement
- Automatic arrays
- Argument attributes including INTENT and OPTIONAL
- CASE construct
- DO and DO WHILE constructs
- Many of the array operation intrinsics
- MIL-STD 1753 bit intrinsics
- RANDOM_NUMBER intrinsic

Microsoft Corp.
One Microsoft Way
Redmond, WA 98052
(206) 882–8080

Fortran PowerStation includes the following Fortran 90 extensions:

- 31-character identifiers
- NAMELIST
- SELECT CASE statement
- INTERFACE blocks
- INCLUDE line
- Floating point model inquiry intrinsics
- CYCLE

Southdale Integrated Systems
3410 South Service Road
Burlington
Ontario L7N 3P2
Canada
(416) 639–1990

FTN77+ Release 2.25 Fortran compiler for the QNX operating system includes these Fortran 90 extensions:

- Inline comments
- Long symbolic names (i.e., up to 16 characters)
- Wide source file lines (i.e., up to 132 columns)
- Bit intrinsic functions

WATCOM
415 Phillip Street
Waterloo
Ontario, N2L 3X2
Canada
(519) 886–3700

WATCOM FORTRAN 77 includes the following Fortran 90 extensions:

- INCLUDE line
- 31-character names including underscore and lower case
- ! to signal an end-of-line comment
- IMPLICIT NONE
- Character and non-character data are allowed in the same COMMON block
- Octal (O) constants
- Most MIL-STD 1753 bit intrinsics
- ALLOCATE and DEALLOCATE statements
- ALLOCATED instrinsic
- Some new OPEN statement specifiers (i.e., ACTION, RECL for sequential files, ACCESS='APPEND')
- ACTION specifier in INQUIRE statement
- NAMELIST

- Hexadecimal edit (Z) in FORMAT statement
- DO WHILE, END DO, EXIT, CYCLE, DO forever
- DO loop block labels

Fortran 90 Fundamental Publications

The Fortran 90 standard was approved on September 21, 1992, by ANSI (X3.198-1992) and in July, 1991, by ISO/IEC (1539:1991(E)). It is available from the following groups:

American National Standards Institute (ANSI)
1430 Broadway
New York, NY 10018
(212) 642 - 4900

PRINT DISTRIBUTION

Global Professional Publications
Global Engineering Documents
3130 South Harbor Boulevard
Santa Ana, CA 92704
(714) 979 - 8135

Global Info Centre
31-35 Rue de Neuilly
92110 Clichy
France
33-1-40871702

Global Info Centre
Suite 1310, Tower 1, World Trade Square
123 Hoi Bun Road
Kowloon
Hong Kong
852-755-6733

ELECTRONIC DISTRIBUTION

Unicomp, Inc.
1123 Marigold Drive NE
Albuquerque, NM 87122
(505) 275 - 0800

International Organization for Standardization (ISO)
1, Rue de Varembé
Case Postale 56
CH-1211 Genève 20
Switzerland

British Standards Institution (BSI)
2 Park Street
London W1A 2BS
England

Standards Council of Canada (SSC)
1200-450 O'Connor Street
Ottowa
Ontario K1P 6N7
Canada
(613) 995 - 4564

Association Franÿaise de Normalisation (AFNOR)
Tour Europe
Cedex 07
92080 Paris la Defense
France
1-42915555

Deutsches Insitut für Normung (DIN)
Burggrafenstrasse 6
Postfach 1107
D-1000 Berlin 30
Germany

Japan Standards Association (JSA)
1-24 Akasaka 4
Minato-ku 107
Tokyo
Japan
03-3583-8001

Selected Source Code Listings

PARTS Program File

This program was used to illustrate array manipulation in Chapter 2, *Array Operations*. Because it shares a good deal of code with the INVERT program in Chapter 2, not all of the code was listed there.

```
      program parts
c
c     Compute matrix inverse by partitions.  Treatment follows
c     pages 86 through 88 of
c
c     Jain, Mahinder K., S. R. K. Iyengard, and Rajendra K. Jain
c     1985 NUMERICAL METHODS FOR SCIENTIFIC AND ENGINEERING
c          COMPUTATION.  John Wiley & Sons.  406 pages.  New York.
c          ISBN 0-470-20143-6.
c
c     Declare variables.
      integer, parameter        :: m = 2
      integer, parameter        :: n = 3
      real                      :: determinant
      real, dimension (n,n)     :: identity, inverse, matrix
      real, dimension (m,  m  ) :: nw,      i_nw
      real, dimension (m,  n-m) :: ne,      i_ne
      real, dimension (n-m,m  ) :: sw,      i_sw
      real, dimension (n-m,n-m) :: se,      i_se
c     data matrix / 1, 4, 3, 1, 3, 5, 1, -1, 3 /
      data matrix / 1, 2, 3, 1, 0, 7, 1,  6, 1 /
c
c     Tell the user what will happen.
      print *, " "
      print *, "PARTS inverts matrix by partitions"
```

```
c
c      Carve up the matrix into four partitions.
       nw(1:m  ,1:m  ) = matrix(1  :m,1  :m)
       sw(1:n-m,1:m  ) = matrix(m+1:n,1  :m)
       ne(1:m  ,1:n-m) = matrix(1  :m,m+1:n)
       se(1:n-m,1:n-m) = matrix(m+1:n,m+1:n)
c
c      Build up the inverse of the original matrix quadrant
c      by quadrant.
       call invert ( se, n-m, determinant, i_se )
       nw   = nw - matmul ( matmul ( ne, i_se ), sw )
       call invert ( nw, m, determinant, i_nw )
       i_sw = - matmul ( matmul ( i_se, sw ), i_nw )
       i_ne = - matmul ( matmul ( i_nw, ne ), i_se )
       i_se = i_se - matmul ( matmul ( i_se, sw ), i_ne )
c
c      Stitch together the four quadrants to form the inverse
c      of the original matrix.
       inverse(1  :m,1  :m) = i_nw(1:m  ,1:m  )
       inverse(m+1:n,1  :m) = i_sw(1:n-m,1:m  )
       inverse(1  :m,m+1:n) = i_ne(1:m  ,1:n-m)
       inverse(m+1:n,m+1:n) = i_se(1:n-m,1:n-m)
c
c      Display the original matrix, its inverse, and a check
c      (i.e., multiplying a matrix by its inverse SHOULD result
c      in the identity matrix ... all zeros but with 1's on
c      the diagonal).
       call echo ( "MATRIX", matrix, n )
       call echo ( "INVERSE", inverse, n )
       identity = matmul ( matrix, inverse )
       call echo ( "IDENTITY", identity, n )
c
c      End of processing.
       print *, " "
       print *, "PARTS is finished."
       print *, " "
       end
c
c      Invert a 1x1, 2x2, or 3x3 matrix.
       subroutine invert ( matrix, rank, determinant, inverse )
c
c      Invert a matrix using straightforward technique of finding
c      minors, cofactors, determinants, and adjoints presented in
c
c          Miller, Ronald E.
c          1972  MODERN MATHEMATICAL MODELS FOR ECONOMICS AND
```

```
c                      BUSINESS.  Holt, Rinehart and Winston, Inc.
c                      488 pages.  New York, NY.  ISBN 0-03-084393-4.
c
c      on pages 17 through 23 and slightly thereafter.
c
c      Declare variables.
       real, dimension (:,:), allocatable :: adjoint
       real, dimension (:,:), allocatable :: cofactor
       real                               :: determinant
       real, dimension (:,:), allocatable :: identity
       integer                            :: rank
       real, dimension (rank,rank)        :: inverse
       real, dimension (rank,rank)        :: matrix
       if ( rank .lt. 1 .or. rank .gt. 3 ) then
            print *, "ERROR! matrix rank not 1, 2, or 3 (INVERT)"
            go to 200
       end if
c
c      Handle the special case of a 1x1 array.
       if ( rank .eq. 1 ) then
            if ( matrix(1,1) .ne. 0.0 ) then
                 determinant = 0.0
                 inverse(1,1) = 1.0 / matrix(1,1)
            else
                 print *, "ERROR! 1x1 matrix has no inverse (INVERT)"
            endif
            go to 200
       endif
c
c      Form the adjoint matrix.
       allocate ( adjoint(rank,rank) )
       call factor ( transpose(matrix), rank, adjoint )
c
c      Compute the determinant.
       call determine ( matrix, rank, determinant )
c
c      If it exists, form and check the inverse matrix.
       if ( determinant .ne. 0.0 ) then
            inverse = ( 1.0 / determinant ) * adjoint
c
c           Form the identity matrix by post-multiplying
c           the matrix by its inverse.  This will result in the
c           identity matrix (i.e., all zeros with 1s on diagonal).
            allocate ( identity(rank,rank) )
            identity = matmul ( matrix, inverse )
            if ( abs ( float ( rank ) -
     -                sum(identity,mask=identity.gt.0.0) )
     -           .gt. 0.05                                    )
     -           print *, "ERROR! sum identity diagonal ",
     -                    "differs from rank (INVERT)"
```

```
              deallocate ( identity )
         else
             print *, "ERROR! determinant zero ... no inverse (INVERT)"
         end if
c
c        Deallocate the various arrays.
         deallocate ( adjoint )
c
c        End of processing.
200      continue
         end subroutine invert
c
c        Echo a matrix.
         subroutine echo ( name, array, rank )
         integer                    :: rank
         real, dimension (rank,rank) :: array
         character(*)               :: name
c
c        Print it.
         print *, " "
         do i = 1, rank, 1
             write ( *,100 ) name, i, array(i,:)
100          format ( 1H , a10, ' row ', i1, ': ', 6f8.4 )
         end do
         end subroutine echo
c
c        Form cofactor matrix.
         subroutine factor ( matrix, rank, cofactor )
         integer                             :: rank
         real, dimension (:,:), allocatable :: across
         real, dimension (rank,rank)        :: cofactor
         real, dimension (:,:), allocatable :: down
         real, dimension (:,:), allocatable :: extract
         real, dimension (rank,rank)        :: matrix
         real                                :: minor
         integer                             :: rankm1
c
c        Allocate necessary workspace.
         rankm1 = rank - 1
         allocate ( across(rankm1,rankm1) )
         allocate ( down  (rank,  rank ) )
c
c        Assess the cofactor array first by column ...
         column: do j = 1, rank, 1
c
c            Copy everything but the J-th column.
             if ( j .ne.   1 )
    -        down(:,1:j-1  ) = matrix(:,1:j-1  )
             if ( j .ne. rank )
    -        down(:,j:rankm1) = matrix(:,j+1:rank)
```

```
c
c          ... and then, within columns, by rows.
          row: do i = 1, rank, 1
c
c              Copy everything but the I-th row.
              if ( i .ne.    1 )
     —        across(1:i-1,   :) = down(1:i-1,   :)
              if ( i .ne. rank )
     —        across(i:rankm1,:) = down(i+1:rank,:)
c
c              Compute the determinant of this new matrix.
              call determine ( transpose(across), rankm1, minor )
c
c              Set this element of the cofactor array.
              if ( mod (i+j,2) .eq. 1 ) minor = -minor
              cofactor(i,j) = minor
c
c              Work on the next element.
          end do row
      end do column
c
c      Free memory.
      deallocate ( down )
      deallocate ( across )
      end subroutine factor
c
c      Compute determinant.
      subroutine determine ( matrix, rank, determinant )
      integer                   :: rank
      real                      :: determinant
      real, dimension(rank,rank) :: matrix
c
c      Calculate the determinant for several cases.
      select case ( rank )
        case ( :0 )
          determinant = 0.0
        case ( 1 )
          determinant =    matrix(1,1)
        case ( 2 )
          determinant = (  matrix(1,1)*matrix(2,2) )
     —                  - (  matrix(1,2)*matrix(2,1) )
        case ( 3 )
          determinant = (  (matrix(1,1)*matrix(2,2)*matrix(3,3))+
     —                     (matrix(1,2)*matrix(2,3)*matrix(3,1))+
     —                     (matrix(1,3)*matrix(2,1)*matrix(3,2)) )
     —                  - (  (matrix(1,3)*matrix(2,2)*matrix(3,1))+
```

311

```
      -                      (matrix(2,3)*matrix(3,2)*matrix(1,1))+
      -                      (matrix(3,3)*matrix(1,2)*matrix(2,1)) )
        case (4:)
          determinant = 0.0
      end select
      end subroutine determine
```

CONCORD Program File

This program was used in Chapter 4, *Subroutines and Functions Revisited*, to illustrate the use of INCLUDE files and other methods of managing procedures. It was not completely listed in that chapter because much of the code was concerned only with implementing the algorithm and did not contribute to the discussion there.

```
      program concord
c
c     Program exhibits "classic" program structure.  Calculates
c     Calculate Kendall's Coefficient of Concordance which measures
c     congruence among judges' ranking of a set of events.  It is
c     described on pages 229 and 230 of
c
c         Siegal, Sydney
c         1956  NONPARAMETRIC STATISTICS FOR THE BEHAVIORAL
c                   SCIENCES.  McGraw-Hill Book Company.  312
c                   pages.  New York, NY.
c
c     Siegal's sample data (Table 9.11, pages 230) for three judges
c     and six events
c
c         1 6 3 2 5 4
c         1 5 6 4 2 3
c         6 3 2 5 4 1
c
c     yields a value of 0.162 for this Coefficient of Concordance.
c     Values of 0 imply perfect discord among the judges' ranking
c     and values of 1 imply unanimous agreement among the judges'
c     ranking.
c
c     This program is structured in a "classic" pattern with
c     twelve subprograms fixed in the following hierarchy with
c     two additional "floating" routines:
c
```

```
c                              concord           || error
c                                 |              || tell
c        +------------+------------+-------------+
c        |            |            |             |
c      init         start       driver        finish
c                                 |
c        +------------+------------+-------------+
c        |            |            |             |
c     limits        input       kencon        result
c                                 |
c                               wtest
c                                 |
c                         +-------------+
c                         |             |
c                       rank          tie
c
c     In olden days, such a program structure would dictate the
c     way build an overlay.  CONCORD, ERROR, and TELL -- along
c     with the two common areas -- would be in the root and each
c     level would be overlaid.
c
      INCLUDE 'concord.int'
      INCLUDE 'concord.ins'
      name  = '.MAIN.'
      call init
      call tell ( name, push )
      call start
      call tell ( name, pass )
      call driver
      call tell ( name, pass )
      call finish
      call tell ( name, pass )
      call error
      call tell ( name, pass )
      call tell ( name, pop  )
      end program concord

      subroutine init
      INCLUDE 'concord.ins'
      name   = 'init'
      crtout = 6
      debug  = .TRUE.
      pass   = 0
      pop    = -1
      push   = 1
      chisqr = 0.0
      crtin  = 5
      degfre = 0
      nullify ( ename )
      events = 10
```

```
          ifile = ' '
          io    = 0
          irec  = 0
          iunit = 7
          nullify ( jname )
          judges = 32
          kendal = 0.0
          mistak = .FALSE.
          units  = .FALSE.
          ofile = ' '
          ounit = 8
          nullify ( scores )
          end subroutine init

          subroutine start
          INCLUDE 'concord.ins'
          character*7 dfile
          name  = 'start'
          call tell ( name, push )
          write ( crtout,100 )
100       format ( / 1H , 'CONCORD is a classically ',
         -                 'structured program.'        )
200       continue
c
c         Use ADVANCE="NO" to arrest the cursor at the end
c         of the prompt so that the user's reponse appears
c         on the same line.
          write ( crtout,300,advance='NO' )
300       format ( / 1H , 'Enter data file name: ' )
          read ( crtin,400 ) dfile
400       format ( a7 )
c
c         Use LEN_TRIM to be sure the user entered some filename.
          i = len_trim ( dfile )
          if ( i .lt. 1 ) go to 200
600       continue
          ifile = dfile(1:i) // '.input'
          ofile = dfile(1:i) // '.output'
          open ( unit=iunit, file=ifile, status='OLD', iostat=io )
          if ( io .eq. 0 ) then
c
c             Use the TRIM instrinsic to give the display
c             of the file name a more professional look
c             since it will remove any trailing blanks.
              write ( crtout,700 ) trim (ifile), iunit
700           format ( 1H , 'Input file ', a,
         -                   ' open on unit ', i2.2 )
c
c             Keep track which unit numbers are attached to
c             files.  In case the program aborts, a later
```

```
c                 routine, ERROR, will close any open files.
                  units(iunit) = .TRUE.
          else
                  write ( crtout,800 ) trim(ifile), iunit, io
800               format ( 1H , 'Can not open existing input file ', a,
          -                      ' on unit ', i2.2, ' (IOSTAT=', i5.5, ')' )
                  mistak = .TRUE.
                  call error
          end if
          open ( unit=ounit, file=ofile, status='NEW', iostat=io )
          if ( io .eq. 0 ) then
                  write ( crtout,900 ) trim(ofile), ounit
900               format ( 1H , 'Output file ', a,
          -                      ' open on unit ', i2.2 )
                  units(ounit) = .TRUE.
          else
                  write ( crtout,1000 ) trim(ofile), ounit, io
1000              format ( 1H , 'Can not open new output file ', a,
          -                      ' on unit ', i2.2, ' (IOSTAT=', i5.5, ')' )
                  mistak = .TRUE.
                  call error
          end if
          call tell ( name, pop )
          end subroutine start

          subroutine driver
          INCLUDE 'concord.ins'
          name  = 'driver'
c
c     This routine is the classic place for the maintenance
c     programmer to begin a study of this program because it
c     shows the overall program structure in just one series
c     of calls.
          call tell ( name, push )
          call limits
          call tell ( name, pass )
          call input
          call tell ( name, pass )
          call kencon
          call tell ( name, pass )
          call result
          call tell ( name, pass )
          call tell ( name, pop )
          end subroutine driver

          subroutine limits
          INCLUDE 'concord.ins'
          name  = 'limits'
          call tell ( name, push )
```

```
c
c       Get the number of judges and events for the problem
c       at hand.  Repeat the prompt if the user enters a number
c       that is larger than the maximum numbers set as JUDGES
c       and EVENTS in the INIT routine.
100     continue
            write ( crtout,200,advance='NO' )
200         format ( / 1H , 'Enter number of judges: ' )
            read ( crtin,*,err=100 ) i
            if ( i .ge. 1 .and. i .lt. judges ) judges = i
300     continue
            write ( crtout,400,advance='NO' )
400         format ( / 1H , 'Enter number of events: ' )
            read ( crtin,*,err=300 ) j
            if ( j .ge. 1 .and. j .lt. events ) events = j
        allocate ( ename(events) )
        allocate ( jname(judges) )
        allocate ( scores(judges,events) )
        call tell ( name, pop )
        end subroutine limits

        subroutine input
        INCLUDE 'concord.ins'
        integer irec
        real    total
        name = 'input'
        call tell ( name, push )
        irec = 1
        rewind iunit
        do j = 1, events, 1
            read ( iunit,100,err=700,end=900 ) ename(j)
100         format ( a6 )
c
c           Keep tabs of what record is being read so that
c           if an error occurs the offending line number can
c           be reported in the error message.
            irec = irec + 1
        end do
        do i = 1, judges, 1
            read ( iunit,300,err=700,end=900 ) jname(i),
     -                                  scores(i,1:events)
300         format ( a6, 10f5.0 )
            total = sum ( scores(i,:) )
            if ( total .lt. events ) then
c
c               This error message will appear if any zero scores
c               are entered.  It will also be tripped if the user
c               entered a wrong number for the number of JUDGES
c               or EVENTS.
                write ( crtout,500 ) i, irec
```

```
500            format ( 1H , 'Invalid scores for judge ', i2.2,
       -                  ' at input record ', i2.2            )
             mistak = .TRUE.
             call error
         end if
         irec = irec + 1
       end do
       go to 1100
700    continue
          write ( crtout,800 ) irec, iunit
800       format ( 1H , 'Input read error at record ', i5.5,
       -                  ' on unit ', i2.2                    )
          mistak = .TRUE.
          call error
900    continue
          write ( crtout,1000 ) irec, iunit
1000      format ( 1H , 'Input premature EOF at record ', i5.5,
       -                  ' on unit ', i2.2                    )
          mistak = .TRUE.
          call error
1100   continue
       if ( debug ) then
          do j = 1, events, 1
             write ( crtout,1200 ) j, ename(j)
1200         format ( 1H , 'INPUT: event ', i5.5, ' name ', a6 )
          end do
          do i = 1, judges, 1
             write ( crtout,1400 ) i, jname(i)
1400         format ( 1H , 'INPUT: judge ', i5.5, ' name ', a6 )
          end do
          do i = 1, judges, 1
             write ( crtout,1600 ) scores(i,1:events)
1600         format ( 1H , 'INPUT: scores ', 10f5.1 )
          end do
       end if
       call tell ( name, pop )
       end subroutine input

       subroutine kencon
       INCLUDE 'concord.ins'
       real, dimension(:), allocatable :: a
       name = 'kencon'
       call tell ( name, push )
c
c    Collapse the two-dimensional raw scores table
c    into a one-dimensional vector.
       allocate ( a(events*judges) )
       a  = pack ( scores, MASK=scores.ne.0.0 )
c
c    Compute Kendall's W.
```

```
            call wtest ( a, judges, events, kendal, chisqr, degfre )
            call tell ( name, pass )
c
c       Make sure that the computation is within range.
            if ( kendal .lt. 0.0 .or. kendal .gt. 1.0 ) then
                write ( crtout,100 ) kendal
100             format ( 1H , 'Coefficient negative or exceeds one!' )
                mistak = .TRUE.
                call error
            end if
c
c       Deallocate the one-dimensional representation of the
c       raw scores matrix.
            deallocate ( a )
            call tell ( name, pop )
            end subroutine kencon


            subroutine wtest ( raw, njudges,    mevents,
        -                         w,    chi_square, ndf        )
c
c       Rewritten from IBM SYSTEM/360 SCIENTIFIC SUBROUTINE PACKAGE
c       PROGRAMMERS MANUAL, Version 3, Program 360A-CM-03X,
c       Publication GH-20-0205-4, Page 76
c
            INCLUDE 'concord.ins'
            real                                         :: avr_rank
            real,                      intent(out) :: chi_square
            integer,                   intent(in ) :: mevents
            integer,                   intent(out) :: ndf
            integer,                   intent(in ) :: njudges
            integer                                      :: nm
            real,    dimension(njudges*mevents)          :: ranked
            real,    dimension(njudges*mevents), intent(in ) :: raw
            real                                         :: rm
            real                                         :: rn
            real                                         :: t
            real                                         :: ties
            real,                      intent(out) :: w
            real,    dimension(mevents)                  :: work
            name = 'wtest'
            call tell ( name, push )
            nm = njudges * mevents
            rm = real(mevents)
            rn = real(njudges)
            t  = 0.0
c
c       Rank the scores on the M events for each of N judges.
            do i = 1, njudges, 1
c
c           Rank the M scores for the I-th judge.
```

```
        call rank ( raw(i:nm:njudges),
    —              ranked(i:nm:njudges),
    —              mevents              )
        call tell ( name, pass )
c
c       Compute correction for ties.
        call tie  ( ranked(i:nm:njudges), mevents, ties )
        call tell ( name, pass )
c
c       Keep a running count of the number of ties.
        t = t + ties
      end do
c
c  Sum the ranked scores given by each of the N judges
c  for the M events.  WORK(J) will be the total ranked
c  scores for the J-th of M events over all N judges.
c  Note that WORK is an automatic array.  It is declared
c  in this procedure and storage is automatically
c  created and discarded when this procedure exits.
   work = 0.0
   do j = 1, mevents, 1
       work(j) = sum ( ranked(1+(njudges*(j-1)):njudges*j) )
   end do
c
c  Compute the average rank assigned to events.
   avr_rank = sum ( work ) / rm
c
c  Square the difference between the sum of ranks
c  for an event and the average rank assigned to
c  events (i.e., a "sum of squared differences").
   s = dot_product ( work-avr_rank, work-avr_rank )
c
c  Complete the somputation of concordance and Chi-square
c  (from Siegal, 1956, Eqs. 9.15 and 9.17, pages 231
c  and 236, repectively).
   w   = s / ( ( ( rn*rn ) * ( rm*rm*rm - rm ) / 12.0 ) - rn*t)
   if ( mevents .gt. 7 ) then
       chi_square = rn * ( rm - 1.0 ) * w
       ndf        = mevents - 1
   else
       chi_square = 0.0
       ndf        = 0
   end if
   call tell ( name, pop )
   end subroutine wtest

   subroutine rank ( raw_scores, ranked_scores, mevents )
c
c  Rewritten from IBM SYSTEM/360 SCIENTIFIC SUBROUTINE PACKAGE
c  PROGRAMMERS MANUAL, Version 3, Program 360A-CM-03X,
```

```
c      Publication GH-20-0205-4, Page 71.
c
       INCLUDE 'concord.ins'
       integer                                :: assigned
       integer                                :: equal
       integer,                     intent(in ) :: mevents
       integer, dimension (1)                 :: min_location
       real                                   :: min_score
       real,    dimension (mevents), intent(out) :: ranked_scores
       real,    dimension (mevents), intent(in ) :: raw_scores
       integer                                :: small
       real                                   :: split
       name  = 'rank'
       call tell ( name, push )
c
c      Initialize the rank vector, find the smallest score,
c      and initialize the number of ranks assigned.
       ranked_scored = 0.0
       min_score    = minval ( raw_scores )
       assigned     = 0
c
c      Examine every score.  Because of ties, perhaps less than
c      MEVENTS examinations need to be made but no MORE than
c      MEVENTS examinations will ever be needed.
       do i = 1, mevents, 1
c
c         A rank is assigned to a give score in RAW_SCORES
c         based on the number of scores it beats or ties.
c         So, count the scores less than or equal to the
c         target value.
          small = count ( raw_scores .lt. min_score )
          equal = count ( raw_scores .eq. min_score )
c
c         If a score is unique, then its rank is one more
c         than the number of scores less than it.  Note that
c         MINLOC is used to find out the matrix location of
c         the smallest value.  Recall that it returns an
c         array, not a scalar value.  That's why there has
c         to be an array, MIN_LOCATION, that only holds one
c         element to receive the result of MINLOC.
          if ( equal .eq. 1 ) then
              min_location = minloc( raw_scores,
    -                        MASK = raw_scores.eq.min_score )
              ranked_scores(min_location) = small + 1
c
c         If a score is not unique (i.e., tied with one or
c         more other scores), then its rank is "split" among
c         it and the other events receiving the same score.
c         As always in Fortran, the presence of a floating-
c         point value on one side of an operator causes the
```

```
c         integer on the other side to be converted to a
c         floating point number so that the results are
c         precise.  Thus, the 0.5 causes (EQUAL+1) to be
c         converted to a real number, and then SMALL in its
c         turn is also converted to a real number.
          else
                split = small + ( ( equal + 1 ) * 0.5 )
                where ( raw_scores .eq. min_score )
                      ranked_scores = split
                end where
          end if
c
c         Determine the next larger score.
          min_score=minval(raw_scores,MASK=raw_scores.gt.min_score)
c
c         Note that the limit of the DO loop, MEVENTS, may not
c         be reached.  Due to ties, all ranks might be assigned
c         before MEVENTS evaluations are required.  That is why
c         this DO loop is terminated when all ranks have been
c         assigned rather han when MEVENTS comparisons have
c         been made.
          assigned = assigned + equal
          if ( assigned .ge. mevents ) exit
      end do
      call tell ( name, pop )
      end subroutine rank

      subroutine tie ( ranked_scores, mevents, ties )
c
c     Rewritten from IBM SYSTEM/360 SCIENTIFIC SUBROUTINE PACKAGE
c     PROGRAMMERS MANUAL, Version 3, Program 360A-CM-03X,
c     Publication GH-20-0205-4, Page 74.
c
      INCLUDE 'concord.ins'
      integer                                    :: assigned
      integer                                    :: equal_ranks
      integer,                    intent(in )    :: mevents
      real,     dimension (mevents), intent(in )    :: ranked_scores
      real,                       intent(out)    :: ties
      real                                       :: min_rank
      name = 'tie'
      call tell ( name, push )
c
c     Initialize the tie correction, find the smallest rank,
c     and initialize the number of ranks examined.
      ties    = 0.0
      min_rank = minval ( ranked_scores )
      assigned = 0
c
c     Examine every rank.  Because of ties, perhaps less than
```

```
c       M examinations need to be made but no MORE than M
c       examinations will ever be needed.
        do i = 1, mevents, 1
c
c           Count the number of ranks equal to the target rank.
c           Here, the COUNT intrinsic is very handy.
            equal_ranks = count ( ranked_scores .eq. min_rank )
c
c           Compute the correction for ties.  Note that if this
c           rank is unique (i.e., EQUAL_RANKS=1), then the entire
c           term in parenthesis is zero and does not contribute to
c           the correction for ties.  The correction, TIES, has
c           these values for different values of EQUAL_RANKS:
c           TIES is 0 for EQUAL_RANKS of 1, 0.5 for EQUAL_RANKS
c           of 2, 2.0 for 3, 5.0 for 4, 17.5 for 6, 28.0 for 7, etc.
            ties = ties+(((equal_ranks*equal_ranks*equal_ranks) -
       -                                  equal_ranks)/12.0)
c
c           Find the next larger rank.
            min_rank = minval ( ranked_scores,
       -                        MASK = ranked_scores.gt.min_rank )
c
c           Note that the limit of the DO loop, MEVENTS, may not
c           be reached.  Due to ties, all ranks might be assigned
c           before MEVENTS evaluations are required.  That is why
c           this DO loop is terminated when all ranks have been
c           assigned rather han when MEVENTS comparisons have
c           been made.
            assigned = assigned + equal_ranks
            if ( assigned .ge. mevents ) exit
        end do
        call tell ( name, pop )
        end subroutine tie

        subroutine result
        INCLUDE 'concord.ins'
        name  = 'result'
        call tell ( name, push )
        write ( ounit,100 )
100     format ( 1H1 //////
       -            13x, 'KENDALL''S COEFFICIENT OF CONCORDANCE' /// )
        write ( ounit,200 ) ename
200     format ( 1H , 6x, 10 ( 1x, a6 ) )
        write ( ounit,300 )
300     format ( // )
        do i = 1, judges, 1
            write ( ounit,400 ) jname(i), scores(i,1:events)
400         format ( 1H , a6, 10f7.1 )
        end do
        write ( ounit,300 )
```

```
        write ( ounit,600 ) kendal, chisqr, events, degfre
600  format ( 1H , 6x, f7.3, " Kendall's Coefficient",
     -       / 1H , 6x, f7.3, ' Chi-squared ',
     -                        '[if number of events, ', i2.2,
     -                        ', exceeds 7]'
     -       / 1H , 6x, i7  , ' Degrees of Freedom'       )
        call tell ( name, pop )
        end subroutine result

        subroutine tell ( what, where )
        INCLUDE 'concord.ins'
        character*6,               intent(in ) :: what
        integer,                   intent(in ) :: where
        integer                               :: depth
        save depth
        if ( where .ne. pop ) then
            if ( where .eq. push ) depth = depth + 1
            if ( debug ) then
                write ( crtout,100,advance="NO" )
100             format ( 1H , "TELL: " )
                do i = 2, depth, 1
                    write ( crtout,200,advance="NO" )
200                 format ( 6x )
                end do
                write ( crtout,300 ) what
300             format ( a6 )
            end if
        end if
        if ( where .eq. pop ) depth = depth - 1
        end subroutine tell

        subroutine finish
        INCLUDE 'concord.ins'
        character*14 dname
        name  = 'finish'
        call tell ( name, push )
        write ( crtout,100 )
100  format ( / 1H , 'Closing files ...' )
        do i = 1, MAXUNT, 1
            if ( units(i) ) then
                inquire ( unit=i, name=dname )
                write ( crtout,200 ) i, dname
200             format ( 1H , 'UNIT=', i2.2, 1x, 'NAME=', a )
                close ( unit=i )
                units(i) = .FALSE.
            end if
        end do
        write ( crtout,400 )
400  format ( / 1H , 'CONCORD is finished.' )
```

```
        call tell ( name, pop )
        end subroutine finish

        subroutine error
        INCLUDE 'concord.ins'
        name  = 'error'
        call tell ( name, push )
        if ( mistak ) then
            write ( crtout,100 )
100         format ( / 1H , 'ERROR! Fatal mistake!' / )
            stop
        else
            write ( crtout,200 )
200         format ( / 1H , 'No errors detected.' / )
        end if
        if ( associated ( ename  ) ) deallocate ( ename  )
        if ( associated ( jname  ) ) deallocate ( jname  )
        if ( associated ( scores ) ) deallocate ( scores )
        call tell ( name, pop )
        end subroutine error
```

CONCORD Insert File

```
c       -----------------------------------------------------------
        integer                                 MAXUNT
        parameter                            ( MAXUNT=10 )
        real                                    chisqr
        integer                                 crtin
        integer                                 crtout
        logical                                 debug
        integer                                 degfre
        character* 6, dimension(:  ), pointer :: ename
        integer                                 events
        integer                               :: i = 0
        character*14                            ifile
        integer                                 iunit
        integer                                 io
        integer                               :: j = 0
        character* 6, dimension(:  ), pointer :: jname
        integer                                 judges
        real                                    kendal
        logical                                 mistak
        character* 6                          :: name = ' '
        character*14                            ofile
        integer                                 ounit
        integer                                 pass
        integer                                 pop
        integer                                 push
        real,        dimension(:,:), pointer :: scores
```

```
      logical                                  units(MAXUNT)
      common / area /  chisqr, crtin,   crtout, debug,  degfre,
      -                events, io,      iunit,  judges, kendal,
      -                mistak, ounit,   pass,   pop,    push,
      -                scores, units,
      -                ename,  ifile,   jname,  ofile
c     ------------------------------------------------------------------
```

CONCORD Interface File

```
c     ------------------------------------------------------------------
      interface
        subroutine driver
          end subroutine driver
        subroutine error
          end subroutine error
        subroutine finish
          end subroutine finish
        subroutine init
          end subroutine init
        subroutine input
          end subroutine input
        subroutine kencon
          end subroutine kencon
        subroutine limits
          end subroutine limits
        subroutine rank ( raw_scores, ranked_scores, mevents )
          integer,                    intent(in ) :: mevents
          real,    dimension (mevents), intent(out) :: ranked_scores
          real,    dimension (mevents), intent(in ) :: raw_scores
          end subroutine rank
        subroutine result
          end subroutine result
        subroutine start
          end subroutine
        subroutine tell ( what, where )
          character*6,                intent(in ) :: what
          integer,                    intent(in ) :: where
          end subroutine tell
        subroutine tie ( ranked_scores, mevents, ties )
          integer,                    intent(in ) :: mevents
          real,    dimension (mevents), intent(in ) :: ranked_scores
          real,                       intent(out) :: ties
          end subroutine tie
        subroutine wtest( raw, njudges,    mevents,
      -                   w,  chi_square, ndf          )
          real,    intent(out) :: chi_square
          integer, intent(in ) :: mevents
          integer, intent(out) :: ndf
```

```
          integer, intent(in ) :: njudges
          real,    intent(in ), dimension(njudges*mevents) :: raw
          real,    intent(out) :: w
          end subroutine wtest
       end interface
c      ------------------------------------------------------------
```

CONCORD Input File

```
event1
event2
event3
event4
event5
event6
JUDGEA  1.0  6.0  3.0  2.0  5.0  4.0
JUDGEB  1.0  5.0  6.0  4.0  2.0  3.0
JUDGEC  6.0  3.0  2.0  5.0  4.0  1.0
```

PART2 Program File

Small pieces of this program were listed in Chapter 7, *Dynamic Memory Management*. The goal there was to show how the program PARTS from Chapter 2, *Array Operations*, could use memory more efficiently if it was adapted to use allocatable arrays.

```
       program part2
c
c      Compute matrix inverse by partitions using pointers.
c      Treatment follows pages 86 through 88 of
c
c      Jain, Mahinder K., S. R. K. Iyengard, and Rajendra K. Jain
c      1985  NUMERICAL METHODS FOR SCIENTIFIC AND ENGINEERING
c            COMPUTATION.  John Wiley & Sons.  406 pages.  New York.
c            ISBN 0-470-20143-6.
c
c      Declare variables.
       integer, parameter            :: m = 2
       integer, parameter            :: n = 3
       real                          :: determinant
       real, dimension (n,n)         :: identity
       real, dimension (n,n), target :: inverse
       real, dimension (n,n), target :: matrix
       real, dimension (m,m)         :: t_nw
       real, dimension (:,:), pointer :: i_nw, i_ne, i_sw, i_se
       real, dimension (:,:), pointer ::   nw,   ne,   sw,   se
       data matrix / 1, 2, 3, 1, 0, 7, 1, 6, 1 /
```

```
c
c      Tell the user what will happen.
       print *, " "
       print *, "PART2 inverts matrix by partitions using pointers"
c
c      Carve up the matrix into four partitions.
       nw => matrix(1   :m,1   :m)
       sw => matrix(m+1:n,1   :m)
       ne => matrix(1   :m,m+1:n)
       se => matrix(m+1:n,m+1:n)
c
c      Build up the inverse of the original matrix quadrant
c      by quadrant.
       i_nw => inverse(1   :m,1   :m)
       i_sw => inverse(m+1:n,1   :m)
       i_ne => inverse(1   :m,m+1:n)
       i_se => inverse(m+1:n,m+1:n)
       call invert ( se, n-m, determinant, i_se )
       t_nw = nw - matmul ( matmul ( ne, i_se ), sw )
       call invert ( t_nw, m, determinant, i_nw )
       i_sw = - matmul ( matmul ( i_se, sw ), i_nw )
       i_ne = - matmul ( matmul ( i_nw, ne ), i_se )
       i_se = i_se - matmul ( matmul ( i_se, sw ), i_ne )
c
c      Display the original matrix, its inverse, and a check
c      (i.e., multiplying a matrix by its inverse SHOULD result
c      in the identity matrix ... all zeros but with 1's on
c      the diagonal).
       call echo ( "MATRIX", matrix, n )
       call echo ( "INVERSE", inverse, n )
       identity = matmul ( matrix, inverse )
       call echo ( "IDENTITY", identity, n )
c
c      End of processing.
       print *, " "
       print *, "PART2 is finished."
       print *, " "
       end program part2
c
c      Invert a 1x1, 2x2, or 3x3 matrix.
       subroutine invert ( matrix, rank, determinant, inverse )
c
c      Invert a matrix using the straightforward technique of
c      finding minors, cofactors, determinants, and adjoints
c      presented in
c
c          Miller, Ronald E.
c          1972  MODERN MATHEMATICAL MODELS FOR ECONOMIC AND
c                BUSINESS.  Holt, Rinehart and Winston, Inc.
c                488 pages.  New York, NY.  ISBN 0-03-084393-4.
```

```
c
c      on pages 17 through 23 and slightly thereafter.
c
c      Declare variables.
       real, dimension (:,:), allocatable :: adjoint
       real, dimension (:,:), allocatable :: cofactor
       real                               :: determinant
       real, dimension (:,:), allocatable :: identity
       integer                            :: rank
       real, dimension (rank,rank)        :: inverse
       real, dimension (rank,rank)        :: matrix
       if ( rank .lt. 1 .or. rank .gt. 3 ) then
            print *, "ERROR! matrix rank not 1, 2, or 3 (INVERT)"
            go to 200
       end if
c
c      Handle the special case of a 1x1 array.
       if ( rank .eq. 1 ) then
            if ( matrix(1,1) .ne. 0.0 ) then
                 determinant = 0.0
                 inverse(1,1) = 1.0 / matrix(1,1)
            else
                 print *,"ERROR! 1x1 matrix has no inverse (INVERT)"
            endif
            go to 200
       endif
c
c      Form the adjoint matrix.
       allocate ( adjoint(rank,rank) )
       call factor ( transpose(matrix), rank, adjoint )
c
c      Compute the determinant.
       call determine ( matrix, rank, determinant )
c
c      If it exists, form and check the inverse matrix.
       if ( determinant .ne. 0.0 ) then
            inverse = ( 1.0 / determinant ) * adjoint
c
c           Form the identity matrix by post-multiplying
c           the matrix by its inverse.  This will result in the
c           identity matrix (i.e., all zeros with 1s on diagonal).
            allocate ( identity(rank,rank) )
            identity = matmul ( matrix, inverse )
            if ( abs ( float ( rank ) -
     -                 sum(identity,mask=identity.gt.0.0) )
     -           .gt. 0.05                                       )
     -           print *, "ERROR! sum identity diagonal ",
     -                     "differs from rank (INVERT)"
            deallocate ( identity )
       else
```

```
               print *,"ERROR! determinant zero: no inverse (INVERT)"
          end if
c
c     Deallocate the various arrays.
          deallocate ( adjoint )
c
c     End of processing.
200       continue
          end subroutine invert
c
c     Echo a matrix.
          subroutine echo ( name, array, rank )
          integer                   :: rank
          real, dimension (rank,rank) :: array
          character(*)              :: name
c
c     Print it.
          print *, " "
          do i = 1, rank, 1
               write ( *,100 ) name, i, array(i,:)
100            format ( 1H , a10, ' row ', i1, ': ', 6f8.4 )
          end do
          end subroutine echo
c
c     Form cofactor matrix.
          subroutine factor ( matrix, rank, cofactor )
          integer                          :: rank
          real, dimension (:,:), allocatable :: across
          real, dimension (rank,rank)       :: cofactor
          real, dimension (:,:), allocatable :: down
          real, dimension (:,:), allocatable :: extract
          real, dimension (rank,rank)       :: matrix
          real                             :: minor
          integer                          :: rankm1
c
c     Allocate necessary workspace.
          rankm1 = rank - 1
          allocate ( across(rankm1,rankm1) )
          allocate ( down  (rank,  rank ) )
c
c     Assess the cofactor array first by column ...
          column: do j = 1, rank, 1
c
c            Copy everything but the J-th column.
               if ( j .ne.    1 )
     -         down(:,1:j-1  ) = matrix(:,1:j-1  )
               if ( j .ne. rank )
     -         down(:,j:rankm1) = matrix(:,j+1:rank)
c
```

```
c          ... and then, within columns, by rows.
           row: do i = 1, rank, 1
c
c              Copy everything but the I-th row.
               if ( i .ne.    1 )
     -         across(1:i-1,    :) = down(1:i-1,    :)
               if ( i .ne. rank )
     -         across(i:rankm1,:) = down(i+1:rank,:)
c
c              Compute the determinant of this new matrix.
               call determine ( transpose(across), rankm1, minor )
c
c              Set this element of the cofactor array.
               if ( mod (i+j,2) .eq. 1 ) minor = -minor
               cofactor(i,j) = minor
c
c              Work on the next element.
           end do row
       end do column
c
c      Free memory.
       deallocate ( down )
       deallocate ( across )
       end subroutine factor
c
c      Compute determinant.
       subroutine determine ( matrix, rank, determinant )
       integer                 :: rank
       real                    :: determinant
       real, dimension(rank,rank) :: matrix
c
c      Calculate the determinant for several cases.
       select case ( rank )
         case ( :0 )
           determinant = 0.0
         case ( 1 )
           determinant =    matrix(1,1)
         case ( 2 )
           determinant = (  matrix(1,1)*matrix(2,2) )
     -              - (  matrix(1,2)*matrix(2,1) )
         case ( 3 )
           determinant = ( (matrix(1,1)*matrix(2,2)*matrix(3,3))+
     -                     (matrix(1,2)*matrix(2,3)*matrix(3,1))+
     -                     (matrix(1,3)*matrix(2,1)*matrix(3,2)) )
     -              - ( (matrix(1,3)*matrix(2,2)*matrix(3,1))+
     -                     (matrix(2,3)*matrix(3,2)*matrix(1,1))+
     -                     (matrix(3,3)*matrix(1,2)*matrix(2,1)) )
         case (4:)
           determinant = 0.0
```

```
      end select
      end subroutine determine
```

DETOUR *Program File*

This program was partly listed in Chapter 7, *Dynamic Memory Management.* It is a generalization of the TOUR program also in that chapter.

```
      module city_list
      type river
            type (river), pointer :: upstream
            character (len=25)    :: city
            type (river), pointer :: downstream
      end type river
      type ( river ), pointer    :: finish
      type ( river ), pointer    :: start
      type ( river ), pointer    :: travel
      end module city_list

      program detour
!
!     Use a doubly linked list to travel downstream and
!     upstream along a river.  The sample input file
!     lists the start and end points and selected cities
!     on the Mississippi.
!
      use city_list
      character (len=25)         :: city_input
      type ( river ), pointer    :: temp
!
!     Initialize the first data element.
      allocate ( start )
      nullify ( start%upstream   )
      start%city = ' '
      nullify ( start%downstream )
      travel => start
!
!     Read the cities along the way.
      print *, " "
      print *, "Enter cities ..."
      do
            read ( *,100,end=200 ) city_input
100         format ( a25 )
!
!           Keep track of the previous city.
            temp => travel
!
!           Record the current city.
            travel%city = city_input
```

```
!
!          Allocate memory for the next city and
!          point to that storage.
           allocate ( travel%downstream )
           travel => travel%downstream
!
!          Link the previous city as "upstream" from
!          the current city.
           travel%upstream => temp
        end do
200     continue
!
!       Keep track of the last city.
        finish => temp
!
!       Clear the end-of-list.
        nullify ( travel%downstream )
!
!       Advise the user that all data have been read.
        print *, " "
        print *, "All city names have been read ..."
!
!       Show the cities going downstream.
        print *, " "
        print *, "LIST the original tour"
        print *, "===================="
        call droute
!
!       Replace Davenport with Dubuque.
        print *, " "
        print *, "REPLACE Davenport with Dubuque"
        print *, "==============================="
        travel => start
        do
            if ( travel%city(1:4) .eq. 'Dave' ) then
                travel%city = 'Dubuque, Iowa'
                exit
            else
                travel => travel%downstream
                if ( .not. associated ( travel%downstream ) ) exit
            end if
        end do
        call uroute
!
!       Insert Hannibal below Rock Island and above St. Louis.
        print *, " "
        print *, "INSERT Hannibal between Rock Island and St. Louis"
        print *, "================================================="
        travel => start
        do
```

```
         if ( travel%city(1:11) .eq. 'Rock Island' ) then
             call city_insert ( "Hannibal, Missouri      " )
             exit
         else
             travel => travel%downstream
             if ( .not. associated ( travel%downstream ) ) exit
         end if
     end do
     call droute
!
!    Delete Vicksburg (below Memphis and above Natchez).
     print *, " "
     print *, "DELETE Vicksburg from between Memphis and Natchez"
     print *, "================================================="
     travel => start
     do
         if ( travel%city(1:9) .eq. 'Vicksburg' ) then
             temp => travel%downstream
             travel => travel%upstream
             deallocate ( travel%downstream )
             travel%downstream => temp
             temp%upstream => travel
             nullify ( temp )
             exit
         else
             travel => travel%downstream
             if ( .not. associated ( travel%downstream ) ) exit
         end if
     end do
     call uroute
!
!    Clear the linked list allocation.
     print *, " "
     print *, "DEALLOCATE the linked list"
     print *, "=========================="
     print *, " "
     print *, "    Cities deallocated going downstream ..."
     travel => start
     do
         print *, "     ", travel%city
         temp => travel%downstream
         deallocate ( travel )
         if ( .not. associated ( temp%downstream ) ) exit
         travel => temp
     end do
     nullify ( finish    )
     nullify ( start     )
     nullify ( temp      )
!
```

```
!       End of program.
        print *, " "
        end program detour
!
!       Show the downstream route.
        subroutine droute
        use city_list
        print *, " "
        print *, "      Cities passed going downstream ..."
        travel => start
        do
            print *, "      ", travel%city
            travel => travel%downstream
            if ( .not. associated ( travel%downstream ) ) exit
        end do
        end subroutine droute
!
!       Show the upstream route.
        subroutine uroute
        use city_list
        print *, " "
        print *, "      Cities passed going upstream ..."
        travel => finish
        do
            print *, "      ", travel%city
            if ( .not. associated ( travel%upstream ) ) exit
            travel => travel%upstream
        end do
        end subroutine uroute

        subroutine city_insert ( city_input )
        use city_list
        character (len=25)        :: city_input
        type ( river ), pointer   :: down, temp
        down => travel%downstream
        allocate ( temp )
        temp%city = city_input
        temp%upstream => travel
        temp%downstream => travel%downstream
        travel%downstream => temp
        down%upstream => temp
        nullify ( down, temp )
        end subroutine city_insert
```

F90OPEN Program File

Output from this program was shown in Chapter 8, *File Handling*. The program exists merely to illustrate all the attributes of files managed by the OPEN statement.

```
      program f90open
c
c     Declare OPEN and INQUIRE statement variables.
      character acc*10, act*09, blnk*04, del*10, dir*07, fin*12,
     -          fmt*09, fm*11, fn*12, pad*03, pos*06, r*07,
     -          rw*07, seq*07, sta*07, unf*11, w*7
      integer  ios,  nr,    num,    recl,  u
      logical  ex,   nmd,   od
c     Declare local subprograms.
      logical  f90openeh
      external f90openeh
c     Initialize OPEN and INQUIRE statement variables.
      acc  = ' '
      act  = ' '
      blnk = ' '
      del  = ' '
      dir  = ' '
      ex   = .FALSE.
      fin  = 'FOPEN.SF'
      fm   = ' '
      fmt  = ' '
      ios  = 0
      fn   = ' '
      nmd  = .FALSE.
      nr   = 0
      num  = 0
      od   = .FALSE.
      pad  = ' '
      pos  = ' '
      r    = ' '
      recl = 0
      rw   = ' '
      seq  = ' '
      sta  = ' '
      unf  = ' '
      u    = 7
      w    = ' '
c
c     Tell the user what's up.
      print 100
100   format ( / 1H , 'F90OPEN exercises file handling.' )
```

```
c
c      Open the file.
       open ( unit=u, file=fin, err=200, iostat=ios )
200    continue
       if ( .NOT. f90openeh ( 'OPEN   ', ios ) ) go to 1000
c
c      Display OPEN keyword values.
       print 300
300    format ( / 1H , 'Fortran 90 OPEN keyword values ...' )
       print 400, acc, act, blnk, del,  fin, fm,
      -           ios, pad, pos,  recl, sta, u
400    format ( 1H , 'access    ', a10,   3x, 'action    ', a9,
      -       / 1H , 'blank     ', a4,    9x, 'delim     ', a10,
      -       / 1H , 'file      ', a8,    5x, 'form      ', a11,
      -       / 1H , 'iostat    ', i5.5,  8x, 'pad       ', a3,
      -       / 1H , 'position  ', a6,    7x, 'recl      ', i5.5,
      -       / 1H , 'status    ', a7,    6x, 'unit      ', i5.5)
c
c      Get the status of the file.
       inquire(unit=u,                   err=500,      iostat=ios,
      -        access=acc,   action=act,blank=blnk,   delim=del,
      -        direct=dir,   exist=ex,  form=fm,       formatted=fmt,
      -        name=fn,      named=nmd, nextrec=nr,    number=num,
      -        opened=od,    pad=pad,   position=pos,read=r,
      -        readwrite=rw, recl=recl, sequential=seq,
      -        unformatted=unf, write=w )
500    continue
       if ( .NOT. f90openeh ( 'INQUIRE', ios ) ) go to 1000
c
c      Display INQUIRE keyword values.
       print 600
600    format ( / 1H , 'Fortran 90 INQUIRE keyword values ...' )
       print 700, acc,  act,  blnk, del, dir, ex,
      -           fin,  fm,   fmt,  ios, fn,  nmd
700    format ( 1H , 'access    ', a10,   3x, 'action    ', a9,
      -       / 1H , 'blank     ', a4,    9x, 'delim     ', a10,
      -       / 1H , 'direct    ', a4,    9x, 'exist     ', l1,
      -       / 1H , 'file      ', a8,    5x, 'form      ', a11,
      -       / 1H , 'formatted ', a9,    4x, 'iostat    ', i5.5,
      -       / 1H , 'name      ', a12,   1x, 'named     ', l1 )
       print 800, nr,   num,  od,   pad, pos, r,
      -           rw,   recl, seq,  unf, u,   w
800    format( 1H , 'nextrec   ', i5.5,  8x, 'number    ', i5.5,
      -       / 1H , 'opened    ', l1,    12x, 'pad       ', a3,
      -       / 1H , 'position  ', a6,    7x, 'read      ', a7,
      -       / 1H , 'readwrite ', a7,    6x, 'recl      ', i5.5,
      -       / 1H , 'sequential', a7,    6x, 'unformatted', a11,
      -       / 1H , 'unit      ', i5.5,  8x, 'write     ', a7 )
c
c      Close the file.
```

```
       sta = 'DELETE'
       close ( unit=u, err=900, iostat=ios, status=sta )
900    continue
       if ( .NOT. f90openeh ( 'CLOSE  ', ios ) ) go to 1000
c
c      Error handling.
1000   continue
c
c      End of processing.
       print 1100
1100   format ( / 1H , 'F90OPEN is finished.' / )
       end program f90open
c
c
       logical function f90openeh ( statement, ios )
       character*7 statement
       integer    ios
       f90openeh = .FALSE.
       if ( ios .gt. 0 ) then
           print 100, statement, ios
100        format ( / 1H , 'ERROR! ', a7, ' statement (',
      -                    'IOSTAT=', i5.5, ')' )
       else if ( ios .eq. 0 ) then
           f90openeh = .TRUE.
           print 200, statement, ios
200        format ( / 1H , a7, ' statement worked fine (',
      -                      'IOSTAT=', i5.5, ')' )
       else
           print 300, statement, ios
300        format ( / 1H , a7, ' statement IOSTAT = ', i6.5, '?' )
       end if
       end function f90openeh
```

POS Program File

This program, which shows all the possible position states that a file can have, was partly listed in Chapter 8, *File Handling*.

```
       program pos
c
c      Declare (and initialize) variables and functions.
       logical    error
       integer    iostat
       integer  :: unit = 7
       character*9 position
c
c      Tell the user what's up.
       print *, " "
```

```
      print *, "POS exercises file POSITION inquiries"
      print *, " "
c
c     Open a file and report on position.
      open ( unit=unit,file='pos.file',status='NEW',iostat=iostat )
      if ( error ( 'OPEN', iostat ) ) go to 300
      inquire ( unit=unit, position=position, iostat=iostat )
      if ( error ( 'INQUIRE', iostat ) ) go to 300
      call location ( 'OPEN', position )
c
c     Write a few lines into file and report on position.
      write ( unit,100 )
100   format ( ///// )
      inquire ( unit=unit, position=position, iostat=iostat )
      if ( error ( 'WRITE', iostat ) ) go to 300
      call location ( 'WRITE', position )
c
c     Rewind the file and report on position.
      rewind unit
      inquire ( unit=unit, position=position, iostat=iostat )
      if ( error ( 'REWIND', iostat ) ) go to 300
      call location ( 'REWIND', position )
c
c     Read a few records and report on position.
      read ( unit,200 )
200   format ( /// )
      inquire ( unit=unit, position=position, iostat=iostat )
      if ( error ( 'READ', iostat ) ) go to 300
      call location ( 'READ', position )
c
c     Close and delete the file and then report position.
      close ( unit=unit, status='DELETE' )
      inquire ( unit=unit, position=position, iostat=iostat )
      if ( error ( 'CLOSE', iostat ) ) go to 300
      call location ( 'CLOSE', position )
c
c     End of processing.
      go to 400
c
c     Error handling managed by ERROR function.
300   continue
c
c     Tell the user its over.
400   continue
      print *, " "
      print *, "POS is finished"
      print *, " "
c
c     Attach subprograms.
      contains
```

```
c
c      Report any error.
       function error ( action, status )
       character(*) action
       integer      status
       if ( status .eq. 0 ) then
           error = .FALSE.
       else
           error = .TRUE.
           print 100, status, action
100        format ( 1H , 'ERROR! status ', i5.5, ' action ', a9 )
       end if
       end function error
c
c      Report file position.
       subroutine location ( action, place )
       character(*) action
       character*9  place
       print 100, action, place
100    format ( 1H , '... position after ', a6, ' is ' , a9 )
       end subroutine location
c
c      End of program.
       end program pos
```

NUMERIC Program File

This test program, which appeared in Chapter 9, *Numeric Models*, shows all the KIND values available on the computer system, and the parameters of integer and floating-point numbers.

```
       program numeric
c
c      Exercise numeric model functions.
c
c      Declare variable types.
       character                  a
       complex                    c
       integer                    current_kind
       double precision       :: d =123.56d0
       integer                    digits_precision
       integer                    exponent_range
       integer                :: i = 789
       logical                    l
       integer                    old_kind
       type kind_structure
           integer precision
           integer range
```

```
      end  type kind_structure
      type ( kind_structure ) :: types(10)
      real                     :: x = 123.56
c
c     Report basic kinds.
      print *,    " "
      print *,    "KINDs"
      print *,    " "
      print 100, "Character (KIND)", kind(a)
  100 format ( a40, ': ', g24.10 )
      print 100, "Complex (KIND)", kind(c)
      print 100, "Double precision (KIND)", kind(d)
      print 100, "Integer (KIND)", kind(i)
      print 100, "Logical (KIND)", kind(l)
      print 100, "Real (KIND)", kind(x)
c
c     Report on the INTEGER model.
      print *,    " "
      print *,    "INTEGER components"
      print *,    " "
      print 200, "Base of model (RADIX)", radix(i)
  200 format ( a40, ': ', g24.10 )
      print 200, "Bits defined in model (BIT_SIZE)", bit_size(i)
      print 200, "Significant digits (DIGITS)", digits(i)
      print *,    " "
      print *,    "INTEGER extrema"
      print *,    " "
      print 200, "Largest value (HUGE)", huge(i)
      print 200, "Decimal exponent range (RANGE)", range(i)
      print *,    " "
      print *,    "INTEGER manipulation"
      print *,    " "
      print 200, "Kind (KIND)", kind(i)
      old_kind = selected_int_kind(1)
      do exponent_range = 2, 128, 1
         current_kind = selected_int_kind(exponent_range)
         if ( current_kind .ne. old_kind ) then
             print 300, "Valid kind (SELECTED_INT_KIND)",
     -                       old_kind, exponent_range-1
  300        format ( a40, ':      ', i5, ' => +/- 10**', i3.3 )
             old_kind = current_kind
         end if
         if ( current_kind .eq. -1 ) exit
      end do
c
c     Report on the REAL model.
      print *,    " "
      print *,    "REAL components"
      print *,    " "
      print 400, "Base of model (RADIX)", radix(x)
```

```
400 format ( a40, ': ', g24.10 )
    print 400, "Significant digits (DIGITS)", digits(x)
    print 400, "Minimum exponent (MINEXPONENT)", minexponent(x)
    print 400, "Maximum exponent (MAXEXPONENT)", maxexponent(x)
    print *,   " "
    print *,   "REAL extrema"
    print *,   " "
    print 400, "Smallest value (TINY)", tiny(x)
    print 400, "Largest value (HUGE)", huge(x)
    print 400, "Decimal exponent range (RANGE)", range(x)
    print *,   " "
    print *,   "REAL precision"
    print *,   " "
    print 400, "Decimal precision (PRECISION)", precision(x)
    print 400, "Negligible value (EPSILON)", epsilon(x)
    print *,   " "
    print *,   "REAL fit"
    print *,   " "
    print 400, "Value of x", x
    print 400, "Exponent part (EXPONENT)", exponent(x)
    print 400, "Scale (SCALE)", scale(x,radix(x))
    print 400, "Nearest + infinity (NEAREST)", nearest(x, 1.0)
    print 400, "Nearest - infinity (NEAREST)", nearest(x,-1.0)
    print 400, "Fractional part (FRACTION)", fraction(x)
    print 400, "Absolute spacing (SPACING)", spacing(x)
    print 400, "Relative spacing (RRSPACING)", rrspacing(x)
    print 400, "Exponent form (SET_EXPONENT)", 
   -           set_exponent(fraction(x),exponent(x))
    print *,   " "
    print *,   "REAL manipulation"
    print *,   " "
    print 400, "Kind (KIND)", kind(x)
    types(:)%precision = 0
    types(:)%range     = 0
    R: do exponent_range = 1, 512, 1
       P: do digits_precision = 1, 128, 1
          current_kind = selected_real_kind(digits_precision,
   -                                         exponent_range    )
          if ( current_kind .gt. 0 ) then
             if ( digits_precision .gt.
   -             types(current_kind)%precision )
   -             types(current_kind)%precision=digits_precision
             if ( exponent_range .gt.
   -             types(current_kind)%range )
   -             types(current_kind)%range = exponent_range
          end if
          if ( current_kind .eq. -1 ) exit
       end do P
       if ( current_kind .eq. -2 ) exit
    end do R
```

```
      do i = 1, 10, 1
         if ( types(i)%precision .eq. 0 ) cycle
            print 500, "Valid kind (SELECTED_REAL_KIND)",
     -                    i, types(i)%precision,
     -                    types(i)%range
 500           format ( a40, ':      ', i5, ' => p=',i3.3,
     -                                   ' r=',i3.3  )
      end do
c
c     Report on the DOUBLE PRECISION data type.
      print *,   " "
      print *,   "DOUBLE PRECISION components"
      print *,   " "
      print 600, "Base of model (RADIX)", radix(d)
 600 format ( a40, ': ', g24.10 )
      print 600, "Significant digits (DIGITS)", digits(d)
      print 600, "Minimum exponent (MINEXPONENT)", minexponent(d)
      print 600, "Maximum exponent (MAXEXPONENT)", maxexponent(d)
      print *,   " "
      print *,   "DOUBLE PRECISION extrema"
      print *,   " "
      print 600, "Smallest value (TINY)", tiny(d)
      print 600, "Largest value (HUGE)", huge(d)
      print 600, "Decimal exponent range (RANGE)", range(d)
      print *,   " "
      print *,   "DOUBLE PRECISION precision"
      print *,   " "
      print 600, "Decimal precision (PRECISION)", precision(d)
      print 600, "Negligible value (EPSILON)", epsilon(d)
      print *,   " "
      print *,   "DOUBLE PRECISION fit"
      print *,   " "
      print 600, "Value of d", d
      print 600, "Exponent part (EXPONENT)", exponent(d)
      print 600, "Scale (SCALE)", scale(d,radix(d))
      print 600, "Nearest + infinity (NEAREST)", nearest(d, 1.0)
      print 600, "Nearest - infinity (NEAREST)", nearest(d,-1.0)
      print 600, "Fractional part (FRACTION)", fraction(d)
      print 600, "Absolute spacing (SPACING)", spacing(d)
      print 600, "Relative spacing (RRSPACING)", rrspacing(d)
      print 600, "Exponent form (SET_EXPONENT)",
     -            set_exponent(fraction(d),exponent(d))
      print *,   " "
      print *,   "DOUBLE PRECISION manipulation"
      print *,   " "
      print 600, "Kind (KIND)", kind(d)
```

```
c
c      End of processing.
       print *,   " "
       end program numeric
```

E

Obtaining Configuration Software

Obtaining the Example Programs

The software is available electronically in a number of ways: by FTP, FTPMAIL, BITFTP, and UUCP. The cheapest, fastest, and easiest ways are listed first. The first one that works for you is probably the best. Use FTP if you are directly on the Internet. Use FTPMAIL if you are not on the Internet but can send and receive electronic mail to Internet sites (this includes CompuServe users). Use BITFTP if you send electronic mail via BITNET. Use UUCP if none of the above work.

FTP

To use FTP, you need a machine with direct access to the Internet. The software may be obtained from any of the hosts below. (The last host is likely to have the most up-to-date distributions.)

Machine	Directory
ftp.uu.net	/published/oreilly/nutshell/fortran90
ftp.ora.com	/pub/nutshell/fortran90
ftp.primate.wisc.edu	/pub/fortran90-book

A sample session is shown, with what you should type in boldface:

```
% ftp ftp.uu.net
Connected to ftp.uu.net.
220 FTP server (Version 6.21 Tue Mar 10 22:09:55 EST 1992) ready.
Name (ftp.uu.net:kismet): anonymous
```

```
331 Guest login OK, send domain style e-mail address as password.
Password: kismet@ora.com (Use your user name and host here)
230 Guest login OK, access restrictions apply.
ftp> cd /published/oreilly/nutshell/fortran90
250 CWD command successful.
ftp> binary (Very important! You must specify binary transfer for
compressed files.)
200 Type set to I.
ftp> get fortran90.tar.Z
200 PORT command successful.
150 Opening BINARY mode data connection for fortran90.tar.Z.
226 Transfer complete.
ftp> quit
221 Goodbye.
%
```

Once you obtain a distribution, extract the files from it by typing:

```
% zcat fortran90.tar.Z | tar xf -
```

System V systems require the following *tar* command instead:

```
% zcat fortran90.tar.Z | tar xof -
```

If *zcat* is not available on your system, use separate *uncompress* and *tar* commands:

```
% uncompress fortran90.tar.Z
% tar xf fortran90.tar.Z    or    tar xof fortran90.tar.Z
```

FTPMAIL

FTPMAIL is a mail server available to anyone who can send and receive electronic mail to and from Internet sites. This includes most workstations that have an e-mail connection to the outside world, and CompuServe users. You do not need to be directly on the Internet. Here's how to do it.

You send mail to *ftpmail@decwrl.dec.com*. In the message body, give the name of the anonymous FTP host and the FTP commands you want to run. The server will run anonymous FTP for you and mail the files back to you. To get a complete help file, send a message with no subject and the single word "help" in the body. The following is an example mail session that should get you a listing of the files in the selected directory and the file *fortran90.tar.Z\fP*. The listing is useful in case there are other files you may be interested in.

```
% mail ftpmail@decwrl.dec.com
Subject:
reply alan@ora.com    (where you want files mailed)
```

```
connect ftp.uu.net
cd /published/oreilly/nutshell/fortran90
dir
binary
uuencode      (or btoa if you have it)
get fortran90.tar.Z
quit
%
```

A signature at the end of the message is acceptable as long as it appears after "quit."

All retrieved files will be split into 60KB chunks and mailed to you. You then remove the mail headers and concatenate them into one file, and then *uudecode* or *atob* it. Once you've got the desired distribution, extract the files from it by following the directions under FTP.

BITFTP

BITFTP is a mail server for BITNET users. You send it electronic mail messages requesting files, and it sends you back the files by electronic mail. BITFTP currently serves only users who send it mail from nodes that are directly on BITNET, EARN, or NetNorth. BITFTP is a public service of Princeton University. Here's how it works.

To use BITFTP, send mail containing your FTP commands to *BITFTP@PUCC.* For a complete help file, send HELP as the message body.

The following is the message body you should send to BITFTP:

```
FTP  ftp.uu.net  NETDATA
USER  anonymous
PASS your Internet e-mail address (not your bitnet address)
CD  /published/oreilly/nutshell/fortran90
DIR
BINARY
GET  fortran90.tar.Z
QUIT
```

Once you've got the desired distribution, extract the files from it by following the directions under FTP.

Questions about BITFTP can be directed to *MAINT@PUCC* on BITNET.

UUCP

UUCP is standard on virtually all UNIX systems. The software is available by UUCP via modem from UUNET; UUNET's connect-time charges apply.

You can get the software from UUNET whether you have an account or not. If you or your company has an account with UUNET, you will have a system with a direct

UUCP connection to UUNET. Find that system, and type the following command (type everything on one line):

```
uucp uunet\!/published/oreilly/nutshell/fortran90/fortran90.tar.Z
   yourhost\!yourname
```

The backslashes can be omitted if you use the Bourne shell (*sh*) instead of *csh*. The file should appear some time later (up to a day or more) in the directory */usr/spool/uucppublic/yourname*. If you don't have an account but would like one so that you can get electronic mail, then contact UUNET at 703-204-8000.

If you don't have a UUNET account, you can set up a UUCP connection to UUNET using the phone number 1-900-468-7727. As of this writing, the cost is 50 cents per minute. The charges will appear on your next telephone bill. The login name is "uucp" with no password. For example, an *L.sys/Systems* entry might look like:

uunet Any ACU 19200 1-900-468-7727 ogin:—ogin: uucp

Your entry may vary depending on your UUCP configuration. If you have a PEP-capable modem, make sure \f(CWs50=255s111=30\fP is set before calling.

Once you've got the desired distribution, extract the files from it by following the directions under FTP.

Index

doubly linked lists, 156–164
DPROD intrinsic, 246
DSPREAD program, 265
dynamic memory management,
    135–173
    allocatable arrays and, 135–136,
        137–141
    pointers and, 141–173
    targets and, 141–169

E

E edit descriptor, 208
Earth's Aura, 125
Edington, J.A., 190
edit descriptors
    Fortran 77, 203–205
ELSE IF statement, 8
ELSE statement, 8
ELSEWHERE statement, 9, 48
EN edit descriptor, 208
encapsulation, 124
END IF statement, 7
END MODULE NAME statement, 121
END MODULE statement, 121
end off shifting, 32–36
END statement, 7, 9
ENDFILE statement, 7
end-of-file, opening files at, 182–184
engineering notation, 208–209
ENTRY statement, 8
EOSHIFT intrinsic, 32–36, 49, 252, 260,
    272
EPSILON intrinsic, 222, 227, 228, 252,
    262
EQUIVALENCE statement, 4, 7
    derived types in, storage of, 81
    modules and, 124, 125
    pointer restrictions and, 172
    sequential storage and, 137
    TRANSFER intrinsic and, 281
Erlang variates, 290
error detection
    ADVANCE program and, 190–194
error handling
    optional arguments for, 100–102
    program structure and, 84

ES edit descriptor, 208
exclamation point (!), 11, 12
exclusive OR, 239–240
execution flow, tracing, 92
EXISTS program, 291–292
EXIT DO loop feature, 77
EXIT statement, 4, 9
EXP intrinsic, 246
EXPONENT intrinsic, 228, 252, 262
extending arrays, 263
extensions, compatibility and, 5
EXTERNAL functions, 7
extracting
    array sections, 27–28
    array sections with vector
        subscripts, 29–31
    bit fields, 241-242
    diagonals, 28

F

F90OPEN program, 177, 186
    source code, 335–337
Fahrenheit conversion, 49
file handling, 175–211
    expanded file options, 176–186
    formats, 203–211
    Fortran 90 facilities, 175–176
    read-only files, 178
file pointers
    in sequential files, 186–188
FILENAME program, 249
files
    attributes, 176–178
    definition of types, 176
    detecting location in, 186–188
    direct access, computing record
        length in, 188–189
    formatted, maximum record
        length in, 185–186
    information about, 186–189
    overwriting, 184–185
    sequential, 180–182
FILTER argument, 269
fixed format source code, 12–13
fixed storage, 137–138

About the Author

Jim Kerrigan works as a consultant for a computer hardware vendor. He has been involved with Fortran in both research and commercial environments for over twenty years. Jim admits to having used Fortran to create programs ranging from socioeconomic forecasting to data parallel algorithms and from a project management package to operating system monitors. Before working for computer companies (first Prime, then Sequent, and now Hewlett-Packard), Jim received a BA in Archaeology from Temple University and an MA in Regional Science from the University of Pennsylvania. He has written one book already, *From Fortran to C*, published by Windcrest/McGraw-Hill.

Colophon

Our look is the result of reader comments, our own experimentation, and feedback from distribution channels.

Distinctive covers complement our distinctive approach to technical topics, breathing personality and life into potentially dry subjects. UNIX and its attendant programs can be unruly beasts. Nutshell Handbooks help you tame them.

A Canada goose graces the cover of *Migrating to Fortran 90*. Canada geese, also called "honkers" because of their horn-like call, are migratory birds. Their range extends from Canada and Alaska in the summer, to the Gulf of Mexico in the winter. Canada geese are highly social, living in groups called gaggles or skeins of 200 to 300 individuals. During the breeding season each pair, which mate for life, split from the larger group. Nesting begins in March or April, depending on latitude and weather. Canada geese preferably nest on the ground near water, but have been known to inhabit the abandoned nests of birds of prey in trees. Clutch size averages 5 to 6, and incubation takes 28 days. The female goose incubates the eggs, while the gander stands guard beside her. They are very protective, as anyone who has approached a nesting pair knows. Their hissing is legendary, and their beating wings can become serious weapons. There is a record of a man being knocked from his horse by a goose protecting its nest; the man recovered but the goose died. There have also been reports of geese beating dogs and other attackers with their wings, and if attacked in the water they've been known to sit on their adversary's head until they drown.

The young are led to water soon after hatching, and in the case of those hatched in trees, are pushed out by their mothers. Goslings have many enemies, including large fish. But for those who survive, maturity comes in only six weeks, in time to assimilate into a group and begin their first migration. Geese fly in distinctive V and W shaped patterns, and their distinctive honking is a harbinger of spring for people who live along their flight path. Geese have been clocked at 60 mph, but take many months to arrive at their summer feeding grounds. They travel only as fast as the temperature rises, and move an average of 9 to 30 miles a day.

Edie Freedman designed this cover and the entire UNIX bestiary that appears on other Nutshell Handbooks. The beasts themselves are adapted from 19th-century engravings from the Dover Pictorial Archive. The cover layout was produced with Quark XPress 3.1 using the ITC Garamond font.

The inside layout was designed by Edie Freedman and was implemented by Mike Sierra in FrameMaker 3.1 using the ITC Garamond Light and ITC Garamond Book fonts. The figures were created in Aldus Freehand 3.1 by Chris Reilley. The colophon was written by Allen Noren.

From the best-selling The Whole Internet *to our Nutshell Handbooks, there's something here for everyone. Whether you're a novice or expert UNIX user, these books will give you just what you're looking for: user-friendly, definitive information on a range of UNIX topics.*

Using UNIX

Connecting to the Internet: An O'Reilly Buyer's Guide **NEW**

By Susan Estrada
1st Edition August 1993
188 pages
ISBN 1-56592-061-9

More and more people are interested in exploring the Internet, and this book is the fastest way for you to learn how to get started. This book provides practical advice on how to determine the level of Internet service right for you, and how to find a local access provider and evaluate the services they offer.

!%@:: A Directory of Electronic Mail **NEW** Addressing & Networks

By Donnalyn Frey & Rick Adams
3rd Edition August 1993
458 pages, ISBN 1-56592-031-7

The only up-to-date directory that charts the networks that make up the Internet, provides contact names and addresses, and describes the services each network provides. It includes all of the major Internet-based networks, as well as various commercial networks such as CompuServe, Delphi, and America Online that are "gatewayed" to the Internet for transfer of electronic mail and other services. If you are someone who wants to connect to the Internet, or someone who already is connected but wants concise, up-to-date information on many of the world's networks, check out this book.

Learning the UNIX Operating System **NEW**

By Grace Todino, John Strang & Jerry Peek
3rd Edition August 1993
108 pages, ISBN 1-56592-060-0

If you are new to UNIX, this concise introduction will tell you just what you need to get started and no more. Why wade through a six-hundred-page book when you can begin working productively in a matter of minutes? This book is the most effective introduction to UNIX in print. This new edition has been updated and expanded to provide increased coverage of window systems and networking. It's a handy book for someone just starting with UNIX, as well as someone who encounters a UNIX system as a visitor via remote login over the Internet.

The Whole Internet User's Guide & Catalog

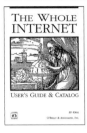

By Ed Krol
1st Edition September 1992
400 pages, ISBN 1-56592-025-2

A comprehensive—and best-selling—introduction to the Internet, the international network that includes virtually every major computer site in the world. The Internet is a resource of almost unimaginable wealth. In addition to electronic mail and news services, thousands of public archives, databases, and other special services are available: everything from space flight announcements to ski reports. This book is a comprehensive introduction to what's available and how to find it. In addition to electronic mail, file transfer, remote login, and network news, *The Whole Internet* pays special attention to some new tools for helping you find information. Whether you're a researcher, a student, or just someone who likes electronic mail, this book will help you to explore what's possible.

Smileys

By David W. Sanderson, 1st Edition March 1993
93 pages, ISBN 1-56592-041-4

Originally used to convey some kind of emotion in an e-mail message, smileys are some combination of typographic characters that depict sideways a happy or sad face. Now there are hundreds of variations, including smileys that depict presidents, animals, and cartoon characters. Not everyone likes to read mail messages littered with smileys, but almost everyone finds them humorous. The smileys in this book have been collected by David Sanderson, whom the *Wall Street Journal* called the "Noah Webster of Smileys."

UNIX Power Tools

By Jerry Peek, Mike Loukides, Tim O'Reilly, et al.
1st Edition March 1993
1162 pages
(Bantam ISBN)
0-553-35402-7

Ideal for UNIX users who hunger for technical—yet accessible—information, *UNIX Power Tools* consists of tips, tricks, concepts, and freely-available software. Covers add-on utilities and how to take advantage of clever features in the most popular UNIX utilities. CD-ROM included.

Learning the Korn Shell NEW

By Bill Rosenblatt
1st Edition June 1993
363 pages, ISBN 1-56592-054-6

This new Nutshell Handbook is a thorough introduction to the Korn shell, both as a user interface and as a programming language. Provides a clear explanation of the Korn shell's features, including *ksh* string operations, co-processes, signals and signal handling, and command-line interpretation. Also includes real-life programming examples and a Korn shell debugger *(kshdb)*.

Learning perl NEW

By Randal L. Schwartz, 1st Edition November 1993 (est.)
220 pages (est.), ISBN 1-56592-042-2

Perl is rapidly becoming the "universal scripting language". Combining capabilities of the UNIX shell, the C programming language, *sed*, *awk*, and various other utilities, it has proved its use for tasks ranging from system administration to text processing and distributed computing. *Learning perl* is a step-by-step, hands-on tutorial designed to get you writing useful perl scripts as quickly as possible. In addition to countless code examples, there are numerous programming exercises, with full answers. For a comprehensive and detailed guide to programming with Perl, read O'Reilly's companion book *Programming perl*.

Programming perl

By Larry Wall & Randal L. Schwartz
1st Edition January 1991, 428 pages, ISBN 0-937175-64-1

Authoritative guide to the hottest new UNIX utility in years, co-authored by its creator. Perl is a language for easily manipulating text, files, and processes.

Learning GNU Emacs

By Deb Cameron & Bill Rosenblatt
1st Edition October 1991
442 pages, ISBN 0-937175-84-6

An introduction to the GNU Emacs editor, one of the most widely used and powerful editors available under UNIX. Provides a solid introduction to basic editing, a look at several important "editing modes" (special Emacs features for editing specific types of documents), and a brief introduction to customization and Emacs LISP programming. The book is aimed at new Emacs users, whether or not they are programmers.

sed & awk

By Dale Dougherty, 1st Edition November 1990
414 pages, ISBN 0-937175-59-5

For people who create and modify text files, *sed*
and *awk* are power tools for editing. Most of the
things that you can do with these programs can be
done interactively with a text editor. However, using
sed and *awk* can save many hours of repetitive
work in achieving the same result.

MH & xmh: E-mail for Users & Programmers

By Jerry Peek, 2nd Edition September 1992
728 pages, ISBN 1-56592-027-9

Customize your e-mail environment to save time
and make communicating more enjoyable. *MH &
xmh: E-mail for Users & Programmers* explains
how to use, customize, and program with the MH
electronic mail commands available on virtually any
UNIX system. The handbook also covers *xmh*, an X
Window System client that runs MH programs. The
new second edition has been updated for X Release 5
and MH 6.7.2. We've added a chapter on *mhook*,
new sections explaining under-appreciated small
commands and features, and more examples showing how to use MH to handle common situations.

Learning the vi Editor

By Linda Lamb, 5th Edition October 1990
192 pages, ISBN 0-937175-67-6

A complete guide to text editing with *vi*, the editor
available on nearly every UNIX system. Early chapters cover the basics; later chapters explain more
advanced editing tools, such as *ex* commands and
global search and replacement.

UNIX in a Nutshell:
For System V & Solaris 2.0

By Daniel Gilly and the staff of O'Reilly & Associates
2nd Edition June 1992, 444 pages, ISBN 1-56592-001-5

You may have seen UNIX quick reference guides,
but you've never seen anything like *UNIX in a
Nutshell*. Not a scaled-down quick-reference of
common commands, *UNIX in a Nutshell* is a complete reference containing all commands and
options, along with generous descriptions and
examples that put the commands in context. For all
but the thorniest UNIX problems this one reference
should be all the documentation you need. Covers
System V Releases 3 and 4 and Solaris 2.0.

An alternate version of this quick-reference is
available for Berkeley UNIX.
Berkeley Edition, December 1986
(latest update October 1990)
272 pages, ISBN 0-937175-20-X

Using UUCP and Usenet

By Grace Todino & Dale Dougherty
1st Edition December 1986 (latest update October 1991)
210 pages, ISBN 0-937175-10-2

Shows users how to communicate with both UNIX
and non-UNIX systems using UUCP and *cu* or *tip*, and
how to read news and post articles. This handbook
assumes that UUCP is already running at your site.

System Administration

Managing UUCP and Usenet

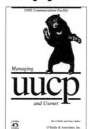

By Tim O'Reilly & Grace Todino
10th Edition January 1992
368 pages, ISBN 0-937175-93-5

For all its widespread use,
UUCP is one of the most difficult UNIX utilities to master.
This book is for system
administrators who want to
install and manage UUCP and
Usenet software. "Don't even
TRY to install UUCP without it!"—Usenet message
456@nitrex.UUCP

sendmail   NEW

By Bryan Costales, with Eric Allman & Neil Rickert
1st Edition October 1993 (est.)
600 pages (est.), ISBN 0-937175-056-2

This new Nutshell Handbook
is far and away the most comprehensive book ever written
on *sendmail*, a program that
acts like a traffic cop in rout-
ing and delivering mail on
UNIX-based networks.
Although *sendmail* is the
most widespread of all mail
programs, it's also one of the
last great uncharted territories—and most difficult
utilities to learn—in UNIX system administration.
The book covers both major versions of *sendmail*:
the standard version available on most systems, and
IDA *sendmail*, a version from Europe.

termcap & terminfo

By John Strang, Linda Mui & Tim O'Reilly
3rd Edition July 1992
270 pages, ISBN 0-937175-22-6

For UNIX system administrators and programmers.
This handbook provides information on writing and
debugging terminal descriptions, as well as terminal
initialization, for the two UNIX terminal databases.

DNS and BIND

By Cricket Liu & Paul Albitz, 1st Edition October 1992
418 pages, ISBN 1-56592-010-4

DNS and BIND contains all you need to know about the Domain Name System (DNS) and BIND, its UNIX implementation. The Domain Name System (DNS) is the Internet's "phone book"; it's a database that tracks important information (in particular, names and addresses) for every computer on the Internet. If you're a system administrator, this book will show you how to set up and maintain the DNS software on your network.

Essential System Administration

By Æleen Frisch, 1st Edition October 1991
466 pages, ISBN 0-937175-80-3

Provides a compact, manageable introduction to the tasks faced by everyone responsible for a UNIX system. This guide is for those who use a stand-alone UNIX system, those who routinely provide administrative support for a larger shared system, or those who want an understanding of basic administrative functions. Covers all major versions of UNIX.

X Window System Administrator's Guide

By Linda Mui & Eric Pearce
1st Edition October 1992
372 pages, With CD-ROM: ISBN 1-56592-052-X
Without CD-ROM: ISBN 0-937175-83-8

This book is the first and only book devoted to the issues of system administration for X and X-based networks, written not just for UNIX system administrators but for anyone faced with the job of administering X (including those running X on stand-alone workstations). The *X Window System Administrator's Guide* is available either alone or packaged with the XCD. The CD provides X source code and binaries to complement the book's instructions for installing the software. It contains over 600 megabytes of X11 source code and binaries stored in ISO9660 and RockRidge formats. This will allow several types of UNIX workstations to mount the CD-ROM as a filesystem, browse through the source code and install pre-built software.

Practical UNIX Security

By Simson Garfinkel & Gene Spafford
1st Edition June 1991
512 pages, ISBN 0-937175-72-2

Tells system administrators how to make their UNIX system—either System V or BSD—as secure as it possibly can be without going to trusted system technology. The book describes UNIX concepts and how they enforce security, tells how to defend against and handle security breaches, and explains network security (including UUCP, NFS, Kerberos, and firewall machines) in detail.

Managing NFS and NIS

By Hal Stern
1st Edition June 1991
436 pages, ISBN 0-937175-75-7

Managing NFS and NIS is for system administrators who need to set up or manage a network filesystem installation. NFS (Network Filesystem) is probably running at any site that has two or more UNIX systems. NIS (Network Information System) is a distributed database used to manage a network of computers. The only practical book devoted entirely to these subjects, this guide is a must-have for anyone interested in UNIX networking.

TCP/IP Network Administration

By Craig Hunt
1st Edition July 1992
502 pages, ISBN 0-937175-82-X

A complete guide to setting up and running a TCP/IP network for practicing system administrators. Covers how to set up your network, how to configure important network applications including *send-mail*, and discusses troubleshooting and security. Covers BSD and System V TCP/IP implementations.

System Performance Tuning

By Mike Loukides, 1st Edition November 1990
336 pages, ISBN 0-937175-60-9

System Performance Tuning answers the fundamental question, "How can I get my computer to do more work without buying more hardware?" Some performance problems do require you to buy a bigger or faster computer, but many can be solved simply by making better use of the resources you already have.

Computer Security Basics

By Deborah Russell & G.T. Gangemi Sr.
1st Edition July 1991
464 pages, ISBN 0-937175-71-4

Provides a broad introduction to the many areas of computer security and a detailed description of current security standards. This handbook describes complicated concepts like trusted systems, encryption, and mandatory access control in simple terms, and contains a thorough, readable introduction to the "Orange Book."

UNIX Programming

Understanding Japanese Information Processing   NEW

By Ken Lunde
1st Edition September 1993 (est.)
450 pages (est.), ISBN 1-56592-043-0

Understanding Japanese Information Processing provides detailed information on all aspects of handling Japanese text on computer systems. It tries to bring all of the relevant information together in a single book. It covers everything from the origins of modern-day Japanese to the latest information on specific emerging computer encoding standards. There are over 15 appendices which provide additional reference material, such as a code conversion table, character set tables, mapping tables, an extensive list of software sources, a glossary, and much more.

lex & yacc

By John Levine, Tony Mason & Doug Brown
2nd Edition October 1992
366 pages, ISBN 1-56592-000-7

Shows programmers how to use two UNIX utilities, *lex* and *yacc*, in program development. The second edition of *lex & yacc* contains completely revised tutorial sections for novice users and reference sections for advanced users. The new edition is twice the size of the original book, has an expanded index, and now covers Bison and Flex.

High Performance Computing   NEW

By Kevin Dowd, 1st Edition June 1993
398 pages, ISBN 1-56592-032-5

High Performance Computing makes sense of the newest generation of workstations for application programmers and purchasing managers. It covers everything, from the basics of modern workstation architecture, to structuring benchmarks, to squeezing more performance out of critical applications. It also explains what a good compiler can do—and what you have to do yourself. The book closes with a look at the high-performance future: parallel computers and the more "garden variety" shared memory processors that are appearing on people's desktops.

ORACLE Performance Tuning   NEW

By Peter Corrigan & Mark Gurry
1st Edition September 1993 (est.)
650 pages (est.), ISBN 1-56592-048-1

The ORACLE relational database management system is the most popular database system in use today. With more organizations downsizing and adopting client/server and distributed database approaches, system performance tuning has become vital. This book shows you the many things you can do to dramatically increase the performance of your existing ORACLE system. You may find that this book can save you the cost of a new machine; at the very least, it will save you a lot of headaches.

POSIX Programmer's Guide

By Donald Lewine, 1st Edition April 1991
640 pages, ISBN 0-937175-73-0

Most UNIX systems today are POSIX-compliant because the Federal government requires it for its purchases. However, given the manufacturer's documentation, it can be difficult to distinguish system-specific features from those features defined by POSIX. The *POSIX Programmer's Guide*, intended as an explanation of the POSIX standard and as a reference for the POSIX.1 programming library, helps you write more portable programs.

Understanding DCE

By Ward Rosenberry, David Kenney & Gerry Fisher
1st Edition October 1992
266 pages, ISBN 1-56592-005-8

A technical and conceptual overview of OSF's Distributed Computing Environment (DCE) for programmers and technical managers, marketing and sales people. Unlike many O'Reilly & Associates books, *Understanding DCE* has no hands-on programming elements. Instead, the book focuses on how DCE can be used to accomplish typical programming tasks and provides explanations to help the reader understand all the parts of DCE.

Guide to Writing DCE Applications

By John Shirley
1st Edition July 1992
282 pages, ISBN 1-56592-004-X

A hands-on programming guide to OSF's Distributed Computing Environment (DCE) for first-time DCE application programmers. This book is designed to help new DCE users make the transition from conventional, nondistributed applications programming to distributed DCE programming. Covers the IDL and ACF files, essential RPC calls, binding methods and the name service, server initialization, memory management, and selected advanced topics. Includes practical programming examples.

Power Programming with RPC

By John Bloomer
1st Edition February 1992
522 pages, ISBN 0-937175-77-3

RPC, or remote procedure calling, is the ability to distribute the execution of functions on remote computers. Written from a programmer's perspective, this book shows what you can do with RPC's, like Sun RPC, the de facto standard on UNIX systems. It covers related programming topics for Sun and other UNIX systems and teaches through examples.

Managing Projects with make

By Andrew Oram & Steve Talbott
2nd Edition October 1991
152 pages, ISBN 0-937175-90-0

make is one of UNIX's greatest contributions to software development, and this book is the clearest description of *make* ever written. This revised second edition includes guidelines on meeting the needs of large projects.

Software Portability with imake

By Paul DuBois
1st Edition July 1993
390 pages, 1-56592-055-4

imake is a utility that works with *make* to enable code to be complied and installed on different UNIX machines. This new Nutshell Handbook—the only book available on *imake*—is ideal for X and UNIX programmers who want their software to be portable. It includes a general explanation of *imake*, how to write and debug an *Imakefile*, and how to write configuration files. Several sample sets of configuration files are described and are available free over the Net.

UNIX for FORTRAN Programmers

By Mike Loukides
1st Edition August 1990
264 pages, ISBN 0-937175-51-X

This book provides the serious scientific programmer with an introduction to the UNIX operating system and its tools. The intent of the book is to minimize the UNIX entry barrier and to familiarize readers with the most important tools so they can be productive as quickly as possible.

UNIX for FORTRAN Programmers shows readers how to do things they're interested in: not just how to use a tool such as *make* or *rcs*, but how to use it in program development and how it fits into the toolset as a whole. "An excellent book describing the features of the UNIX FORTRAN compiler *f77* and related software. This book is extremely well written." — American Mathematical Monthly, February 1991

Practical C Programming

By Steve Oualline
2nd Edition January 1993
396 pages, ISBN 1-56592-035-X

C programming is more than just getting the syntax right. Style and debugging also play a tremendous part in creating programs that run well. *Practical C Programming* teaches you not only the mechanics of programming, but also how to create programs that are easy to read, maintain, and debug. There are lots of introductory C books, but this is the Nutshell Handbook! In the second edition, programs now conform to ANSI C.

Checking C Programs with lint

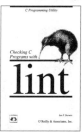

By Ian F. Darwin
1st Edition October 1988
84 pages, ISBN 0-937175-30-7

The *lint* program is one of the best tools for finding portability problems and certain types of coding errors in C programs. This handbook introduces you to *lint*, guides you through running it on your programs, and helps you interpret *lint's* output.

Using C on the UNIX System

By Dave Curry
1st Edition January 1989
250 pages, ISBN 0-937175-23-4

Using C on the UNIX System provides a thorough introduction to the UNIX system call libraries. It is aimed at programmers who already know C but who want to take full advantage of the UNIX programming environment. If you want to learn how to work with the operating system and to write programs that can interact with directories, terminals, and networks at the lowest level you will find this book essential. It is impossible to write UNIX utilities of any sophistication without understanding the material in this book. "A gem of a book. The author's aim is to provide a guide to system programming, and he succeeds admirably. His balance is steady between System V and BSD-based systems, so readers come away knowing both." — SUN Expert, November 1989

Guide to OSF/1

By the staff of O'Reilly & Associates
1st Edition June 1991
304 pages, ISBN 0-937175-78-1

This technically competent introduction to OSF/1 is based on OSF technical seminars. In addition to its description of OSF/1, it includes the differences between OSF/1 and System V Release 4 and a look ahead at DCE.

Understanding and Using COFF

By Gintaras R. Gircys
1st Edition November 1988
196 pages, ISBN 0-937175-31-5

COFF—Common Object File Format—is the formal definition for the structure of machine code files in the UNIX System V environment. All machine-code files are COFF files. This handbook explains COFF data structure and its manipulation.

Career

Love Your Job!

By Dr. Paul Powers, with Deborah Russell
1st Edition August 1993
210 pages, ISBN 1-56592-036-8

Do you love your job? Too few people do. In fact, surveys show that 80 to 95 percent of Americans are dissatisfied with their jobs. Considering that most of us will work nearly 100,000 hours during our lifetimes (half the waking hours of our entire adult lives!), it's sad that our work doesn't bring us the rewards—both financial and emotional—that we deserve. *Love Your Job!* is an inspirational guide to loving your work. It consists of a series of one-page reflections, anecdotes, and exercises aimed at helping readers think more deeply about what they want out of their jobs. Each can be read individually (anyplace, anytime, whenever you need to lift your spirits), or the book can be read and treated as a whole. *Love Your Job!* informs you, inspires you, and challenges you, not only to look outside at the world of work, but also to look inside yourself at what work means to you.

How to Get Information about O'Reilly & Associates

The online O'Reilly Information Resource is a Gopher server that provides you with information on our books, how to download code examples, and how to order from us. There is also a UNIX bibliography you can use to get information on current books by subject area.

Connecting to the O'Reilly Information Resource

Gopher is an interactive tool that organizes the resources found on the Internet as a sequence of menus. If you don't know how Gopher works, see the chapter "Tunneling through the Internet: Gopher" in *The Whole Internet User's Guide and Catalog* by Ed Krol.

An easy way to use Gopher is to download a Gopher client, either the tty Gopher that uses curses or the Xgopher.

Once you have a local Gopher client, you can launch Gopher with:

    gopher gopher.ora.com

To use the Xgopher client, enter:

    xgopher -xrm "xgopher.rootServer:
    gopher.ora.com"

If you have no client, log in on our machine via telnet and run Gopher from there, with:

    telnet gopher.ora.com
    login: gopher (no password)

Another option is to use a World Wide Web browser, and enter the http address:

    gopher://gopher.ora.com

Once the connection is made, you should see a root menu similar to this:

```
Internet Gopher Information Client v1.12
    Root gopher server: gopher.ora.com

->1. News Flash! -- New Products and
     Projects of ORA/.
   2.About O'Reilly & Associates.
   3.Book Descriptions and Information/
   4.Complete Listing of Book Titles.
   5.FTP Archive and E-Mail Information/
   6.Ordering Information/
   7.UNIX Bibliography/

Press ? for Help, q to Quit, u to go up a
menu                         Page: 1/1
```

From the root menu you can begin exploring the information that we have available. If you don't know much about O'Reilly & Associates, choose About O'Reilly & Associates from the menu. You'll see an article by Tim O'Reilly that gives an overview of who we are—and a little background on the books we publish.

Getting Information About Our Books

The Gopher server makes available online the same information that we provide in our print catalog, often in more detail.

Choose Complete Listing of Book Titles from the root menu to view a list of all our titles. This is a useful summary to have when you want to place an order.

To find out more about a particular book, choose Book Descriptions and Information; you will see the screen below:

```
Internet Gopher Information Client v1.12
    Book Descriptions and Information

->1.New Books and Editions/
   2.Computer Security/
   3.Distributed Computing Environment
     (DCE)/
   4.Non-Technical Books/
   5.System Administration/
   6.UNIX & C Programming/
   7.Using UNIX/
   8.X Resource/
   9.X Window System/
   10.CD-Rom Book Companions/
   11.Errata and Updates/
   12.Keyword Search on all Book
      Descriptions <?>
   13.Keyword Search on all Tables of
      Content <?>
```

All of our new books are listed in a single category. The rest of our books are grouped by subject. Select a subject to see a list of book titles in that category. When you select a specific book, you'll find a full description and table of contents.

For example, if you wanted to look at what books we had on administration, you would choose selection 5, System Administration, resulting in the following screen:

```
           System Administration

   1.DNS and BIND/
   2.Essential System Administration/
   3.Managing NFS and NIS/
   4.Managing UUCP and Usenet/
   5.sendmail/
   6.System Performance Tuning/
   7.TCP/IP Network Administration/
```

If you then choose Essential System Administration, you will be given the choice of looking at either the book description or the table of contents.

```
       Essential System Administration

->1.Book Description and Information.
  2.Book Table of Contents.
```

Selecting either of these options will display the contents of a file. Gopher then provides instructions for you to navigate elsewhere or quit the program.

Searching For the Book You Want

Gopher also allows you to locate book descriptions or tables of contents by using a word search. (We have compiled a full-text index WAIS.)

If you choose Book Descriptions and Information from the root menu, the last two selections on that menu allow you to do keyword searches.

Choose Keyword Search on all Book Descriptions and you will be prompted with:

Index word(s) to search for:

Once you enter a keyword, the server returns a list of the book descriptions that match the keyword. For example, if you enter the keyword DCE, you will see:

```
Keyword Search on all Book Descriptions:
                   DCE

-> 1.Understanding DCE.
   2.Guide to Writing DCE Applications.
   3.Distributed Applications Across DCE
     and Windows NT.
   4.DCE Administration Guide.
   5.Power Programming with RPC.
   6.Guide to OSF/1.
```

Choose one of these selections to view the book description.

Using the keyword search option can be a faster and less tedious way to locate a book than moving through a lot of menus.

You can also use a WAIS client to access the full-text index or book descriptions. The name of the database is

O'Reilly_Book_Descriptions.src

and you can find it in the WAIS directory of servers.

Note: We are always adding functions and listings to the O'Reilly Information Resource. By the time you read this article, the actual screens may very well have changed.

E-mail Accounts

E-mail ordering promises to be quick and easy, even faster than using our 800 number. Because we don't want you to send credit card information over a non-secure network, we ask that you set up an account with us in advance. To do so, either call us at 1-800-998-9938 or use the application provided in Ordering Information on the Gopher root menu. You will then be provided with a confidential account number.

Your account number allows us to retrieve your billing information when you place an order by e-mail, so you only need to send us your account number and what you want to order.

For your security, we use the credit card information and shipping address that we have on file. We also verify that the name of the person sending us the e-mail order matches the name on the account. If any of this information needs to change, we ask that you contact order@ora.com or call our Customer Service department.

Ordering by E-mail

Once you have an account with us, you can send us your orders by e-mail. Remember that you can use our online catalog to find out more about the books you want. Here's what we need when you send us an order:

1. Address your e-mail to: order@ora.com
2. Include in your message:
   - The title of each book you want to order (including ISBN number, if you know it)
   - The quantity of each book
   - Method of delivery: UPS Standard, Fed Ex Priority...
   - Your name and account number
   - Anything special you'd like to tell us about the order

When we receive your e-mail message, our Customer Service representative will verify your order before we ship it, and give you a total cost. If you would like to change your order after confirmation, or if there are ever any problems, please use the phone and give us a call—e-mail has its limitations.

This program is an experiment for us. We appreciate getting your feedback so we can continue improving our service.

How to Order by E-mail

E-mail ordering promises to be quick and easy. Because we don't want you sending credit card information over a non-secure network, we ask that you set up an account with us before ordering by e-mail.

To find out more about setting up an e-mail account, you can either call us at (800) 998-9938 or select `Ordering Information` from the Gopher root menu.

O'Reilly & Associates Inc.
103A Morris Street, Sebastopol, CA 95472

(800) 998-9938 • (707) 829-0515 • FAX (707) 829-0104 • order@ora.com

How to get information about O'Reilly books online
• If you have a local gopher client, then you can launch gopher and connect to our server:
`gopher gopher.ora.com`
• If you want to use the Xgopher client, then enter:
`xgopher -xrm "xgopher.rootServer: gopher.ora.com"`
• If you want to use telnet, then enter:
`telnet gopher.ora.com   login: gopher    [no password]`
• If you use a World Wide Web browser, you can access the gopher server by typing the following http address:
`gopher://gopher.ora.com`

WE'D LIKE TO HEAR FROM YOU

Company Name

Name

Address

City/State

Zip/Country

Telephone

FAX

Internet or *Uunet* e-mail address

Which O'Reilly book did this card come from? _____

Is your job: ❏ SysAdmin? ❏ Programmer?

❏ Other? What? _____

Do you use other computer systems besides UNIX? If so, which one(s)?

Please send me the following:

❏ A free catalog of titles

❏ A list of bookstores in my area that carry O'Reilly books

❏ A list of distributors outside of the U.S. and Canada

❏ Information about bundling O'Reilly books with my product

O'Reilly & Associates Inc.

(800) 998-9938 • (707) 829-0515 • FAX (707) 829-0104 • order@ora.com

How to order books by e-mail:

1. Address your e-mail to: order@ora.com
2. Include in your message:
   - The title of each book you want to order
     (an ISBN number is helpful but not necessary)
   - The quantity of each book
   - Your account number and name
   - Anything special you'd like us to know about your order

O'Reilly Online Account Number

Use our online catalog to find out more about our books (see reverse).